The Autobiography of Jane Brakhage

The Autobiography of Jane Brakhage

Jane Wodening

With P. Adams Sitney and David E. James
As Told to and Edited by David E. James

Sticking Place Books
New York

Table of Contents

Acknowledgements

I am deeply grateful to Jane Wodening for agreeing to the conversations that comprise this book and for her candor, forthrightness, unwavering support, and good humor during them. The entire process was a pleasure and an honor for me. Her enthusiasm for the prospect of publication only makes her death two years ago—two years after we finished talking—the more regrettable.

Jane's grandchildren, Desirae Brakhage and Iona Bartek, have been wonderfully supportive throughout, generously answering my questions and supplying illustrations.

P. Adams Sitney inspired and then guided and assisted the process from its very beginnings. He and I (as well as he and Jane) were in regular communication almost to the end. His despair at the values of the academic publishing industry persuaded him that I would never be able to arrange publication, an insight that seemed to be proven true by the complete disinterest of all the university presses I contacted when the conversations were completed. Unfortunately, he too died before I was able to effect the present publication.

My freedom now to imagine his joy at seeing it in print is due entirely to Paul Cronin of Sticking Place Books; I am grateful to Paul's vision for this book and all his work on it.

Grateful acknowledgments to the following for permission to reproduce specified materials: Adam Hyman for photograph, "Jane Wodening Visits Los Angeles Filmforum, 2020 iii 8"; photographs "Jane with Goose, c 1970s" and "Jane Wodening with the Family's Pet Pigeon, Fanny, 1977" are licensed under the Creative Commons Attribution-Share Alike 4.0 International and have been slightly edited; the Brakhage Family Estate for photographs "Jane and Betsy with Their Mothers," "Jane and Stan at Their Cabin in Lump Gulch," "Jane with the Table She Made," and "Myrrena, Neowyn, Crystal and Jane"; the Estate of Stan Brakhage and Fred Camper (www.fredcamper.com) for frame enlargements from *Thigh Line Lyre Triangular*, *Mothlight*, and *Creation*; Carolee Schneemann Foundation/Artists Rights Society (ARS), New York, Courtesy Lisson Gallery and P•P•O•W, New York, for "Portrait of Jane Brakhage, Carolee Schneemann, oil, 1958," and photograph "Stan, Baby Myrrena, Jane, Carolee Schneemann, and Jim Tenney, Illinois," © 2025; Sky Sitney for photograph "P. Adams Sitney, circa. 1964"; and Anthology Film Archives for permission to print "The Birth Film" by Jane Brakhage from *Film Culture*, 31 (Winter, 1963-64); rpt., P. Adams Sitney, ed., *Film Culture Reader* (New York: Praeger, 1970), pp.230-33, © Anthology Film Archives.

All items © copyright; all rights reserved.

Introduction

Jane Wodening is known today primarily as a prose writer. Her first extended publication, *Lump Gulch Tales* in 1993, was a collection of stories gleaned from her neighbors in the Colorado Rocky Mountain township where she lived, some of their recollections stretching back to the Depression when it was a mining center. Its success encouraged her to continue with brief autobiographical essays, many of them exploring her relationship with animals both domestic and wild. After her divorce from her husband, to whom she had been married for thirty years, she embarked on two major adventures: first, an almost three-year-long series of solo travels mainly around the western half of the US; and second, a ten-year retreat in which she lived alone in an isolated cabin at 10,000 feet in the Fourth of July Canyon in the Rocky Mountains. Drawing on her extensive journals, she documented these respectively (though not in chronological order) in the books *Living Up There* (2009) and *Driveabout* (2016). In these, she enlarged and linked earlier short stories, essays, and journal entries into extended narratives that elaborated her observations of the people she met but also of the flora, fauna, and landscape. Eventually her concern became the entire biota, the environment, and even nature as a whole, conceptualized within an increasingly comprehensive and passionate vision of what she saw as the threat posed by a contemporary civilization that then—and now—seemed willfully and uncomprehendingly bent on destroying life on earth.

These, her mature achievements, had been foreshadowed by miscellaneous projects, several of which are described in her own recollections below, among them, a high school short story involving a visitor from outer space and a book about the history of the planet that would explain everything. But her first completed writing and her first publication was "The Birth Film," an account of the birth of her first child that was filmed by her husband.* At her death she left several unfinished manuscripts including an ambitious project, *The Tablets*, that had occupied her for a number of years. This was to have been her ecological summa, a novelistic dramatization of her accumulated insights on the destructiveness of civilization that "would clarify the problem between humanity and nature, show what changes ought to be made by humanity that would make it possible for the species to continue indefinitely on Earth."† Unable to resolve this into literary form, she finally abandoned it. Though it is never linearly summarized, these writings as a whole comprise a richly realized spiritual autobiography.

---

* "The Birth Film," *Film Culture*, 31 (Winter, 1963-64), rpt., P. Adams Sitney, ed., *Film Culture Reader* (New York: Praeger, 1970), pp.230-233. See below, Appendix 3.
† *Living Up There*, p.16; see also pp.214-15 and 236. Full bibliographical details of all Jane's books may be found in Appendix 2.

Born into a peripatetic Middle American family as Mary Jane Collom, she had a lonely, uneventful childhood in the Midwest, relieved primarily by strong friendships with local dogs. As a teenager, excruciatingly shy and helplessly unpopular among her peers, she attended various schools and colleges, interspersing them with temporary jobs. Though she had a few minor romantic encounters, she was depressed, directionless, and even suicidal until she met an equally distressed though aggressively ambitious artist, Stan Brakhage, an aspiring filmmaker. They married precipitously and she replaced her father's surname with his and so became Jane Brakhage. During the next three decades, she played multiple roles in their creation of one of the most radically original and seminal oeuvres in the history of cinema. Even while she was the pillar of their family that grew to include five children, she was simultaneously the Muse of Brakhage's vision, a collaborator in his photography and editing, an amanuensis and the distributor of his work, and, most essentially, the chief protagonist and imagistic focus of his films. Testifying to the importance of her role in their work, Brakhage claimed that the "By Brakhage" signature with which he identified his films, "should be understood to mean 'by way of Stan and Jane Brakhage,' as it does in all my films since marriage."* Correlatively, according to another important filmmaker, she became "the most profoundly differentiated and individuated woman in the history of film."†

At the same time, as through her husband she met some of the most important poets and other artists of the era, she developed an awareness of her autonomous creative potential. Initially manifested as a variety of domestic craft projects, this first flowered as three innovative scrapbooks that documented her family life and her and her husband's social circle. Eventually, her ambitions revealed themselves as an urgent commitment to writing. The death of a close friend with whom she had made a pact that they would assist each other in becoming writers produced a life-changing epiphany: "I visited her as she lay dying... That night I woke in wild terror and my head on the pillow was her head on the pillow, and for the first time in my life I knew I would die someday, and if I didn't do something, I would die without having done anything."‡

This crisis approximately coincided with the final collapse of her marriage which, formerly inspirational and productive, had become toxic and psychically destructive. Despite Brakhage's use of her and his frequent proclamations of her fundamental importance to his work—"bragging on her," as she sometimes put it—he had long been cruel and unfaithful, and after thirty years he left her. With her children mostly grown and independent, she set out to live without him, "to pull myself together into a singularity, an individual person."§ The quest for an autonomous selfhood led her to the two projects mentioned, in the course of which she created herself individually as an artist but also as its dialectal complement, a member of several kinds of community: first, she

---

* Stan Brakhage, *Metaphors on Vision*, ed. P. Adams Sitney (New York: Anthology Film Archives, 2017), p.96.
† Hollis Frampton, "Stan and Jane Brakhage, Talking" *Artforum* (January 1973), p.77.
‡ "Transformations" in *The Lady Orangutan and Other Stories*, p.7.
§ *Ibid*, p.7.

re-established her relations with her children and her Colorado neighbors, then renewed and expanded her friendships with some of her old acquaintances and also made new friends on her travels and by becoming involved in ham radio. The growing reputation of her work gave her a place in the fellowship of other writers, largely women, and of her readers. Crucial in her public self-realization was the matter of her name.

As recounted below, while visiting a writer friend in Boston in the late 1980s, she gave a reading in Cambridge, where among her audience she met a man knowledgeable in Old English. Explaining to him that her family's English genealogy could be traced back to King Arthur, she asked him to find her a new name to replace both "Collom," her brother's name, and "Brakhage," her husband's, with which she no longer wished to be identified. He proposed one that combined the Norse god Odin or Woden with a suffix indicating "child of." Accepting this, she went to the local District Court to legalize her new surname, and at the same time removed the "Mary" that associated her given name of "Mary Jane" with marijuana. Jettisoning both Mary Jane Collum and Jane Brakhage, she discovered herself as "a child of God": Jane Wodening.

Now entirely freed from its dependency on her former life as Brakhage's wife, the full elaboration of her mature art resonated with the 19th-century imaginative self-discovery recounted by Wordsworth and other English Romantic poets and Thoreau and the New England Transcendentalists.* Her visionary realizations were not expounded in one major summary event but rather accumulated in ongoing local epiphanies that resonate among each other, described especially in *Living Up There*, *Driveabout*, and *Wolf Dictionary*. (In a striking parallel to her husband's distribution of his films outside commercial channels, these and her other books were all published by small, provincial, and essentially non-profit presses.) As well as her discovery of an autonomous identity in her writing and in herself as a writer, these entailed the extension of the kinship with domestic animals that dated back to her first childhood dog friends to include all the animal life she encountered in the Colorado wilderness: wolves, coyotes, possums, bears, and so on, as well as many kinds of birds. Though this identification initially appears to anthropomorphize these animals, the insight (provided by filmmaker Peter Kubelka) that people are themselves animals inverts it, (re) placing humans within the totality of insects, birds, and wild animals, big and small. She extended her joyful acceptance of this commonality to include all living things and thence to all the created world into a vision of nature as a `luminous interactive and interdependent organic whole: "I came to realize that living

---

* Jane occasionally mentions Thoreau, for example: "I've been thinking about Thoreau" (*Driveabout*, p.49) but nowhere elaborates her thoughts about him. Though her references to Buddhism are also undeveloped, the concept of "dependent origination" (*pratītyasamutpāda*) is fundamental to her mature sense of the interconnectedness of all phenomena. The Hindu concept of *Vanaprastha*, the third stage of life which involves a withdrawal from worldly affairs for a more solitary, contemplative life in the forest, is clearly parallel to her retreat to the mountains.

in the world is always a multiplicity of choices, worlds upon worlds, interlaced, a living mosaic. It was a revelation of life on earth, even just as it is."[*]

The present tracing of Jane's autobiography to this point of spiritual self-discovery began in 2018 with what I called the "Stan Brakhage Biography Project." Distressed by the fact that no one was writing a biography of Brakhage and by the death of many of the people most closely associated with him, I resolved to interview as many of those who had known him as possible to form a resource for some future biographer.[†] I and several colleagues were able to preserve the recollections of more than a dozen of Brakhage's most significant friends and collaborators. But these did not include Jane, obviously the most important informant, who had expressed enthusiastic interest in the project. Failing to find a woman or indeed anyone to interview her, I tried to persuade P. Adams Sitney, the premiere scholar of U.S. avant-garde film, to undertake it. His knowledge of Brakhage and his achievement was unequalled; he had known Jane since 1962 and was in regular communication with her. Adamantly refusing, he advised me to do it myself, while also indicating that he would assist by indicating areas of discussion that he believed would be especially generative and by making transcripts of our meetings. So I did. Jane was generously accommodating, and right away we found an easy rapport. I quickly began to enjoy my role in our conversations that in effect were three-way, including P. Adams by way of his input and his annotations to the transcripts. Since I began the first conversation by asking Jane about her own childhood memories rather than her first encounter with Brakhage, what I had envisaged as a means of gathering information about him was spontaneously re-routed into Jane's autobiography.

After some preliminary conversations, Jane (who was living in Denver at the time) and I decided that we would meet weekly over Zoom usually on Tuesdays from 10:30 to about noon, beginning in January 2021, at the height of COVID. After each discussion, I emailed that week's audio file to P. Adams, who transcribed it and sent the transcription to Jane, who in turn amended or added to it. I have incorporated these amendments into the present text, which consequently differs somewhat from the preserved tapes of the discussions.[‡] Apart from a few days when he was hospitalized in March 2021, P. Adams was in regular telephone contact with Jane throughout. I understood that they discussed the interviews and Jane's amendments, sometimes disagreeing with each other. Finally, they quarreled sufficiently seriously that he refused to continue his involvement, and the last conversation was transcribed by another friend of Jane's. I based the present text on a new AI transcription of the original tapes, continuously cross-referencing it against the original files and P. Adams' version of them. Glitches in the Zoom made some words or even phrases unclear, and in the text I have noted a few instances where Jane's words are unintelligible.

---

[*] *Driveabout*, p.7.

[†] In fact, a biographer appeared much sooner than I anticipated. John Powers is progressing on what I am sure will be a complete and authoritative critical biography.

[‡] These may be consulted at the Brakhage Archives at the University of Colorado at Boulder (https://www.colorado.edu/brakhagecenter).

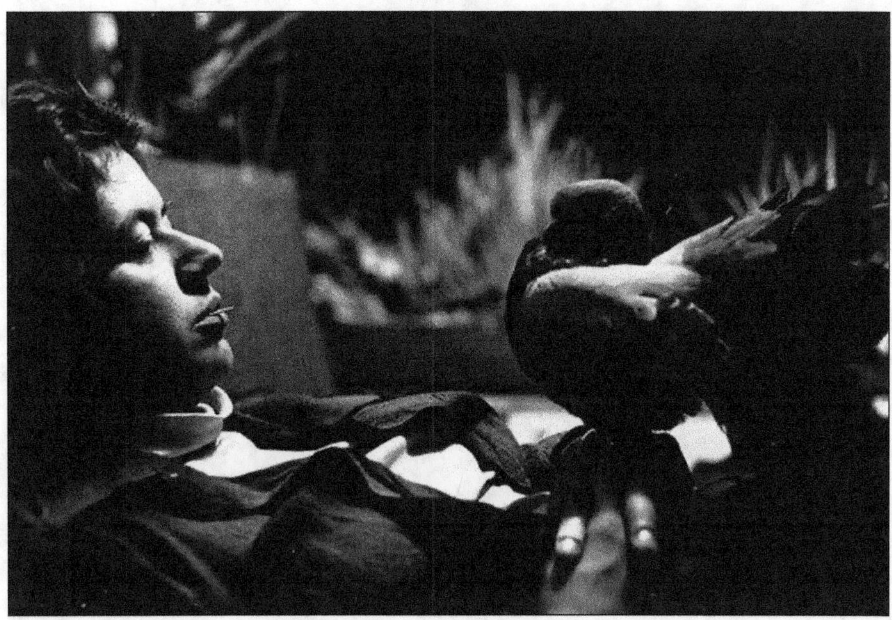

Jane Wodening with the Family's Pet Pigeon, Fanny, 1977.

Painfully aware of the implications and dangers of editing Jane's informal spontaneous oral expression through the linguistic priorities of a male academic, I initially planned a verbatim transcription. I hoped at least to some degree to forestall my rationalization of the movements of her mind to formal grammaticality and instead to preserve the rhythms and textures of her speaking voice, including its hesitancies, false-starts, self-corrections, repetitions, filler-words and so on—not to mention her frequent peals of laughter.

It quickly became clear that this was unfeasible. At the time of our conversations, Jane was over eighty-five years old, recalling events long in the past, some of them still painful. A precise word-for-word transcription would have been around twice as long as the present text and, I felt, unproductively verbose and protracted. I eliminated what I thought detracted from the clarity of her story and generally shaped her spontaneous recollections into sentences, though my choice between a period, a semi-colon, or a comma was often more or less arbitrary. I have retained some grammatical idiosyncrasies and a peppering of colloquialisms, in hopes of preserving at least echoes of the articulation and rhythms of Jane's voice. Nevertheless, her speech is reproduced here only as it has been subjected to several levels of mediation: the technology of Zoom, her discussions with P. Adams, rev.com's transcription, and my final editing. Fortunately, a closer, less mediated, form of her story may be found on the original tapes.

Unless specifically attributed to P. Adams Sitney (PAS), all notes are by me.

David E. James, Los Angeles, 2025 x 20

Prologue

I was thinking the other day, not long ago, about when my daughter, Crystal, and I went for a hike. It had been a cold night, but it was warming up and it was in the morning. So we went and there was this wonderful swamp in the middle of Denver. This is because we have to control the snow-melt in the spring when we have mad scenes of lots and lots of water running through town, and all the basements get washed out. So we have these flood control places, and this one is a big swamp and, of course, it becomes a smallish lake in the spring. We were there walking on the ice, and the grasses were up to the armpits. Crystal was breaking trail and I was following with two ski poles, and we were suffering along. It was a struggle.

And then we'd stop, we'd see footprints and there was one place where there was a whole display of different types of footprints. There were coyotes, there were mice, actually shrew, prints, I think. And there were maybe crows and then very small bird feet. The day was wearing on, it was getting warmer, and we came within maybe fifty yards of the shore and there was no more ice to walk on. So there we were in the middle wading up to our knees and got up onto shore. It was fun, but it was a comedy of errors the whole way.

And I think that's what we're doing too. So there's a big hunk of words for you to work with and I hope it's working out all right.

Good, we've accomplished what I wanted to accomplish today. I suggest that we end this meeting now, I'll look at the video and verbal transcripts to see that they're working OK. Then I'll email you in preparation for our next meeting, which will begin the interviews proper. Thank you so much. Happy New Year! I look forward to speaking with you next week after my technological investigations.

I mean, now the image of that walking in the swamp is like you and me walking through this world of technology, that was what the symbol was for me anyway.

One

2021 January 12. Childhood in Illinois and Colorado; Mom and Daddy were teachers; brother Jack; some dogs.

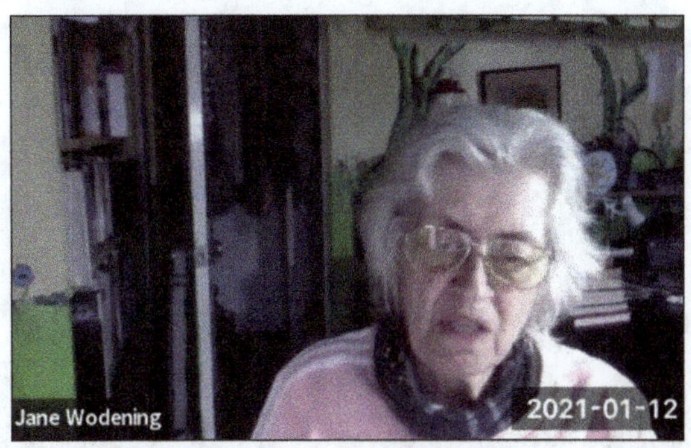

Jane Wodening [*reading from computer screen*]: This meeting is being recorded. OK. I've just been trying to figure out my childhood.

David E. James: *We're making this recording as part of a historical project with the intention of archiving it at the University of Colorado at Boulder. Do you agree that it may be made public, and that people may have access to it?*

Yes. Yes. If you don't mind. I mean, there's no telling what I might say.

That will be at your discretion. If there are parts that you would like to conceal, that will be totally fine. There's also the possibility that this might be published in some way. Do you have any feelings about that? Do you give your consent?

Yeah. I mean, you go ahead. That'd be fine.

We agreed that you would talk about your life before you met Stan Brakhage. My point of departure would be, could you talk about your very earliest memories? But if you want to start at a different place, I'll be quiet and intervene only if you ask me to.

I would prefer that you jump in and say, "Ooh!" and "Ah!" and smile and laugh and stuff.

OK. I'll do that.

The very earliest memory I have is lying on my back in the crib, my little fat legs kicking above me. I was crying for my mother to come up. I knew that she was busy, and it irritated me that she was busy. So I called her by crying and she had to come upstairs, and she knew what I wanted. I wanted her to sing to me. She had a beautiful voice, to my mind, the most beautiful thing on earth. And kind of gruffly, she picked me up and sang to me a few lines and then put me down. As she was going downstairs, I started crying again. That's my first memory.

Did she come back up and sing some more?

No, she did not.

Where was this?

This was in Western Springs, Illinois.

And that's where you were born?

I was born in Chicago, and we lived in Western Springs until I was eleven. I've written a couple stories—at least one story, anyway—about the importance of dogs in my childhood, dogs really made a tremendous effect on me. But since I've written that story up already, I'll let it go for now, but it is kind of basic, called "Wagsy" and it's in the book, *Animals I've Neglected to Mention.*

My parents were both very quiet, very demure, very shy. They met in college, and she got her BA and he got an MA in education. He didn't have any place to teach in Western Springs, and she was busy raising my brother and me. My brother was five years older than I was, and he was rough on me. He was not my playmate except for word games he would play with me since there was no one else around. Sometimes in these word games, we'd get to laughing uproariously. I adored my brother.

You asked for genealogy, and I don't know how much to give you. Both sides of the family have an enormous, massive genealogy. I'll give you just a glimpse on either side. My mother was very into genealogy and enjoyed searching. She even went to England to see the castle and, thirty miles away, the miners' town. Thomas Hungerford in the castle and Thomas Miner from the miners' town of Chew Magna had both come to America at about the same time and their grandchildren married.* So they were thirty miles apart for generations and finally married in New England. I think the son of those two that married wrote a diary. And his name, of course, was Thomas Miner. I'm afraid I gave my copy to a grandchild and it's vanished. He was a farmer so that's what he wrote about. There was one day when the pig got run over by a carriage and had to be

---

* The extensive ruins of Farleigh Hungerford Castle, begun in the 1370s, are in Farleigh Hungerford, Somerset. Some twenty miles away, the village of Chew Magna lies within the Somerset Coalfield. Though coal had been mined in the area since Roman times, the industry grew in the 18th and 19th centuries.

butchered on the road. It was all quite exciting, but most of the days were pretty boring.

This was in New England?

Yeah, Connecticut, I think. My mother was following her genealogy in England particularly. She was thrilled with her great grandfather or maybe great, great, grandfather, who was a captain in the American Revolution. He had a lame hand from being shot by somebody, whether it was in the war or by Indians, I don't know. But he could drop his hat from his galloping horse and then go galloping by and pick it up with, I guess, his good hand and put it back on his head. That's the main thing I remember about him.

But you never saw him do this?

Oh, no, no, no. This was recorded. There are other little stories like that that she found. There was a page, a sheet of paper about four feet square that has my Aunt Grace in one corner and out from it is line after line. Each line has got somebody in it and they're related. Her daughter, Marsha, made it. On my father's side— my mother could work as hard as she wanted but she would never compete with my father, who wasn't doing any genealogy—there is a book telling one line from the people on the Mayflower that came over. There was this little boy who was on the Mayflower, eight years old or so, and he was the father of all this line. Then you can go up from the Mayflower to King Edward I, climbing slowly up the aristocracy that evidently we were climbing down in real time. From Edward I, we can go up through the Plantagenets to King Alfred the Great. If you'd like, you can go out to the ancestor god, Woden. That's where I got my name, but it was given to me by a scholar in Cambridge, Massachusetts.

Had your father researched this genealogy, going back to the Mayflower?

No, no. There's this book, and of course he knew about it, but he was not into researching it or anything.

What is the book?

The book? I don't know the name of it. I saw it in New London, Connecticut. There are four copies of it. Unless that little building burned down, it's still there. I spent some time there sitting on the floor with a wolfhound, talking with two ladies about other lines. I could look it up, but I didn't. I just continued on my travels. But the book was there. So I've got a lot of English people in my ancestry, going way back.

How did your parents meet?

They met at the University of Illinois where they were studying education. Daddy was a year behind because he had caught tuberculosis in high school and took a year off, so he was a year late. It turned out when he was forty-five that he still had a cyst in his lung somewhere, so he was still positive for tuberculosis.

My mother loved to dance, she loved to dance and sing. And Daddy couldn't do either one. It was too bad, but she could dance. She was always singing "do di do do" as she was doing the dishes. And she had a lovely voice, as I said before.

They met at the university and graduated, and then one or both of them got a job?

Well, Mom got a job first, and I don't know what she was doing. I never considered what she might've been doing or considered asking her what she did. But he went on and studied for his master's while she was working. And then Jack was born at about the time that he got his master's. And then she quit and he started working.

And then you were born in 1936?

Yeah. Yeah.

When did they graduate?

Jack was five years older than I, so they graduated in about '30, '31.

You've talked about your earliest memory of your mother singing to you. Could you talk any more about your childhood memories in Illinois?

I could go on and on about the dogs, but I will talk about the town a bit. It was a quiet little town on the Burlington Route of the train going straight west of Chicago and it ends up in Denver. It goes up and actually ends up in Rollinsville, Colorado, where we lived for some time. It goes through Rollinsville and up over the divide, so we were not far from the tracks, which was nice. I always thought it was nice because I liked the train howling. I liked to hear it howl, it was very pretty. And just across the tracks was downtown, but on this side, there was a candy shop, I know that. You could buy a sack of little bits of bad-tasting sugar, beads or something stuffed into paper for a penny. I was born into the Depression and we were typically poor. Pinching pennies was something my mother, I think, always did, and so I learned to do that early on. But then, the war!

Well, there was a day when I was roller-skating up and down the sidewalk, and I learned something really exciting and new. I invented a technique and it was great. It was marvelous. I ran to my parents to tell them how smart I was and they said, "Shush! Shush!" They were both hunched over the radio, one of those grand old radios. It was a fake, of course—can't even been made of plastic. I don't know what it was made of, cardboard or something. But it was a beautiful old thing. They were hunched over it, listening to President Roosevelt saying that he hated war, and that Eleanor hated war and that we had to go to war.

I didn't know what he was talking about. I couldn't figure it out, and I was just irritated that they wouldn't listen to me, so I put my head down and left the house. After that, we had rationing. Sometimes there were strange-looking airplanes flying over town and everybody would duck and worry, but it was always the good guys. There was rationing so we had to be very careful about how much bread and how much meat so that we could eat decently all through the month. You just had to pinch and scrape. Just when the war broke out, bananas started emerging from South America; we kept getting them because it was possible to move them up here, but it was very sparse. We got one banana for the family, and both my brother and I liked to cut a banana into our breakfast cereal and eat it. I saw that it was just one, and I was reaching for it, but my brother came to the door and said, "Oh no, you don't." And I ran and tripped over a stump and cut my leg badly. There were seven stitches, and I didn't see the banana again.

You got another banana?

[*laughs*] No, no, no, no, no, no. It was weeks later before I saw another, it wasn't that easy. Maybe if we did get another next day, Jack got it. He was more skilled at that sort of thing. He could run faster backwards than I could run frontwards.

I was a lonely child. There were a couple of little girls that would play with me sometimes. They were not interested in things that I was interested in, but it was awfully nice to have somebody to play with, even if I wasn't playing what I wanted to play. There was a thing that we did, we didn't knock on the doors to ask for the child to come out. We would go under their bedroom and shout, "Oh, Kay! Oh, Maryanne!" Those were the two, Kay and Maryanne. Maryanne left pretty soon, and I didn't see any of her again. But Kay stayed for quite a while.

Another thing was baseball in the vacant lot. Now the vacant lot was just catty-corner through the back corner of our backyard. And so that was easy to get to, but all the kids were older than me. But there was this great thing: to play baseball, you have to have how many, nine people on each team? Of course, we didn't have that. We might have five or six kids all together, so we played piggy-move-up: there's the third and there's first, there's the pitcher, there's the catcher, and there's you, the batter, and one person on first base. That's how many kids there were, and so that's what we played. That made me acceptable in the baseball games because every child was really an important thing to fill a spot that needed filling. They taught me how to bat right-handed, which is too bad because I'm left-handed. I can't bat left-handed. I can't run the computer left-handed either for the same reason, because it was set up for a right-handed person.

Let's see, I went to school, I was unpopular, I was lonesome. My only friends were the dogs, not my dog, it was other people's dogs. I didn't have a dog, so the one next door was a big deal. And that's Wagsy, and that's in the story. I guess I liked school at first, but then later it was, I dunno. I always found something interesting there, but I was staring out the window a whole lot and spacing out and dreaming and not listening much. But I got pretty steady B's. B for boring, I think. Anyway, I can't remember the grade school much.

Can you remember any of the teachers?

I can't remember the teachers in grade school. I remember some in high school. I remember the science teacher. Very nice, very kindly. And I don't remember the math… [*unidentified noise*] What?

Oh, it's just my computer telling us what time it is. It's no problem.

Oh, have we talked for an hour? No, half an hour. Half an hour. Yeah. How long should we talk?

As long as you feel like it. I couldn't be here for twenty-four hours, but twenty-three would be OK.

Is that right? [*laughs delightedly*] Maybe I should piss you off. [*laughs*]

Why were you unpopular?

As I think about it now, I was unpopular because I was so involved with dogs and socializing with dogs that I never learned how to socialize with kids. That was partly because my parents were shy and didn't bring me out to whatever fun thing was going on or introduce me to neighbors' kids.

Your father wasn't teaching at this school?

No, my father was doing bookkeeping. Before the war, it was for the city of Western Springs in the little city hall, which had previously been a water tower at the railroad and was just round and cute and small, and probably not too efficient. That's where he worked, it was just a block away. But then when the war started, he got a job at the aluminum company, I suppose he was doing bookkeeping there too. He was good at math; he was really quick at adding and subtracting and doing all that. He did that waiting for his draft card. Every day he would expect his draft card, and he never got it. I suppose that was because he was married and had a job working for the aluminum company.

So what else? Oh, the thing about the war, of course, was that there were hardly any cars, because it was bad enough to buy a car, but you just couldn't buy gas. You couldn't go, I don't know how many miles it was, but it wasn't very many miles that you could go in a car and then you were stuck for the rest of the month, you couldn't buy more. Some people had a car because they had to have it for work or something. But if you had to go somewhere, you took the train if it was possible. And there was Chicago on the other end of the train.

Did your father consciously decide not to become a teacher after he'd been educated to become one?

No, he just didn't get a job. He was an eccentric also, and when he talked, he had this deep, slow voice, and he would hesitate often and sound like an idiot. But he was quite intelligent and very sharp, actually, but talked slowly and he was not sociable. He was shy, so he wouldn't get jobs. When the war ended, he lost his job at the aluminum company. I remember he brought home a complete set of pots and pans made out of aluminum for my mother.

Then he got sick and wanted a dryer location, needed to live in a dry place. So he and Mom sent out letters to see if they could get jobs in Colorado or Arizona or someplace like that, and he got this job in the little town of Fraser, Colorado. I clearly remember driving across the country on Highway 66, I believe. It wasn't very well traveled at that time, but it was great fun: all the world going by and miles and miles and miles of cornfields and whatnot. And playing the game with my brother, like, OK, what color is that car that's coming? And neither one of us was all that good. Anyway, Fraser was a different world.

So now you are leaving Illinois to go to Colorado. It's 1946 or so and you are about 10. Any other things about Illinois that we haven't talked about? I wonder if you might want to talk a bit more about your relationship with dogs.

Yeah. Well, OK, I should talk about the dogs. The one dog I don't remember, of course, was the one in my infancy. And I believe that she was with me more than my mother was, because my mother was very busy when I was an infant. I'm not sure what she was busy at, but she was busy downstairs, and I could hear her singing, "Do di do!"

She sounds like she was a happy woman.

Not really. She just loved to sing. She didn't exude happiness; she exuded discipline, to me anyway.

You were talking about the first dog.

Yes. Points was her name, she was a little female. Yeah, she had pointy ears. I was alone with her for long periods in my crib, and I assume that I learned dog language from her. So one of my problems—or maybe it's just my descent from my father—is a difficulty in speaking English. I know all the words, and Daddy had a huge vocabulary. It was just to use the words and put them in a sentence that would be relevant to the conversation, that was just a lot of work. It takes doing things that I never learned how to do really, to converse. I learned how to converse after I was fifty, when I was a ham radio operator. I learned to converse on ham radio.

Well, I did some conversing of course, I don't know, going out on dates or whatnot. I usually like philosophy and to figure out the philosophical notions people have. Points got me learning, well, essentially body language and subtleties of dog language that aren't usually noticed. Then when I was five, my mother didn't notice that I was tight with Points, so when she had puppies, she sold or gave away Points as well as the puppies. So that was it, so I don't have any memory of Points. But when I was five, my mother was busy and nobody was around, and I wandered off lonely and kicking stones and went up the alley. There was that little dog next door, Wagsy, who never wagged his tail because he was so busy barking and snarling at everybody who passed by. I said, "Ah, here's somebody who wants to talk to me." So I stood there and slowly moved towards him, just very slowly moved towards him and slowly raised my hand way outside of his reach. Slowly, slowly, slowly, while he was barking and snarling and telling me what a bad person I must be and so on. Then I saw his eyes looking at my hand with intense interest that maybe a little girl could pet him. Then I realized that I had almost conquered him and pretty soon I was scratching his cheek. We were dear friends for a few years there, so that was my friend. My neighbor Kay or Maryanne, they were people I could play human things with. But I don't know, I was a lonely girl. My loneliness shows there in the Wagsy story. It solved it for a time, but really it aimed me in the direction of hanging out with dogs all through my childhood. I just hung out with dogs when I could, actually, in Fraser.

I should think of more of Illinois. What else can I say about Illinois? Well, I should mention Bemis Woods. We could actually walk down our street and enter Bemis Woods, which is a long narrow woods that goes along Salt Creek, I believe it's called. It goes along for several suburbs there. It was quite a wonderful park, just a wilderness area, just a woods that was left alone. Which I am sorry about, parks aren't usually that way anymore, but it was. Daddy wanted us to learn to love nature so he took us down to Bemis Woods quite often. We would walk there and, in his typical fashion, he would see something and he'd say, "Oh." And he'd point and we'd look at it and we would get the vibes of his enthusiasm. He would then talk, tell us about what kind of an animal it was. Jack actually went into becoming a well-known birder, somebody that hunts for birds and names them, so he knew all the names. He had a long list for his annual count. I never got into it. For one thing, he had better eyes than I did so he could say, well, "There's a pied-billed woodpecker with one feather missing in the left wing." That's the way he went, and the way I went was to reach out to them as I reached out to dogs. That's like two different personalities, I guess. But Bemis Woods was a good, wonderful influence on me, and I was really happy to know some little patch of wilderness.

Did you establish any relationship with specific animals there the way you'd done with Wagsy?

Not in Illinois. Actually, I was sticking to dogs altogether pretty much until Lump Gulch. I met some cats and some horses, and somehow I liked donkeys very much. I didn't get into squirrels or robins or anything like that. But Jack and his lifelong friend, Gerard, had an easy time catching friends, he was always making friends. Gerard had a Red-Tailed Hawk or a Golden Eagle or some big raptor. I never saw it, so I can't really say. I don't know in what way they exercised it or anything, but they had it. They probably just kept it in a room or something. So he had a bird, but I didn't. He never had pets, actually ever, that I know of.

Except for this bird?

That was Gerard's, at Gerard's house. He had to go there to visit Gerard's bird.

Did you read as a child?

Avidly! I read a lot, and I can recite several entire poems from *Alice in Wonderland* and *Alice through the Looking Glass*. I loved, of course, *Dr. Doolittle* and, getting older, it was Terhune who wrote about dogs.* But there were other books I've read. Let's see. I read *Robinson Crusoe* and *Treasure Island*, and I think I read all the classics really.

What about Little Women?

No, I don't think so. But I did love Jane Austen. *Little Women* was too ladylike for me. I was so thrilled when we got to Fraser and I didn't have to wear a dress to school. I could wear pants, like a boy. I could just go, it wasn't a rule anymore. I had been a Brownie, I guess, a Scout and a Brownie Scout. Just as we left, I was eleven, and we left in '47, just in time for me to turn twelve, I think.

So now we've got you in Fraser, Colorado. You arrived there after the endless cotton fields on Route 66.

They were not cotton fields. They were cornfields [*laughs*], corn fields and wheat and alfalfa and sugar beets and other things, of course. And yes, that was a great ride.

And now you could wear pants to school in Fraser?

Yeah, we got a little place to rent and lived there. It was across the highway and across the tracks, and there was the school. But between the highway and the tracks was a chicken yard, and in the chicken yard was a weather station. The guy who lived there, whose name was Pullini, only had one arm. One arm was missing up to the elbow from, I guess, World War II. I'm not sure, it might've been World War I, I don't know. He seemed like awfully old to me, but maybe he was not. And he had a couple of dogs. He had two littermates, so two puppies growing up, and he let me play with them, it was kind of wonderful.

---

* Albert Payson Terhune, 1872–1942, a U.S. writer and dog breeder, especially of collies.

There's the house and the road and the chickens and the weather station and the tracks and the school and beyond that was Byers Peak. It's a mountaintop, a really beautiful mountain and I just fell in love with it. It was something I just would look at, just sit and look at it. I don't know how long at a time, but it was a beautiful thing.

So I loved the mountain. I was in fifth grade, I think, and Jack was in high school. As he said, he didn't learn a thing in Fraser. But anyway, he was there and he went to school. One problem was, of course, Daddy taught English and math and was the principal of the school also. So that was how little the town was. And Mom taught third and fourth grade. She much preferred first grade, she asked for first grade, but she got third and fourth. And Daddy got this job in the high school.

I was not only unpopular, I couldn't understand their dialect. It wasn't that different, I guess, but I somehow couldn't understand people very well. And so of course, I went to those two puppies growing up, Spot and Tippy, and played with them a lot. And there was a ski run just actually across the creek, behind the house. The hill was shaved of trees, and so it was a place to go to somehow. We went there and I learned the very basics of skiing, like, don't fall down, you know, and stuff. Or if you do fall down, fall down correctly, that was the main thing. If you're going to fall down, you got to fall down correctly. And so I learned how to fall down correctly, and I think it's served me all my life because one falls down and it hurts.

So there was that. But then later in the year, my parents got me going once a week to the beginner's slope at Winter Park, which was a big, beautiful ski area carved out of a mountain that was higher than the one behind us. It was much higher, but I was happy with the beginner's slope and learning to ski on that. I got good enough towards the end of the year that I thought that, since my name was Mary Jane, I should ski down the Mary Jane slope. It was terrible, but I did survive it. It was straight downhill, like the one behind us only about ten times steeper and higher. It was not fun, I don't like to go fast, but I made it down. And I only fell down maybe once or twice and of course I rolled properly and got right up and went on. That was a great thing, to learn how to ski while I was there.

Oh, I forgot to mention, in Western Springs, I did spend about a year trying to learn the piano, and I did all right until I came to a certain little song in Bach's collection of little songs to teach children with. It was a little song that I hated. And I know that Bach didn't write that because I was becoming very fond of Bach, but I know he didn't write that, and I've heard that he didn't write all of them. So that relieves my mind because I was so absolute about that I was not going to learn that song. "I'd love to learn the next song, please, let's go on." And the teacher got rid of me, I wasn't disciplined enough.

So we left Fraser and found a little cabin in Boulder Canyon where we could spend the summers, and there's Boulder just five miles away, so I went to Boulder High School. Well, no, I wasn't going to high school yet. The next year we went to the cabin, and I took the one called Spot. Spot and I went hiking up the hill behind the house. We went all the way to the top, we went all around, and we hiked and had a grand time in that place called Silver Spruce. There were other cabins, it was a no-fishing gathering or something like that, they were selling it piece by piece. So that was that summer; we'd just lock up the cabin and go to Yampa, that was the next place. We didn't go back to Fraser, we went to Yampa.

That's another town in Colorado? Was your father moving to a different job?

It was pretty much the same thing, only Mom got to be a first-grade teacher. It was a little bit bigger, maybe two or three times bigger than Fraser was. Fraser was a dying copper-mining town, it's now a kind of a tourist trap. But what was Yampa? I don't know. It's amongst the Flat Tops, the hills there are flat-topped. So Spot and I would go on weekends, we'd pick up all the dogs along the road that wanted to come with us, and we would go in a great crowd to walk around in the mountains. [*laughs*] And I think everybody appreciated having their dogs walked, but I don't know if that's true. They never complained because when we'd come back, I would look seriously at that dog and I'd point to his porch and he would go obediently to his porch so they all got home again. I think that was important, but nobody spoke to me about it. Maybe they were shy too, I don't know. Schoolteachers are scary people, I think, generally and especially in small towns.

How did you enjoy school in this period?

I hardly remember it. I only remember two things. There was one time, I think it was Halloween or something, when everybody was chasing around and playing hide-and-seek, or I don't know what it was. Anyway, there were a bunch of kids at that time; I don't remember being friends with them but they wanted a lot of kids. I think they knocked on my door and said, did I want to play? And that was amazing. I went out and played, and it was kind of rough and difficult and I failed the test, I guess.

But there were two teachers who were happy to play canasta with my family sometimes. I think it was once a week that they would come and play canasta with us. So I learned canasta, which I can't remember how to play anymore. But the other thing is that Daddy was teaching a psychology class, and in this psychology class he talked about hypnotism, and they all said they didn't believe in hypnotism. He fell for it and said, "Well, I want you all to come to my house tonight and I'll give you a demonstration. Who wants to be the person, my client?" And somebody, some little girl, I think, said that she would love to do it. So they all arrived, and with his low, dusty voice, he said "Now you're going to sleep and now you're getting tired and your head is sagging. Alright, you're going to sleep." And finally, you could stick a pin in her, and she didn't jump or whatever. He proved that she was hypnotized by sticking a pin in her. I remember he burned it with a match or something. Then there was something else that he said. He said, "When you wake up, you're not going to remember anything we said or did." Then she woke up and she said the thing that she was told to say, and then they were asking her, "Well, do you remember it?" "Well, no!" So he had shown that hypnotism existed. The problem with that was, he should have shown them something thrilling in athletics or something, but I don't know.

Oh, there was another thing. Before we moved into the big house—we actually bought that house and shouldn't have—we were living in a little shabby shack, and there was this dog that used to come and play with me and Spot. And then one time he came and his nose was full of porcupine quills and Daddy made him go away, shooed him away. And we never saw him again, so I assume he was killed for having porcupine quills in his nose. I don't think I was old enough to pull all of them out properly. I would've had to have help, but I don't know. I feel sorry about that dog, he was an Airedale. I don't remember any friends from there. I don't remember school much. There was some fun stuff in the school, I can't remember what, maybe it was a play or something, or maybe it was a book. Maybe that was when I read *Treasure Island* for a class.

So that was Yampa. And we went back to the cabin and I discovered wading in the creek with two sticks; I could wade in the creek and go across it. That was wonderful, except that there was always poison ivy to walk through, and I always did it without paying attention. I should have gone into botany because I could have learned what a poison ivy patch was, but I never seemed to learn. I always got poison ivy, and it itched terrible. And we went up the hill too.

So you are fourteen, fifteen by now?

Something like thirteen maybe? No, let's see. I was twelve in Fraser and thirteen in Yampa. And so since my birthday is in September, I turned fourteen in Wray, Colorado. That was on the plains, except that it had a cliff. I think it had been a lake, yeah, must've been a lake. Anyway, there was a cliff, and the cliff was kind of washed-out too so there was sort of little caverns, little caves in the cliffs. I could go walk over there with Spot and we could hike up there amongst the caves and stuff. It wasn't near as nice. I mean, you could look down on the city of Wray, which was not much, wasn't that interesting.

The only thing I remember to talk about, well, is I did a piece of writing there. I was being two people. I was at the top of the page. I was saying that I found this note, I found this note out in the field and I thought, I'd bring it as my story that you asked me to write. And then I tell the story: I was kidnapped and picked up by my people in some weird space rocket. And they were not really people that were funny looking creatures, but they got me, and I'm just going up now into the spacecraft, so goodbye. Anyway, I told it much more wordy and much better, I assume, because I got an A, even though the teacher scolded me for using a pencil for what the kidnapped child wrote. Somehow that was a pleasure to write it and to be praised for it.

Had your father moved to a different job now in Wray?

Oh, he was teaching, he was the principal in Vernon now. It's just a little farming community. That was where he was tested for tuberculosis. This truck was coming around and they were going to test everybody for tuberculosis. So Dad, he said, "Well, I'll go first, so then they won't be scared." And later, when we received the information, it turned out that he had tuberculosis. He was positive, nobody else was, of course, in that rural area. But yeah, Mom taught first grade, and Daddy was the principal and the teacher of English and math, and God knows what else in Vernon. I believe they had somebody else for coach, although in college, he got some honors for short sprints. He could run fast for brief periods; he was perfectly capable but he was not an athlete. I can't think of anything else there. Well, I don't know. I could talk about joining the church, but it has a kind of a bad ending.

There was a friend, Carolyn, she made friends with me, and she one time took me home for supper, I think it was. I was accustomed to slathering my jam onto the toast and they were horrified to see me doing that and said, "We only just put a little bit of jam on our toast, just a littlest, thinnest coat of jam." So I was ashamed, but then they said, "Oh, you can go ahead and eat it the way you like it." It didn't really help my loneliness at all. The father was a preacher. It was the Presbyterian, I believe, church. And he was really a sweet man. He said that he was going to teach classes once a week and tell stories from the Bible. In Western Springs, I had gone for a while with a neighbor to learn those stories from the Bible, and my parents who were more or less atheists, they said, "Sure, go ahead." Mom liked to go to church, actually, because then she could sing the hymns with people. And she liked that, she liked to sing the hymns, but the rest of it, I don't know. I went to these classes and it was really fun. One time there was a field trip, and I don't remember what happened, but I remember riding in the car, and I know it was all quite sociable. But then it of course came to an end.

The reverend had come to class a few times, and at one point he was standing with his back to the window, and I was sitting in a chair facing the window, and he was telling me—he was standing and he was quite tall—and he was telling me about how Jesus saves. I was having trouble squinting at him because the sun was right behind him, and finally my eyes were watery, and he thought that I had been—what do you call it—I had been saved. I hadn't, it was all a mistake but I really liked him. He was just such a sweet man. Then there was the time when I had to get up in front of the church and he put oil on me for something in different places. Then he said, "Do you take Jesus Christ as your savior?" I didn't want to lie in front of him and these wonderful people in church. I didn't want to lie in church because I respected the church, I revered it, but I didn't… my savior, I don't understand. So I looked at him in desperation, and he said, "Just say yes." [laughs] So, I did.

Shall we halt there. The transcript has been appearing on my screen, and it's just horrible.

Why don't you just send it to P. Adams and have it done right?

I don't think he'll do it.

I bet he would, because he's curious.

OK, well, I'll email him and see what he says. But let's halt there, we've done almost the first fifteen years of your life, and we'll come back next week and do the period when you considered going to college, and then perhaps your meeting with Stan.

We've almost done an hour and a half, haven't we? OK. I just have high school, and it goes on being lonely in a way, although I did have dates, not with boys in school, of course.

Let's pick up that next week. Same time, same place?

OK. Bye. See you next week. It's been a pleasure, you almost wore me out. Thank you.

OK, great. Thank you. Take care.

You too. Take care. Bye.

Two

2021 January 19. Daddy builds a house; high school; swimming, dancing and musicals; cousin Betsy; boyfriends; college math; New York.

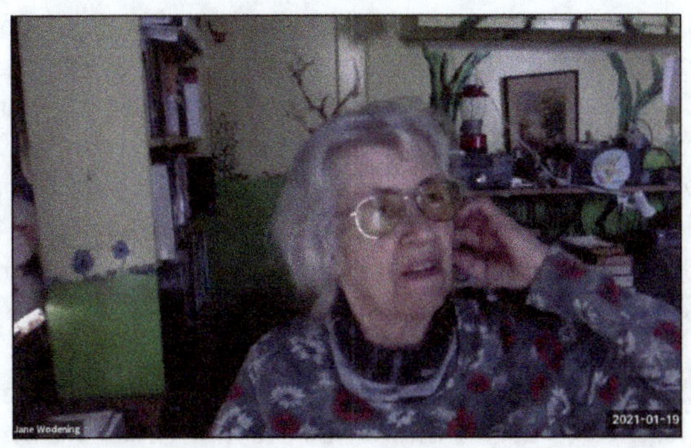

Hello, can you see me?

There you are. Now I can both see and hear you.

How are you?

Well, I'm OK. I'm OK. How are you?

Very well, thanks, trying to get a vaccine.

Yeah, me too. Yeah, I think I'm on the list.

Shall we start?

Oh, start? Yes. Where are we? Let's see. I made a list. Yes. We left off at Wray and we were there for two years.

Could I pick up on a few questions from last time? Is that OK?

Yeah.

Last time you mentioned the pleasure of your mother's singing. Do you sing like her? Are you a good singer?

No. No. I am not near so bad as my father, but I'm just OK.

So you and Stan never sang together?

No. That was a tragedy, I feel. I have a family of friends that sing together, and I just think it's beautiful. It is just a wonderful thing, a family singing together. It's a great bond and it's a beautiful thing, so I'm really sorry that he didn't want to sing. If he was asked to sing, he would sing "Ave Maria," which he learned when he was twelve. In a falsetto voice, which he did very beautifully.

But there's something I want to put in here, an image of Boulder when we came to it in 1948, summertime, and my parents each had things to do. I was eleven going on twelve. There were swimming lessons I could go to but they were later, so they dropped me off at the Court House so that I could loaf around the shops. The Court House had benches all around the outside of a lawn with a fountain close in front of the door. The benches were mostly inhabited by people with TB who had been sent to Boulder because it had wonderfully clean air and wonderful pure glacial waters. Neither of these are so now, but they were then. I liked to sit on a bench and flirt with the gardener, whose name was Louie. Then I'd walk through town to the swimming pool. There were dogs on the way, one in particular went with me for a couple of blocks to protect me from this one dog who came out snarling. The swimming was a treat; I learned to swim underwater and I learned to dive. I didn't like the high dives; I'd dive off the edge and swim underwater clear across the pool. I remember one time walking back to the Court House, seeing a neighbor and desperately trying to remember how to say "Hi" in English.

Last week when we talked about music, it ended when you were six, when you refused to learn to play that Bach song...

Not a Bach song, it was somebody else's song!

So that was at six years old. Anything else about music later in your youth?

I can't think of a thing, except that my mother cared about it. But she was also not interested in working up a family singing. She just missed doing it the way she did it as a child, with her family. There were times when people would gather around the piano and sing. I remember very early a group would gather after my bedtime and sing "Roll Out the Barrel," although I don't remember my parents ever drinking. Mom played the piano. Once or twice if more than one of her siblings showed up, they would sing a few old songs that she had the score to.

Last week you said, "What I call dog language extends to the composition of music too; I hear the person." Would you say a little more about that?

Well, yeah. I don't know how to articulate that or go on about it. It just seems like you see a person's walk, you recognize them; you hear their voice, you recognize them; you hear their composition, you recognize them. Whatever they do, you can recognize them just by watching that.

OK, let's go back to Wray.

Well, I wanted to say goodbye to Wray, but I also wanted to say we were there for two years. We went home to the cabin and Daddy had not gotten another job teaching. The superintendent of schools did not do the usual thing he was supposed to do, that is, write a letter sending him on and saying he was OK. So he couldn't go on teaching. So he started building the house beside the cabin, and he built a house pretty much by himself. It was simply built, it was cement blocks all the way down to the ground or below the ground and on up to ceiling, the roof, actually. He dug the trench, he laid the blocks, he made spaces for pipes, and he did all the things. He must have been reading in a book at the same time, doing it and not making a mistake. He made a big wide space for a big, big fireplace, made of brick, and he was laying the blocks and he was laying the bricks. And my brother came one summer; it was all done, I think, in a summer. Anyway, my brother was trying to dig the trench and a rock hit him in the middle of the forehead so he quit working on the house. He had the scar, I think he kept the scar all his life, just like I kept the scar of the banana fiasco.

I helped Daddy when I could, or in whatever way I could, but it was all heavy work, and I couldn't do most of it. I was fourteen or fifteen by then, so I was getting a little stronger. But when the wall was up to its full height, which was one story of course, so that'd be like eight or nine feet, I got on the top of it and somebody handed me bags of vermiculite and I poured it down through the holes of the cement blocks. So I was filling the house with insulation, and I just scooched around the whole house and did that. And that was really fun because I had sort of a boyfriend. No, that couldn't be? Well, I don't know.

Anyway, Willie was a boyfriend and he drove the grader and he drove it standing up. He was very striking-looking as he stood and drove the grader down the road. And I was hopefully as striking as I sat on top of the wall. Anyway, I was very self-conscious at that time, looking at boys. He was a bit older, but I dated him for two or three years, off and on. He was Wild Willie Weaver. He had a couple of horses, and he was a wild man, and everybody was worried about me going out with him. But he was a delight. He was unpredictable and charming and quite polite in some ways, but not in others.

So the house got made. We had made the roof and everything, and Daddy was working away on that big fireplace with too many bricks. It was a bad idea, it was too wide, but it was also too high. And he had to put a ladder upon another ladder, and it was very dangerous. When he finally finished it, he came into supper and said, "I'm never going to do that again." And I felt the passion in that phrase, in that sentence. But it was a very fine chimney, and it worked, it drew the air up and it was built right. Let's see, what else about that summer?

1950, when you were about fifteen?

I was approaching my fifteenth year, but I know I started dating Willie Weaver when I was fifteen, he was twenty. In high school I was totally unpopular. I started high school there in Boulder. There was a school bus, Gertrude drove it.

There were three other kids in the canyon, and we all got picked up by Gertrude, she took us in her own station wagon and dropped us off at our various schools. I remember, I was hopeful. I wasn't thinking of socializing because I didn't know how or didn't know anything about it. But it seemed like a big school for one thing, and that was interesting, and at least it was big to me. I was a sophomore there. They call 'em, "oneies." So I had three years of high school there, and I guess I did the ninth grade in Wray. I don't know if that counts up correctly or what, anyway.

So we have you as a "oneie" around 1950 beginning high school in Denver and still socially insecure.

Yes, '51. I graduated in '54. There were good things about high school. There was finally, after several months of being a oneie, this other oneie. A girl named Celia came up to me and she was an outsider too, and she said, "You and I are both unpopular, so why don't we just run around together as if we are friends and then we can look like we aren't so unpopular." I said, "OK." So we went to the games together and things, and she invited me over to her house. I don't think I invited her to my house because I'd have to take her home again in the car, because I did have a car. I learned to drive as soon as I could because I wanted to be able to go to town, to see the games and shout and so on like other kids, as if I was a normal high school girl.

I am trying to remember my classes. I know you keep asking me about scholastic things, like "Do you remember the teachers or what you learned?" And I don't remember much. I tried to learn Spanish and I didn't do very well with that, so I quit after one semester, but I still actually have a little Spanish, some understanding of how it works and so on. That's kind of interesting. But the teacher didn't like me either, she was impatient with me. There's kind of a music to learning languages. I'm good at rhythm, very good at rhythm, but I'm not good at music. I learned morse code, but I didn't learn how to work the technology in my ham radio career, which was much much later.

Let's see, I was good in English, and the history class started with the caveman. I was really excited to learn about the caveman and the teacher spotted me as like, "This is a promising student." The next thing was ancient Egypt, and there was no caveman left. There was nothing wild so I lost interest, and she was very disappointed in me. That's what I remember about history class. Let's see if I can think of an upper, not all downers really. Well, my science teacher, I remember him. He was glorious, just wonderful, and he was kind to me and patient. He was brand new, maybe just fresh out of college. He was really not that much older than we were, maybe four or five years older, or maybe three, one of us in a way. I think he was married and I don't know if he had any kids, but he wanted to interest us in science. That was his main purpose, he felt, in his job. He managed to order about one dead cat for each two of us from New York City slums. The cat that my partner and I got, we named her Beulah. As we explored in her insides, we found that not only was she pregnant—which everybody gathered around us to see how she was pregnant and what it looked like and all—but also her stomach was full of cat food, so we realized that she was not a feral cat. All the others had things like tin cans and whatnot in their stomachs, but ours had just cat food. That showed she was caught by mistake, but we went on cutting her up and learning about the insides of creatures. That was very educational, quite fun and exciting. My partner and I talked like friends, although not when we were not working on a cat; but we got along well and the teacher was very helpful.

You mentioned him last time also. Do you remember his name?

Yeah, John, I might think of it. Something like Stark, but that can't be it.

Did you make any connection between your biology classes and your relationships with dogs?

Not really, although I was glad to know what the insides of anybody looked like and how they worked a little bit. That was very interesting, it was additional information about living creatures: here's the heart doing its thing and pumping and the stomach and so on. It was so exciting to see that Beulah was pregnant. So yeah, that was the most exciting class.

I always did well with math, particularly algebra. Algebra was fun because it was like games. It's like, here's a problem, here's some numbers and they're a problem, and if you can straighten it out, you can know what X and Y are. I would straighten it out and I would find out what X and Y were, so I was doing well in math. I don't think I did all that well with geometry. The geometry teacher, I remember her visually very sharply because she stood in a strange way. I thought she was in pain in her back and that she had some kind of brace holding her up; she stood very straight, but not the way people stand somehow. I was interested in her body problems that I perceived just by looking at her in a dog sort of way more than the geometry, although I liked geometry fine. Then there was history—that was quick—and English. English I was good at, and I may have gotten A's in English.

What were you reading at this time?

I think I was reading adventure stories—Scott, perhaps.

Still Jane Austen?

Jane Austen. My mother loved *Pride and Prejudice* so much that she would take a day off every year at Christmas, Christmas vacation. She would lock herself in the bedroom and read *Pride and Prejudice* from cover to cover for one day. That was her own personal annual vacation. And I liked *Pride and Prejudice*, that's my favorite of Jane Austen's. I like Jane Austen very well, she's a really jolly and friendly girl, and so musical. She's got good rhythm in her writing. I felt related to her. And the dog stories of course.

What about painting? Did you do any arts in high school?

I don't think so. There were some kids that took art, but I don't remember taking art, not seriously anyway. Of course, I couldn't march in the band, but I wanted to become a cheerleader, but I couldn't do the splits that was necessary, so I couldn't do that. But I certainly I had a lot of energy and could do things, I was strong. What else? In the high school itself, just walking down the halls and nobody saying "Hi." There was one boy that would smile at me sometimes, and his name was Jack also. And interestingly, he was the first kid from that high school or from my class that died. He died in his twenties or thirties. I don't know what he was into or doing, but he was a nice fellow, open-minded and polite to me. I don't know. Can't think of any clubs I joined or anything.

What about outside of high school?

Of course, connected with high school were the games. As I say, Celia and I would go to the games together and jump and shout and do all the proper things that girls do. Although I wasn't that interested in football particularly [*laughs*], basketball I could do. I knew how to play basketball. I played basketball in gym class, and I was pretty good at it. I had this peculiar quirk where I could go into an empty gymnasium and stand in the middle of the room and throw the basketball over my head into the basket behind me. A swisher quite often, more than 50:50. But the place had to be empty. [*laughs*] And then of course, nobody knew it, nobody knew it.

Was there a movie theater in Boulder?

Yes, there was.

Could you talk about your youthful movie experiences?

Well, I got dates from people outside of the high school, and I believe that maybe one of my first partners for dancing, actually it was square-dancing, was with this guy named Van who had a motorcycle. He would come and get me, and I would take my square dance dress, big and long, with a full circle when I turned to spin, so it was a huge amount of cloth. I'd put it in a grocery bag and go and change in the ladies' room. We would do square dancing, and there were several squares. That was a lot of fun, I enjoyed it, and I got pretty good. I knew what the caller was telling us to do and so on, and it was just a delight. And then afterwards, we would go to the Timber Tavern, which was a bar, obviously, and we would jitterbug to the jukebox. So I did a lot of dancing for hours at a time with this square dancing and the jitterbugging. That was a really good thing that I did, or at least I felt it was good.

Movies?

Movies? I don't think he took me to movies. There was another folk dancer that took me to things, maybe it was movies. I have to say that my favorite movies were musicals. My friend Nancy and I whispered to each other, we used to believe in musicals, like it was the truth, and that was the way life is or should be. I went to other things, whatever was passing by. I saw a lot of Humphrey Bogart and Katharine Hepburn. I didn't see much of Elvis, although I jitter-bugged to him a lot. He was just about my age, actually. So he was a big deal there. But I think the movies I'd go to would be things like *Gone with the Wind* or the Hollywood classic types. I know there was no thought of experimental film or anything like it at all.

Since I'm such an Elvis fan, could you maybe talk a little bit more about Elvis?

Are you an Elvis fan? That's so interesting. [*laughs heartily*]

Oh, yeah. Elvis was a pivot of my whole life.

A pivot of your whole life, really? He was not the pivot of my life. If I may digress momentarily, Buddy Holly was. I liked him very much too, and it turned that he was born at very nearly the same moment that I was born.

Wow!

So he and I were twins, but he died young. That was so sad. I remember, I knew somehow that it was the day the music died, and I felt bad about Buddy Holly. But Elvis, I did not have a crush on Elvis. Everybody seemed to have a mad crush on him, or they found him disgusting, one of the two. And I just thought, "He's good. He's got a good voice, he really knows how to sing, and he's got a lot of emotion in his voice, and he's cool. He looks quite splendid in a way." But I didn't understand the screaming and fainting and so on. I didn't get involved with that.

We're jumping in front of ourselves because Elvis didn't start recording until 1954, and we were at about '51, '52.

I guess we were '50, '51 and '52. I don't know what happened in those years except that I did learn to drive as soon as I could. I was fifteen, a student driver, so I had to have a grownup with me. And about the time I had a license, I got a job briefly in the summer working in a dress shop, folding up handkerchiefs and things and putting them neatly away. I was very embarrassed because I was doing it so that I could go and visit with my cousin, Betsy. Have I mentioned my cousin, Betsy?

You haven't mentioned Betsy.

Well, Cousin Betsy was born four months after I was, and her mother and my mother went shopping once together, both pregnant, and so we were hanging out together before we were born in a way. She was an Air Force brat, and so she was living in Texas and Ohio and Utah, and I don't know, all kinds of places. She kept moving because her father kept being moved from one place to another, he became a major in the end. We would correspond mainly, and once in a while, we would hang out together. I remember hanging out in the backyard playing in my sandbox, we played in my sandbox once, and we did other things together. We played games, maybe Monopoly or something.

She was a friend, and that was good. So I got mail, and that was wonderful, and I would have to write back and she could draw so that when she'd get a crush on a boy, she'd draw a little boat. At the end of the line where she mentioned him, she would draw a little boat, so then I knew that he was a very acceptable boy. She was very nice to have in the background, though I seldom saw her. When we were fifteen, I guess, our mothers decided that that would be a good thing for [us to take a vacation together]. She was going with her family, I don't think her elder brother Bob was coming along. I don't think her dad was there, so it was just her and her mother and me, and we were there.

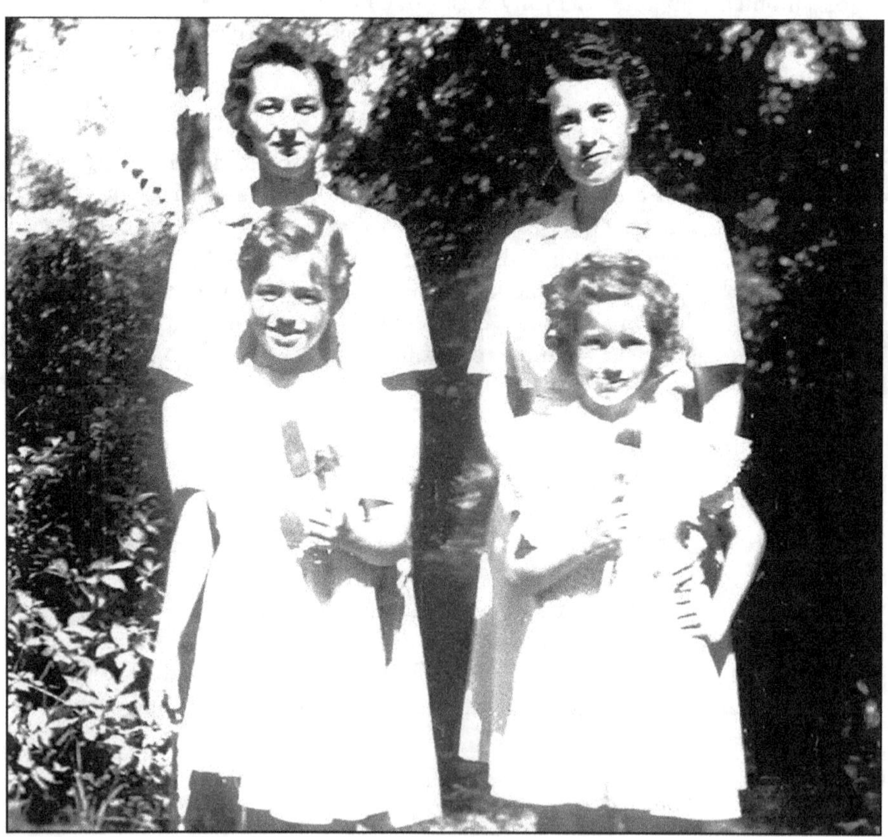

Jane (left) and Betsy with Their Mothers.

We had rented a little cottage on the shores of a little lake that jutted out from Lake Michigan, Portage Lake, so it was quieter, and it was good for keeping the boats out of the wind and violence of the big lake. We could play in Portage Lake and I could swim. Oh, I forgot to mention that Mom taught me to swim, and she brought along two or three other kids that paid their way so that she could pay for all of us without spending money. I was by far the best swimmer of the group, and I don't know why, I just jumped in the water and swam. She said, "You got to learn to put your head in the water." So I learned to swim in Naperville, Illinois, which is a little further west from Western Springs, and I was a good swimmer for a kid and in Portage Lake I would jump off the pier. Betsy told me decades later that she never learned to swim, and that I thought she was just a wimp and wouldn't swim out. I'd say, "Come on out, it's great," and she would say, "No, I'm just going to stay here."

But we chased boys together. There was one that had a yellow convertible, and I can't remember anything more about him. Yes, I can, I remember his license plate. So does she, because that's what we saw as he went by. Our boy-chasing was very minimal, but that was fine. Before that, I had to pay my way on the train at least. So I worked in this dress shop, not waiting on people but putting clothes back on a hanger and generally keeping the place in order. Then I quit. I was very embarrassed and ashamed and told the owner of the store, "I'm so sorry, I have to quit." I knew it all along because I got this job so I could pay my way to Illinois and have a vacation with my cousin. And she said, "It's all right." She was very sophisticated, and I was very not sophisticated. That was that first summer, I believe, that I went to Portage Lake with Betsy. And what was I mentioning about Betsy?

You just mentioned Betsy as the reason why you were working in the clothes shop.

Yes, right! So I don't think I had another job that summer anyway, or maybe the next summer. I don't think I had a job, but definitely the next summer I must have met Wild Willie Weaver, who was really an important influence on my life. I was going with him off and on, sort of now and then through two or three years.

Why was Willie so influential?

Because he was so wild and free. He was so unpredictable and able to do anything that jumped into his head, and he loved finding something really wild to do. He told me about how the little town of Rollinsville, which I didn't know very well at all at that time, had a bar, the Stage Stop, and he once rode his horse, Snuffy, into the bar. It is funny, I can remember horses' names, but not the teachers'. Anyway, he rode Snuffy in and was standing there, and the bartender was saying, "Willie, you get out of here right now, turn that horse right around and get out of here." And he slowly turned the horse around and it shat a big one right on the floor and then trotted out. He had to duck way down, he was kind of tall and sat straight on his horse and he stood straight on his grader, and he had style. That was one thing I liked about him. He had style, and they said he could never come back into the Stage Stop with or without the horse, but I don't know if he ever got past that. There was no other place to get drunk in Rollinsville. The problem with him, he drank too much but he didn't do so when he was taking me out. I was his sober and proper evenings, or at least the first half of them.

It was Gertrude, the bus driver, who got me involved with him; he was her nephew. She knew I needed some fun. And it was Gertrude who warned me about him, that he was already a divorcé and that he drank too much. "Promise me, don't get serious about him," she said, and I never did. But I enjoyed his company, for sure.

You'd be getting close to being a senior and graduating from high school now, around '54, '55.

Yeah, I did. I took typing in my senior year. I just had the feeling that I needed to know how to type, that it was important to me. I had no idea why, but I followed the feeling and I took typing and of course the teacher didn't like me because I was not secretary fodder, I was just not going to be a good secretary. That's what she was trying to work on, teaching people how to become a secretary. But I wanted to type, I wanted to know all that stuff. I did rather badly, did I get a D? I might've gotten a C or D, and I was not content with my skill yet. Typing was not easy for me, really, so I took it again when I went to college in Fort Collins and got a C or a D again. But anyway, that's jumping the gun.

At some point in there, I got a job with a woman who was making cheap jewelry at home. All I had to do was glue a little piece of semi-precious stone onto a ring and then stand it up to dry in a tray of rice. Once, we went down to New Mexico to buy more polished rocks and I drove the whole way. That was a delight. I could buy a used car for about $50 in those days and when it went bad, I'd sell it to the junkyard for $25 and get another. I had to do it all with my own money, so I'd have a job I could drive to.

What else happened in my senior year? I was a driver, I could drive. I could drive to school if I wanted to, I don't think I did generally. I would go to school with Gertrude in the bus, which was really her station wagon. And then after school—and this happened for the whole three years, I believe—I would go to the town library, which was a little building crammed with books There were books in stacks, on the floor, and all over the place, and it had this wonderful smell of moldy old books, which I love. Daddy would pick me up there after an hour or something. Anyway, I had a good amount of time there, and I could find a book and start reading it, and then I could just leave it and come back the next day and go on with it. That would be my place for reading that book. That's where I found immediately P. G. Wodehouse. I would sit there laughing uproariously, and the librarian of course would shush me, and it would be very hard to go on laughing uproariously, but I would sit and shake. Nobody recommended P. G. Wodehouse or who else I discovered there, the bunch of authors you read. The title was always so artificial, so I wanted a secret title. I would look at the first word and the last word of the whole text. I recommend it, it works. You look through your whole library, you will find that that is a respectable title for each book. And if it isn't a respectable title or if it looks mushy or messed up, then you can figure that the book is not well made, that it's not built. It isn't made right, it's not worth reading.

So I did a lot of reading there, and that was really a great little section of my day. It was quite wonderful. And walking through the streets, it was I guess a mile or a mile and a half to the library. And so I had a nice walk through town, and I enjoyed that after-school thing. I guess Mom was teaching first grade in a suburb of Denver and Daddy, I don't remember what he was doing. He was not teaching. It was trying to... Oh God... [*extended technical interruptions*] I told you about Daddy and me—Daddy and I—making the kitchen cabinets for the house in Western Springs. He worked hard on that, so that was the beginning job, and then the next job was building that house. Then he felt that he would be able to be a carpenter, and he read up on how to be a carpenter, and he passed the test. And then he was sitting in this waiting room with all these muscular people, and he was like very scrawny and not really muscular. He got a job on a roof and he wrecked his back, and so he quit trying to be a carpenter and got a job through the employment bureau teaching English to tubercular Navajos in a TB sanitarium. I think that was happening in the summer because he was always picking me up an hour after school at the library. I had thought he had something to go to, a meeting or something.

Your relationship with your parents was reasonably good in your teenage years?

I guess so, yeah, they were letting me think for myself, and I really feel that they should have gotten me to where I would learn social skills because they were very shy, and I grew up very shy and shy means that you don't know how to do a lot of things. And so it took me a long time... anyway.

How did the decision to go to college come about?

Well, Jack had gone to college at Fort Collins, and Fort Collins was the A&M school at that time.* So it was assumed that I would go to college, and so I went, signed up to go to college and study about animals as much as I could. I thought the A&M school would be a good place to do that, but actually not. Jack took forestry there, and he almost had a nervous breakdown in his senior year because he discovered that forestry was not his idea of what to do about a forest, so he didn't want to be a forester. His roommate was so upset that he came to tell my parents not to berate him for quitting college in the middle of his senior year. They got together with him and the three of them together decided that Jack should finish in something like liberal arts. You can just change to liberal arts and not graduate as a forester. And he always said afterwards that he never learned a thing in those four years. I was following in his footsteps, I guess, and going to the place. Of course, I was unpopular there. I lived in the dorm, and there's a

---

* What is now known as Colorado State University in Fort Collins was formerly Colorado Agricultural and Mechanical College (Colorado A&M).

couple things about the dorm. One was that my roommate didn't think well of me either. I must have been really somehow appalling, although I don't know.

Appalling?

Somehow I must have been appalling. Yeah. I don't know, because everybody seemed to dislike me. But finally she reached out to me because she was starting to smoke, and she offered me a cigarette. I thought, "Oh, this is very friendly, my roommate is being friendly to me. I must accept it." So I did, and I spent thirty years of my life smoking and all to be polite to my roommate.

Another thing that happened in the dorm was that somebody was having fun cutting people's hair, and they said, "Why don't we cut Jane's hair? Jane, come and we'll cut your hair." "OK, wow, you want me pretty or something?" So they cut my hair, and I looked in the mirror and I screamed and cried, and it was terrible. And then I was so embarrassed about going out on the campus and being seen with my hair so short and so unattractive, and it was months before I felt like I was able to walk down the street without being embarrassed.

In the meantime, there was an Iranian prince or something, a very ugly guy, I'm sorry to say. He wanted to date me, and I was thinking, "Oh, he's looking for a wife to take home to Iran to be a princess or part of his harem. You can have an American girl that's part of his harem." I may have had a prejudice there, but really, he was not cute, he was not attractive. He didn't say anything when he spoke. Well, he'd call me up, and it was nice to get a phone call, but it was him. So I'd say, "No" and "No." I would say "I'm busy." And finally he called me up and I said, I was busy. And he said, "When you say you're busy, does that just mean no, you don't want to go out with me?" I was very scared and ashamed to say, "Yes." I knew that I had to say the truth and I would never get any more phone calls. That would be too bad, but anyway, I would be telling the truth. So I didn't hear from him again. There were a couple other guys, but they just wanted somebody to take to bed, and I didn't want to do that quite yet.

There was the zoology class in the morning just before lunch. I would go and steep myself in formaldehyde and dead things. I remember particularly the dead, enormously long earthworm. It was as long as a garden snake, it was really long. And I spread it out on the board, and I started copying it, and I thought I was doing extraordinarily well with all my copying of things. I did a shark's eye. Did you know that earthworms have five hearts?

I didn't.

Well, they do, and I drew each one. There were other things too: parts of animals and whatnot, shark's eye, did I say some part of a rat? I can't remember what. I drew the pictures well and accurately, and I was really wanting to make a good impression but evidently I made no impression at all. And he gave me a C+ at the end of the year, which crushed me, it crushed me. Well, OK, nobody, I haven't met any friends there, and the teacher dislikes me, and I can't get along in the dormitory, obviously, and the boys are not my type. I was really depressed that

I had failed again to become popular. I thought with a new crowd of people, I could just start fresh. They wouldn't have a bad rep to lean on. But I built my bad rep quickly, I guess. So I left in some despair at the end of the year and thought, "Well, what should I get into?"

So you only finished one year of college?

Yeah, I only finished that. But I thought, well, I'll go to CU and I'll do math.* I don't like math very much, but I'm good at it so I can do math. So I asked somebody, "What do you do for math?" He said, "Well, there's two kinds of math. There's engineering math, and that's where you become an architect or something like that." I had just read *The Fountainhead*† so that kind of stirred me. "The other way is theoretical math and probably, since you're a girl, the only thing you could do with that would be to teach." So I went to engineering math because I didn't want to be a teacher, although my parents were both teachers, more or less. Actually Mom's father was a teacher, but anyway, I didn't want to be a teacher. I went to class, and there I must have met Susie that summer. There was Susie's dad, Jack Britton; finally, I know a teacher's name.‡ He was a very kind of dry and orderly fellow, but it was nice to be the second-best student in the class. The first one was this wild genius that I couldn't possibly come close to, but I was the second-best student in a class! But it was so boring, it was so boring; algorithms are not anything to get people excited about mathematics. And then my brother came home from the Air Force, and he wanted a ride to New York City. So I quit school and drove him to New York City. But I did leave out the whole thing about being a soda jerk for two or three summers, I think it might've been three summers at the university, the Indian Grill.

This is at the University of Colorado at Boulder.

Yeah, yeah. They have a community center that has this big eating place. And I was a soda jerk there, and I made the best limeades. We sold limeades, but there were ice cream things and whatnot. So I made those and looked across the big room, huge room full of chairs and tables and looking at all these students, and there was a guy there, Clancy. I do want to mention Clancy; he's such an important person in Boulder and a great person. He was a dwarf. He was the cashier, not in that room, but in the next room, the cafeteria, so that he would take money from people with a tray of lunch. And he was so nice. He was just a wonderful person, very kind and warm, enlightening because he was so crippled. He was thinking of taking off one leg because it hurt so much. His sickness was that his bones were weak and breakable, very easily broken. All through his childhood, he'd have a broken bone and be in the hospital, and he wouldn't be

---

* The University of Colorado at Boulder.

† The hero of Ayn Rand's 1943 novel, *The Fountainhead*, is an architect.

‡ Dr. Jack R. Britton taught at the University of Colorado at Boulder in the mid-1950s. He authored *University Mathematics* (San Francisco: W.H. Freeman, 1965) and several other books about math.

putting his energies into growing. So he just stayed little, four-and-a-half or five feet tall and extraordinarily sociable. Everybody loved him. Later on, he became a leprechaun in parades, and he became a puppeteer. I could tell about many years later, working with him as a puppeteer briefly on one occasion, when he had a broken rib at the time and didn't mention it. He was just a magical person. I don't know how I can explain that. I wanted to write a little piece on him, but I didn't know what to say.

Another person was Lala. He was a Burmese, and he was my friend, and he would talk to me, and that was very nice. His name was Mulang La Shwe, and I called him Lala for his middle name. He would always come to me and give me big words to spell or define, and he was always sort of suggesting that he was better at English than I was. But he did that because he liked me, and so we would talk sometimes. That was my job for three years, I think three summers, just for the summer. I'm just jumping around so much.

You got to the point where your brother asked you to drive him to New York.

I said yes and dropped out of school forever. Jack Britton was disappointed, he said I was his second-best student, and I was very touched that he would say that.

He said you were his second-best student ever?

I don't know about ever. I think it was just in the class. I don't know about ever, but in the class that we were in. Anyway.

So you drove your brother to New York?

Yes, I had a Nash, and the seat folded back so somebody could sleep, except that he had brought along Paul Swearingen, who had an extraordinarily high IQ. He was interesting too, he was OK. Anyway, "Swearingen," that's a name.

So you set off in the Nash for New York?

Set off in the Nash for New York. And we took turns driving and we'd stop for food. I don't remember ever sleeping, except that we would take turns sleeping in the fold-down seat, and the others would whisper. And I guess that would be how we'd sleep, that we'd just keep going and somebody would be trying to sleep. But it's not a very deep sleep when you're riding in a car and there's people talking and stuff. Anyway, we arrived, and there was Tom and Gloria, Jack's friends, Tom and Gloria Bartek, and they're the ones who sang, the family sang. When the kids grew up, there were six of them singing. It was run by Gloria, and Gloria was really the singer of the group, but she taught them to harmonize, and they sounded wonderful. But at that time, they had their first baby, Aaron, and we looked for places. Jack found a place on 14th, and I found a place on East 11th. It didn't have a bathroom in the apartment, it was out in the hall, so that was constantly irritating. I never got the key, so I got a screwdriver and undid the hinges so that I could use the bathroom.

Let's see. There was a lot about New York. I think we've skipped some essential things from earlier, but we can look through and put them in, I guess.

It's ten-to-twelve, we should be winding up.

Well, I could just talk about New York. We—Jack—felt that I should become educated, and so he took me to lots of operas and it was very nice. You could pay only $3 and go in. It was five stories high, the old Met building. I don't know if you'd know about that being from England, but it was a really grand old building made in the 18th or 19th century or something. It had five balconies, and the fifth balcony was, I don't know how many feet above. The acoustics were fabulous. It was as though they were singing right beside us. So that was a wonderful, amazing and magical thing to go to the operas. And then finally he took me to something else.

He took me to the Metropolitan Museum of Art, and it was there that I discovered Rembrandt. I just went crazy over him. I just fell in love with Rembrandt because of his eyes, partly because he was looking at me through everybody's eyes. And most particularly, there was one painting there, which I've been told ever since was not one of the paintings that he made, but it had his name there on the painting and on the frame, called, I believe, "The Buccaneer."[*] It was a man who obviously had been out in the wild, and he was looking at me as so many Rembrandt paintings do, they look at you. And he really had a good thing with the eyes. He knew how to make expression and talk with his eyes. He lives forever in those eyes. Then I understood what art was and how the artist could reach inside and relate to one's insides, something beyond doing an accurate job on copying an earthworm's insides. I'm pleased to stop there. I think that's a good place to stop. I am glad to put Rembrandt in and end on that.

That's terrific. Next week, I assume, we'll be coming to the point where you meet Stan, that's very close.

I could have mentioned the first two times, and we could start earlier in high school and pick up some things that I left out. The two times that I met him and he didn't meet me.

---

[*] No painting with this title exists in the Metropolitan Museum of Art's collection, nor indeed in the entire Rembrandt catalogue. It is possible that Jane confused it with reproductions of the oil painting, "The Buccaneer," by the U.S. author and illustrator, Howard Pyle (1853–1911). The print of it first appeared as "The Fate of a Treasure Town" in *Harper's Monthly Magazine*, December 1905 and later as "The Buccaneer was a Picturesque Fellow." After his death, some of Pyle's stories about pirates accompanied by illustrations of them, including "The Buccaneer," were collected as *Howard Pyle's Book of Pirates*. Given her interest in adventure stories mentioned above, it is likely that Jane had seen it. Like many of Rembrandt's subjects, the pirate wears a large hat and has long hair and also stares fiercely out of the painting.

I'd like to hear about those first two meetings There's one other thing: you went with Stan to England twice?

Once to England, twice to Alaska, once to Amsterdam and Utrecht. I don't think there were any more trips where I was brought along.

But you did go to England once. Perhaps you might think about that and at some point I'd like to talk about your time in England. Thank you so very much. I'll send this to P. Adams. We'll correspond and we'll look forward to meeting again next Tuesday. OK.

OK, David. Thank you, bye.

Three

2021 January 26. Meeting Stan Brakhage; depression; marriage; *Wedlock House: An Intercourse*; *Anticipation of the Night*; Jim Tenney and Carolee Schneemann; *Cat's Cradle*; Princeton; Myrrena born; *Window Water Baby Moving*.

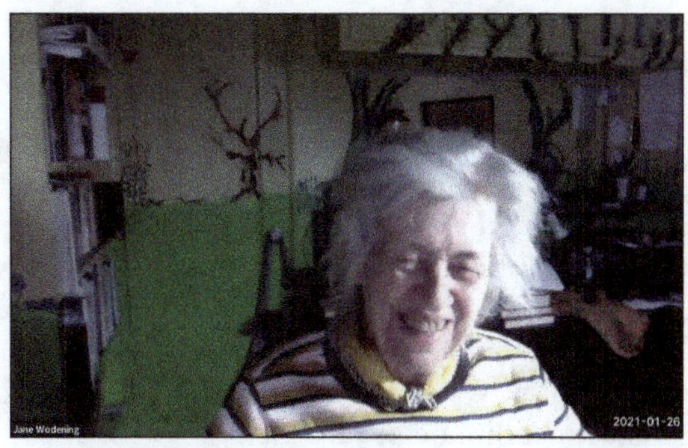

OK. The meeting is being recorded, it says.

Perhaps you could start with the first time you heard of Stan Brakhage.

Well, I was at a matinee in Central City. Central City has always had the highest level of operas. Plays and things from New York City came straight to Central City. It just always has been and it was still going on then. I don't know if it is now. I don't think so, but it was a great tradition. What was that?

That's just my computer.

Oh my goodness. Your computer is participating quite a bit. I was there with one of the folk dancers in the matinee, and we came out and in front of us on the street were two people dueling with obviously wooden swords and one was beating the other one back into the street. Later I heard that Stan and Larry Jordan did that every time the matinee let out to get the audience to come down to their tent theater there, which they had that year in Central City. So that was the first time I met him, and that was very brief.

Did you talk to him on that occasion?

No, I didn't talk to him at all. I said, "Oh, let's go to that," and Ron said, "No, sorry, I have another date this evening." So we missed out. When I went to New

York, I got a job at Rockefeller Center, adding up columns of figures for, I can't think what reason. I would go out for lunch in Rockefeller Center and sit on a bench and eat my sack lunch. Then I'd have a little time after that and one of those times I went down into the basement of Rockefeller Center, where there's a mall and a Brentano's bookstore. I went in and bought up some D.H. Lawrence that I was interested in. There was this wonderful glum-looking black-haired guy at the cash register looking down and refusing to look at me in a very blatant way. He must have looked at me before and decided not to look at me anymore. He sold me my book and handed me the change. All I could do then was walk out the door. I couldn't stand around and say, "Well, what do you think of the weather?" So that's the second time I met him.

And you recognized him from...

No, no, I didn't recognize him. I didn't recognize him at all either time and I didn't put it together until—I think it was years later—we discussed this when he was talking about the tent theater that he had. And he also mentioned, of course, working at Brentano's bookstore for Charles Boultenhouse.* Then I put the three together, or maybe I did them one at a time, I'm not sure, but I think I put it all together at one moment. That was him that I had seen both times and that he had in a very general way, just not rejected me, but ignored me. So those were the two times that I met him before we met.

Last week I talked about working at the Indian Grill as a soda jerk and it must've been there that I met Gladney Oakley, who is one of your mysterious people that you don't know much about.† We started dating and that's when I was first introduced to the films. We dated for quite a while and then he was saying, "I think I can respect you and trust you so that I can introduce you to this genius. I know a genius and I'd like to introduce you to him." I was kind of giggling, I don't know why. I just thought that was silly because my brother and I had ridden across country with a man who had a very high IQ. I assumed that he was a genius and that I knew what a genius was and it's just a person.

I said, "Sure, I'll go." I dressed up in my best outfit and Gladney took me to this little house, tiny little house in Denver. We went in and there was this sickly looking person, looking not grumpy but kind of desperate or something. He introduced me and I wanted to sit down and there was a comfortable chair. I was really nervous and wanted to sit in a really soft chair, but that chair was inhabited by a cat. And I said, "I wonder if I could sit in that chair." And he said, "No, the cat is sitting in it." And I said, "You have a neurotic cat." That was about the first thing I said to him, and he never forgot it.

---

* Charles Boultenhouse (1925–1996), poet, actor, film critic, and filmmaker, best known for his *Dionysus* (1963). The partner of critic Parker Tyler, he worked at Brentano's bookstore in Manhattan for many years. Both Boultenhouse and Tyler befriended Brakhage when he first went to New York.

† Along with Carla Selby, Gladney Oakley began the series "The Experimental Cinema Group" at the University of Colorado at Boulder in 1955. The longest running university program screening avant-garde film and video, it is now called "First Person Cinema."

Did you say erotic or neurotic?

Neurotic, neurotic, yes; neither he nor I were thinking of erotic thoughts. So that's the third time I met him. And then he actually heard my name, and we looked into each other's faces. So that was the first meeting.

He began teaching a class, "How to Make Films," and he gave each of us a strip of white leader. We were to scratch a little thing on each little frame, and I understood 24 frames was a second. And so I had a leaf moving along slowly, slowly curving to turn in the wind in 24 frames, and he was very impressed with that. He ran it through and it worked, so that was good. But beyond that, I didn't really participate much. I mean, we listened to him talk. He liked to talk.

You said you went with Gladney to see the films. What films were these?

I can't remember what films we saw. I went several times and there were different films, and I don't remember names of people or anything until I get to know them. The people, then their films.

Were they Hollywood films?

No, no, no, no. This was the experimental film group. It was Stan and Maya Deren* and Willard Maas† and James Broughton‡ and that gang.

This was in New York?

No, this was in Boulder. I deliberately added James Broughton because he was in California.

Maya Deren was there?

No, but the films... Gladney was in charge of the film society, like you have Adam, isn't that his name?§

---

* Born Eleonora Derenkovskaya in Ukraine, Maya Deren (1917–1961) was the single most important progenitor of the post-war U.S. avant-garde film, as well as one of its most important theorists. Made with Alexander Hamid, her *Meshes of the Afternoon* (1943) reconstructed 1920s Parisian surrealism to inaugurate what P. Adams Sitney designated as the "trance film" (*Visionary Film: The American Avant-Garde* [New York: Oxford University Press, 1974], p.11). Reproducing their overwrought protagonists' subjective visual experience, Brakhage's early films utilized this mode until he sublated it in *Anticipation of the Night*. Deren befriended Brakhage when he first went to New York and he stayed in her apartment.
† A member of Deren's circle in New York, Willard Maas (1906–1971) was a filmmaker and poet. *Geography of the Body* (1943), made with his wife Marie Menken, is his best-known film. The two of them photographed Boultenhouse's *Dionysus*.
‡ James Broughton (1913–1999), poet and poetic filmmaker prominent in the San Francisco Beat scene.
§ Adam Hyman, Executive Director of the Los Angeles Filmforum since 2003. Jane appeared at Filmforum on 2020 March 8, speaking about her life with Brakhage and presenting a program of films by Brakhage and others that featured her.

Yes, yes.

He did Adam's job. He would rent the films and he would get the theater prepared, and he would be sure there was a projectionist and all that stuff. He was very responsible with that, and he had a good collection. I don't know who all he worked with. I'm sure he worked with Amos Vogel to rent films in '56.[*]

Was that film group associated with the University of Colorado or was it an independent group?

It was associated with the University of Colorado, and I know the professor who sponsored it, Forrest Williams, a professor of philosophy.[†] He was the sponsor of it and he worked with Gladney for a number of years from before I arrived until he went away in '57, I guess. Maybe it was '55 when I took up with Gladney, I don't know.

Did you not say a moment ago that you met Stan in a little house? Was that also the theater where they screened the films?

No, no, the little house in Denver was his own little house where he was renting, and he had that cat; he had just come home from the hospital where he had been having a severe asthma attack and so he spent some time in the hospital. He had just come home and we went to visit him, and that's partly why he looked so sickly. He was less sickly later on.

The occasion when he was teaching you to make films, can you describe that?

That was at the university and Gladney had set it up so that he could teach a class and run films. Well, I'm not sure if he was allowed to run films. I think he was really to talk and have us work on films, and particularly the sense of working on white leader and seeing what 24 frames made. But my cousin, Betsy, was with me there. She and I went together to Stan's class. We sat in the back row and we giggled. Stan was always so… It was always very important for him to look like he was great and we were whispering about "the Great Brakhage." But we were listening and learning and he was doing a good job inspiring us. I'm very sorry, the only thing I remember is the thing I did. And that's really a shame.

Had you seen any of Stan's films at this point?

---

[*] A refugee from Nazi Germany, Amos Vogel (1921–2012) founded the important New York screening club, Cinema 16 (1947–1963). He wrote the seminal account of progressive films, *Film as a Subversive Art* (1974). He co-founded the New York Film Festival in 1963, serving as its program director until 1968.

[†] Professor Forrest Williams (1924–2014) joined the philosophy department at the University of Colorado in 1952. He translated and published Sartre and Merleau-Ponty and co-edited the important anthology, *Marxism and Art: Writings in Aesthetics and Criticism* (1972).

No, I think that we saw them soon enough. Some of them, what was the name of the one up in Nevadaville?

Unglassed Windows...

Unglassed Windows Cast a Terrible Reflection. Yes, and others, I think, that we saw of his.

What did you make of his films when you first saw them?

Well, I just thought, "Well, that's something he made." And he did mention that Stan Phillips* had done the photography of all of them, and that he had this group of friends that he worked with.† I thought it was interesting that somebody all by himself would want to make films. These were psychodramas; he hadn't come to *Anticipation of the Night*, which really impressed me. But we hadn't come to that yet until after we were married.

Finally we had a field trip where we went and photographed the tree, maybe that's what we did. We photographed into the branches of a tree, and he was showing us how to run the camera. We were out on Mapleton Avenue; boy, I've even forgotten the streets in Boulder, that's really shocking. I swore I would remember that tree for the rest of my life, and I actually lost it because a lot of the trees are alike right along that area.

He and I stood under a tree and we had this kind of exchange. I knew he was going to call me up that evening. And then he didn't. He did feel strongly about it, he really needed a woman who had money, and I didn't really have money, although as P. Adams pointed out—finally, how many years later?—my parents bought a cabin for us up in the mountains, so his wishes for at least a dowry of some sort came true. He had just given up this woman in Denver who was quite wealthy. The problem was that he was invited to dinner and there were several forks and spoons and whatnot, and he had no idea which one to use. It was very troubling to him and I'm sure he used the wrong one, he started from the inside out or something. But he lost that one. He was not really presentable to the rich, I guess, he was too crazy. I don't know. My parents, of course, didn't like him either.

So we have you there together looking up at the tree. You feel Stan is going to call, but he doesn't.

---

* A high school friend of Brakhage's, Stan Phillips was one of the founders of Western Cine Motion Picture Laboratory, a film-processing lab in Boulder. Brakhage's personal relationship with him and with the lab's president, John Newell, facilitated many of the experimental procedures that were unavailable to his contemporaries.

† In Denver, Brakhage was part of a group of arts—especially drama—oriented young people initially formed in high school known as "the Gadflies." Notable members included Robert Benson, Yvonne Fair, Larry Jordan, Walter Newcomb, Stan Phillips, Morton Subotnick, and James Tenney. Some of them assisted him on his first films.

Yes. Yes. Then I go into a deep depression; weeks and I don't know how long go by, a great deal of time to my mind went by. It was certainly weeks and maybe it was months, and there was absolutely nothing in my life, absolutely nothing. My parents were silent. They tiptoed around, as a matter of fact, because I was depressed. What they should have done is turned on the fast music and let me dance or something. But I found myself going home up Boulder Canyon and Boulder Canyon has some cliffs along the way, and my eyes saw my hands turning the steering wheel towards the cliff, and my eyes told my brain to tell my hands to move the wheel. I was all in pieces and trying to communicate with myself. I did straighten the car, and I didn't go off the cliff, and I went home, "all shook up," speaking of Elvis. [*laughs*]

I wrote a letter to Stan, and I said, "I've got this problem. I don't know, I just seem to be terribly depressed and it's awful. Is there anything you can do to help?" He must have called me up. I think he called me up and said that he loved me. And I said, "I'll be right there." So I started visiting every day, and my parents thought that I was having lessons from the Great Brakhage that Betsy and I had been giggling about. But then one day I called up and said, "I am eloping with the Great Brakhage." [*laughs*] And "Oh dear, no! No! Are you sure?" They were upset.

So across the weekend, Angelo di Benedetto,* the artist, the sculptor, he lived up in Central City and he was close friends with the justice of the peace in the county of Gilpin. So we went up to Central City and got married, and I was wearing my Levis and an army shirt because that's what I had on. Nobody thought I was serious, but I was, I just didn't care about dress. We went up and got married there in that office, and we had three witnesses that were friends of Stans. Let's see, it would be…

Larry Jordan?

No, no, Larry wasn't there. Oh, yeah, I missed that: there was a meeting with Larry Jordan that I skipped over here.

Walt Newcomb?

It might've been Windy.† And it was probably Bobby Benson, Robert Benson, the actor, Shakespearean and et cetera, he was in *Blue Moses*.‡ And one other, probably Stan Phillips, I don't know. We had a little reception at Angelo's place in Central City, and he served us spaghetti and I don't know. There's a little film

---

* Angelo di Benedetto (1913–1992), abstract painter, sculptor, and graphic designer. He and his wife moved to Central City in 1947 and opened an art school there

† Walter "Windy" Newcomb, one of Brakhage's high-school friends, he appeared in *Desistfilm* (1954) and several other early Brakhage films.

‡ Robert Benson (b. 1934) became a successful actor and producer in Hollywood, known for films including *By Design* (1981) and *Emily of New Moon* (1998). As well as in *Blue Moses* (1962), he acted in several of Brakhage's early films including *Unglassed Windows Cast a Terrible Reflection* (1953), *The Extraordinary Child* (1954), and *Desistfilm*.

that Stan Phillips made in which Stan and I were toasting each other with the two glasses of, I think it might've been, champagne. Anyway, a spark jumped from one glass to the other, I think it was from mine to his, but it might've been from his to mine. It's on film, we were up against the fireplace. So it was just a normal occasion in the fireplace, but it happened to show up just right in it with our glasses in that little film by Stan Phillips. I don't know if it still exists, but I bet it does somewhere. It's probably in Stan's and my archive.

Can you say any more about the period between your sending the letter and your decision to elope?

Yeah. Well, that's when Larry* showed up and said he wanted to make a film of me. So we went to the football stadium and couldn't get in, of course. We were kind of slouching around the outside and he made a film of me there. And that film does exist. Shortly after that, he and Stan had a long discussion and Stan won and so Larry went to Petaluma, California; is that where he lives? Let's see, anything else in that time?

So you wrote a letter to Stan saying, you were depressed, and he called saying he loved you. Did you ask him why he loved you or how long he had loved you? Or if he did love you, why hadn't he contacted you?

No, I didn't do that. [*laughs*] I don't think he would've known. Well, I'm sure he would've found an answer that would've satisfied him. But I felt like he was just reaching out to me and saying, you know, "Come over, I'll see what I can do"... that he cared. We stood under the tree together, and then there was that electricity between us that I was talking about, and that was all.

Did you talk about that? Did he tell you that he'd felt the electricity as well?

Nope. He never did. I assumed he did. I mean, of course he did.

Approximately how long was it between the letter and the marriage?

I believe it was six weeks. I'm not sure whether it was between the letter... Yeah, I think it was between the letter and the elopement to Central City, which isn't that far away. But we also went and bought a rock, we couldn't buy a ring. We wanted to buy a ring so that I would have a ring on my finger when I came back. But we just bought a rock, and it said that the ring was being made; that was kind of silly. We went to dinner at my parents' house, and they put on kind of a formal

---

* Lawrence "Larry" Jordan (b. 1934) attended high school with Brakhage. They began making films around the same time and he appeared in Brakhage's *Unglassed Windows Cast a Terrible Reflection* and *Desistfilm*, while Brakhage appeared in his *The One Romantic Venture of Edward* (1956). Like Brakhage, he moved to San Francisco and met Robert Duncan; later he was one of the founding members of the Canyon Cinema Cooperative. The animated *Our Lady of the Sphere* (1969) is his best-known work.

dinner just for the four of us. My parents greeted my husband, they were trying to be friendly and open and nice. So was Stan, I guess, but it was, I don't know… They never really related to each other very much. His parents didn't approve of him, and I don't know what he felt about them. He felt they were all too prudey and he wanted to tease them with naked bodies and stuff.

After your marriage, did you live together in the little house in Denver?

We did, yeah. We lived there for a while, but as soon as we got married, he was talking about, "Let's go to New York City. I want to go to New York City." That sounded fine to me, and I guess we had my car; I don't remember what car we had. Anyway, we had a car and it was surely mine. He didn't drive much. He had bad eyes; that's kind of the funny thing about him. He had bad eyes, bad eyesight, and he had worn thick glasses as a boy. When he felt finally like he wanted to be a good-looking boy for the girls, he threw away his glasses and lost a lot of weight and gave up singing in a beautiful soprano voice. They were trying to teach him how to switch to becoming a tenor instead of a boy soprano. He was very slow at maturing. He got very upset with that because he really felt that he could sing better as a soprano than anything else. He was just horrified and stormed out of the singing building or the teacher's room, whatever that was, and never went back. He threw his glasses in the mud, and went stalking across the street with cars screeching, I assume, and survived that and lost weight.

So he'd thrown the glasses away before he met you?

Yeah.

Would you have any idea when he threw the glasses away?

Well, I would say that he might've been 16 or 17, in high school.

So it was '50 or '51, something like that.

Well, he was a few years older than me.

Stan was born in '33.

Might have been 1953, no, he would have been 20, wouldn't he?

Yeah.

Ha! Well, I don't know the dates on when he went up and had this tent theater in Central City. I don't know truly. But it wouldn't have been '52 or '53. I don't think I was folk dancing, least of all with Ron, until I was at least between my junior and senior year. That'd be '53 or '54 would be more like, I think it would be '54, because I think shortly after that, yes, I went to New York.

And the meeting with Stan in Denver took place in about 1956?

Well, let's call it '55. Give me a little time to go.

So it was a year or more after that first meeting in Denver before you were married?

No, no, no. We met when Gladney introduced me to him. The third meeting, you mean?

Right? Yeah.

The third meeting when Gladney introduced me to him must have been 1957.

OK.

The summer of 1957, and we got married in the end of December. December 27th.

OK. So there's a period of about four or five months between your being introduced to him by Gladney and your marriage to him.

Yeah. Yeah. December 27th, 1957.

Some would say that that was a fairly precipitous marriage.

Yeah.

Would you care to talk about what you saw in each other or what you saw in Stan that made you decide to marry him?

Well, one thing that I've thought about was that I was crying out for somebody to tell me what to do, and he would tell me what to do; I mean, it would be his pleasure to tell me what to do. He was saying, "Let's go to New York." And of course, that would have me driving and because I was a better driver than he was, or at least, I could see better at that time, so I could take care of a lot of things. As I said, I didn't bring a dowry, I didn't bring any money, I didn't have any income. But I had a car and I could drive. I wasn't good at cooking, but I was open to learning and I could wash dishes and clean house. So there I was. And also, while we were still in the little house on Marion Street in Denver, he said his famous line: "OK, now take off all your clothes. I want to make a film about us having sex." I said, "I'm a good girl, I am," and that kind of thing, and he said, "I'm an artist and artists have naked ladies." [*laughs*] "That's always the case, and so I need a naked lady." I think he threatened me, he said, "If you don't do it, I'll find another that will take her clothes off," although I don't remember any in his earlier films that did. But anyway, I took my clothes off and we made

Wedlock House: An Intercourse, which was made there in that little house on Marion Street.

Are you sure it was Marion Street in Denver?

It was South Marion Street in Denver. I believe that's the name. Sometimes when I go downtown or across town, I cross it.

So Wedlock House *was not made in Princeton?*

Wedlock House made in Princeton? No, it was made in Denver.

And that was the first film that you made with Stan?

As best I can remember.

Could we talk about Wedlock House?

I don't know. I can't remember it very well, and I didn't look at it. But I just remember that I was kind of relieved that there wasn't a whole lot of stuff. Everything was out of focus and soft focus and a lot of, I don't know, just kind of feeling about sex. I dunno. I did notice also that there was no sex in the act of making that film. There was no sexuality to it. It seemed like that was purely making a film. It was not a sexual act, that film?

Well, there are prolonged periods of sexual activity in the film. They were all shot in negative with a tripod.

Yeah, OK, OK. Well, maybe it was just me that was not open to it, but he was… Yeah, so I was doing what I was told, but it was not… I don't know.

Most of the filmographies indicate that Wedlock House *was not made till 1959.*

That's because they wanted to put it in Princeton. He probably didn't edit it until '59, but he photographed it in Marion Street.

So Stan persuaded you not only to take your clothes off, but also to become a filmmaker. He persuaded you to hold the camera and shoot. Do you want to talk about this? Because you became an expert photographer very quickly.

I was not an expert at running the camera, that's for sure. I had no technical ability, except I knew what button to push and where to look through and some adjustments to the lens and the distance, how close I had to get or far away or whatnot. But the first time that I said, "Give me the camera" was right after Myrrena was born, and I wanted to get Stan's face.

This is in Window Water Baby Moving?

Yes, in *Window Water Baby Moving*. I don't remember, maybe he told me to do some camera work in *Wedlock House*. I don't know. But I do remember taking the camera from him and photographing him, and that was my contribution. [*laughs*] Well, that was one of my contributions to *Window Water Baby Moving*.

I don't want to claim any prerogatives, but your photography in Wedlock House *is very good.*

Oh, is that right? Well.

Especially your photography of Stan. I don't know how much footage he threw away, but the footage that remains is very powerful imagery of Stan.

Well, that's good.

All in focus, all lit perfectly, and all revealing a great deal about Stan. Your photography is very expressive.

Thank you. Thank you. I really, really appreciate that. And yes, I have forgotten it, but I suppose if I saw it, I would remember it. But yeah, I am not surprised that I would do a good job, and he did appreciate that I was capable of running the camera in a good way.

So you don't remember whether he set the distance and chose the f-stops and things like that?

He probably did. Then he stayed that distance away, and so he did the acting and I photographed. I don't know how much credit you want to give to him and how much you want to give to me about those shots. But I think that's very good that you brought that up because I've forgotten it. What I forget, of course, is the most important stuff, but we worked together always. We worked as one and he was very aware of that and he mentioned it a zillion times. And so it was really a partnership. Of course, he led the dance.

I wasn't actually, in folk dancing, accustomed to being led exactly, although a lot of the folk dancing and the square dancing had to do with following, and I became a very good follower. I could feel which way I was to go and so on. And following is something that is a really creative act in a way, because you have to go into the partner and figure out where he is going to move to and how to move in relation to that. That transferred onto working with Stan with the camera, and I found it very enjoyable working with him and following him. It was usually an act of following, but I mean, Fred Astaire is certainly a great dancer, and Ginger Rogers is amazing that she can keep up with him. So that's what I get. But yeah, I had an eye. I still have an eye, even though I can't see very well, I have an eye.

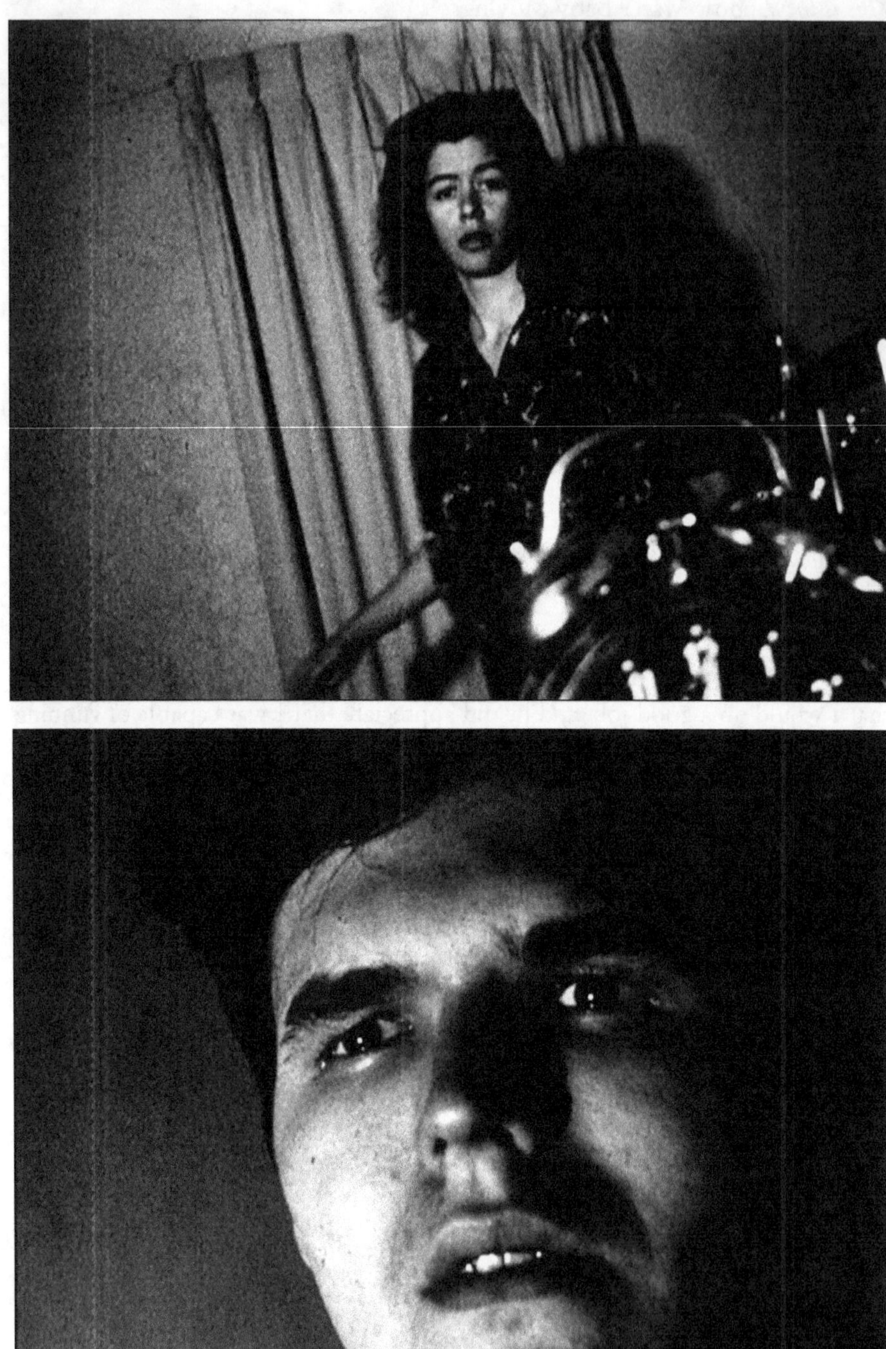

Jane and Stan in *Wedlock House: An Intercourse.*

Could I talk a little bit about Wedlock House *and see if you remember more?*

OK.

There are two kinds of material in the film. There's material of you and Stan making love, which is shot in negative with the camera, I assume, on a tripod.

Yes.

That begins the film, and then there are shots of the house, and I'll talk more about that. Then there's more lovemaking, then there's shots of more house, and then there's more lovemaking. Then there's a prolonged period when you and he are drinking coffee and smoking cigarettes and looking at each other. That's when most of the really first-rate photography of Stan appears. Before that, the shots are very short shots of the house, of the windows, of the curtains, of mirrors, which are in and out of black. It seems that you or Stan were holding a lamp, and that this light occasionally illuminated, but most often failed to illuminate, these rather furtive images that he took of you and that you took of him. You should look at it; it's a very good film.

Hang on. I didn't think it was. I'm glad and I will look at it, and I'm glad it's a good film. That's amazing. I am very pleased if you like my photography.

It's very impressive. But of course Stan had control of the editing, you didn't?

No, I didn't have control of the editing. I would comment once I got to know how to look at these tiny little pictures on the filmstrip and then to look at it through the… He had this viewer that was hand-run. It was, "Wait a minute, it goes like this." "OK." So I could see the film in this little square there in the middle. I would say, "That one shot is too long" or "It's a shock that you break it up." I would say things and he would either ignore me or make changes. He would look at it and see what I was talking about, and then he would maybe forget it or maybe fix it. So that was my influence on his editing, always, because I was interested in what we were doing.

Why were you interested in what you were doing?

Well, it was kind of the center of our life. We were living for the films. We were living for the Muse; we were servants of the Muse. And that was kind of like some of the wedding vows, I guess, that was that "I will serve the Muse with you; I will give everything we've got to the films." That was what he lived for.

I think you became an accomplished filmmaker very quickly. I've asked you several times about your interest in painting and arts and music, and you've never expressed a great deal of interest. But suddenly, you matured as a filmmaker so quickly.

I did express a passionate interest, I hope, in Rembrandt and his eyes looking at me, and I was looking back at him, and we were like conversing eye-to-eye in his paintings. Even if it was somebody else's eye, it was still his eye looking at me and I knew it.

That's so similar to Wedlock House's *prolonged period when you're just looking at each other and the camera goes back and forth. You were looking at him and him looking at you with your eyes both being quite prominent.*

There you go. Yeah. I'm just thrilled that you consider me a good filmmaker. Actually, when we divorced, he put into the divorce papers that I was not to make films. [*laughs*] I said, "I'm not the least interested in making films, so that's easy." But he was afraid that I would make films. And so I don't know, I guess he saw something that you saw, but I was not interested in making a film. I was working with him; and without him, I would want to do something more my style. I mean, film was his style, and I was with him. So that's what I was doing, working on his films. Then when we divorced, why then I was… Well, I had been picking up writing as he'd been drifting away from me, and then I went more deeply into writing, I guess. And that was kind of hard…

Anything else about Wedlock House?

Well, God, you're the one that knows the film more than I do, but I'm really, really pleased.

There were a couple of shots of an alarm clock. Do you remember that?

I remember that. I do remember that, yes. A couple of shots of a clock.

Are they just arbitrary or was there any thought going into placing the alarm clock in the film?

The film, of course, the alarm clock would be wake up, change, do something you have to do.

Great, OK. So you've moved straight away to the first film in which you were primarily involved, and we've scooted over Anticipation of the Night. *I wonder if you want to say anything about that.*

There were a lot of things about that. Yeah, he was still working on it. I think he didn't finish it when we were there, he finished it in Princeton perhaps. He had done all the shots and he was editing all that other stuff that's in the rest of the film, except for the last little bit, the Shadow Man.* I would look at it through the

---

* Photographed when Brakhage was in the grip of various psychosomatic illnesses, *Anticipation of the Night* (1958) was the pivotal film in the evolution of his mature art. Depressed virtually to the point of suicide, he projected what he saw as his impossible future as a night

little editing machine and it was good. Then he called up Bobby Benson—who was really a big strong guy, even though he was quite fat, he was still strong—to come and shoot the Shadow Man. I said, "I thought I was supposed to help you," and he said, "No, in this case it's got to be Bobby." I think it was because he was going to step off the chair with the rope around his neck and see if he got picked up. If I tried to pick him up, it might not work because he was kind of heavy for me to pick up. So when he was photographing from the chair and the Shadow Man was waving around on the ball, and then he handed the camera to Bobby and stepped off the chair. I don't know what Bobby did with the camera, but he grabbed Stan and put him back up on the chair and saved his life, I guess, because the rope was still around his neck. That was all told to me when they came home. Whether that was a true story, I couldn't say, but that was the one they told me.

So you weren't there for that?

No, I was not invited. I was crabby about that, but that's all right.

Were you present for any of the other shooting of Anticipation of the Night, *or was it all shot before you…*

It was all shot before we got together, I think mainly it was shot. He had this glass bowl with the rose in it and, I don't know, there were other things. I used to have the list pretty well memorized, and I could tell you what came next. I saw it quite a few times at that time. And I got that way with all the films. I could just rattle off all the shots, how long the thing was, all the information about it, and how much it cost to sell it. That was a lot of stuff. When we divorced, it was a lot of stuff to forget. Yesterday, I was going through the list of all the places we went in those first seven years of marriage, and we went to like about, I don't know, one every six months or something like that. We just kept moving and we kept going back to my parents' place as kind of a hub. We'd go back there, and they'd take care of us, and then we'd go off somewhere.

So I'm remembering them pretty well now. And I'm seeing that really going through this and actually also doing it last spring in that speech that I gave in LA which kind of started this all off, I guess.*

I feel like it's good for me to go over it and awaken things out of my long-forgotten marriage.

You were talking about the projected suicide at the end of Anticipation.

---

that "could only cast one shadow for me, could only form itself into one black shape, and that was the hanged man. That is the shadow seen on the wall at the end of *Anticipation of the Night*" (Stan Brakhage, *Metaphors on Vision*, ed. P. Adams Sitney [New York: Anthology Film Archives, 2017], p.99). He had planned to complete the film with a shot made while hanging himself and (according to Jane's account here) would have succeeded had it not been for Benson's intervention.

* Though I had met Jane earlier, the Filmforum event was the first time I had an extended conversation with her.

Yeah.

Stan often said that he was not really very interested in living at this time.

Right.

Weren't you a little apprehensive about marrying a person who seemed to be potentially suicidal?

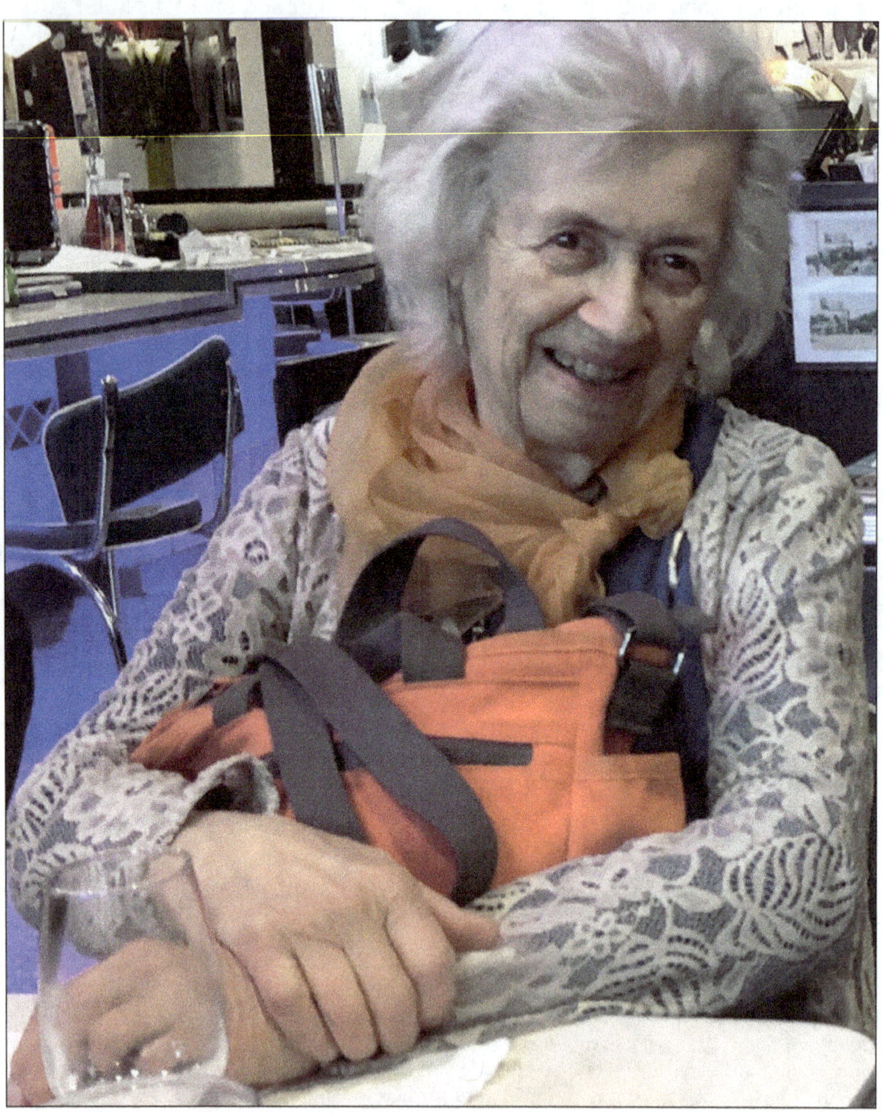

Jane Wodening Visits Los Angeles Filmforum, 2020.

I was also [suicidal]. I mean, if you remember the thing with the steering wheel and the cliff. Yeah, I was also, so I didn't mind that at all. It was just that we were both in a kind of a pickle, or two pickles. So I wasn't bothered. I wasn't looking for a solid future, I was looking for someone to be with.

Stan said about Wedlock House *that the two of you were both in pretty bad ways emotionally and didn't really know what was happening. But at the end of the film, there is a moment of hopefulness. Does that coincide with your recollection?*

I don't, as I say, remember the film, but I do feel that that would be a correct statement about that time. OK, we were both miserable and suicidal and whatnot. He was more consciously suicidal, it was all in my subconscious, and that occasion brought it to the surface in a way. But yeah, it was hope. I mean, we didn't want to kill ourselves anymore. We wanted to see how it was going to go.

And that making the film was something of a breakthrough through the despair. There was a little bit more hope after the film than perhaps there'd been before.

It may have been because of my work with the camera, I was joining him. I was joining him in this work and was doing a good job.

OK, you are married, living in the house in Marion Street. You've shot Wedlock House, *and soon after that you were off to New York. Do you remember that sequence?*

Yes. We drove off and went to New York. I don't remember the drive. We went back and forth so many times. I just remember little specks of this and that drive, and this one, I don't remember very well at all. We did end up at Willard Maas and Marie Menken's house, their shack on the roof. There was a penthouse, but it was really two shacks on a roof in Brooklyn Heights. That was where I remember being again and again in that visit and meeting people there with them. There was some big gathering that we went to, it was all the film people. There was Maya Deren up on the balcony, so I went up. I guess I had already had Myrrena at that time. She had expressed that she disapproved of the secrets of womankind being shown, something like that.* She was mad at him and so I went to meet her; I was all friendly, I reached out my hand to shake hands and she reached out her hand. [*deep breath in*] We didn't shake hands because we were both witches and didn't want to hurt each other, that kind of feeling.

OK, we'll come to that, but before we get there, we've got Cat's Cradle. *This was also completed in 1959, shot in Bennington. When did you first meet Carolee*

---

* Jane is confusing this first meeting with Deren with a later one. Myrrena was born a year later, in Princeton. Deren did object to *Window Water Baby Moving* when she first saw it. (PAS)

Schneemann and James Tenney?†*

We went there first. Is that right? We went to visit them first before we went to New York, I think that's right. We went there and spent a couple weeks, staying with them at Bennington. And Carolee was very helpful with my cooking. I was like, "How do you cook?" because I really didn't know. I was kept out of my mother's kitchen because I was in her way all the time if I went in there. So I didn't know at all how to cook, and Carolee helped me out a lot and got me onto health foods, of course, and whatnot. She was very, very into health foods.

Had you met them before you went to visit?

Yes, I believe so. I think they came to visit us [at Marion Street] and then they went to Vermont and got that house. We had a huge front yard because we were way in the back by the alley. Our house was like a shop or something, a tiny little house in the back of the whole property, and there was this long front yard that was not really anything except a barrier from the street.

And Carolee and James Tenney visited you there?

That's possible. And I remember there's a picture of them sprawled out on the lawn there or something.

Yes. Of the four of you.

Well, who would've taken the picture? I wonder? Maybe Bobby would've, Bobby Benson probably.

So that we've got you on this trip now, you're going to Vermont in 1959, and you arrived there in their cottage in Vermont.

Wait a minute, '59—no, we didn't go in '59. It was three days before 1958 happened that we got married and we stayed in Denver for I don't know how long after that. Not long, a month or two. And then we drove to Bennington in '58, not '59. You're looking at when the film is done, and that's never when it was made. It was always photographed before, and it could be years; for instance, *Creation* was made like twenty years after it was photographed. He was thinking, "Oh, I don't know what I'm ever going to do with that footage." Because he was

---

* Carolee Schneemann (1939–2019), painter and dancer who made great innovations in body and performance art. Featuring sexually explicit footage of her and her husband, James Tenney, her film *Fuses* (1967) was repressed for many years. She claimed to have made it in response to what she saw as Brakhage's misrepresentation of her relationship with Tenney in *Cat's Cradle*.
† James Tenney (1934–2006), composer and pianist. A high school friend of Brakhage's, he composed the music for several of his early films and also for Schneemann's film, *Viet-Flakes* (1967).

frugal and because he was broke all the time, he wanted to use every scrap of film. Other people had a different viewpoint on the footage; they'd throw it away and take what their idea was. But he had to follow what he had because that was a whole lot cheaper than trying to make more film to follow his own idea.

So '58, you're going to Vermont to stay with Carolee and James for a couple of weeks. Do you remember the film Cat's Cradle *that you made there?*

I remember the film, and I remember that the cat was in heat the whole time, which is totally unnatural for the cat to continue being in heat. I don't know if she got pregnant or not. Maybe she didn't get pregnant, and so she was maintaining the heat, I don't know. But anyway, I think there were two couples and there was a sense of sexuality gone mad amongst the four of us. We did not do anything about it, obviously, but the cat was expressing it, and there was all this, as I was saying, witchy feelings amongst us. Where were the powers moving and what was being exchanged?

Stan wrote, "Sexual witchcraft involving two couples and a medium, the cat."

Yeah, the cat was just going on big in heat. My feeling is, well, probably Stan was witching the cat to stay in heat so that he could make a good film about sexuality amongst four people. But I don't know. I mean, we just stayed, obviously, two couples.

Did you all get along or did you fight and argue?

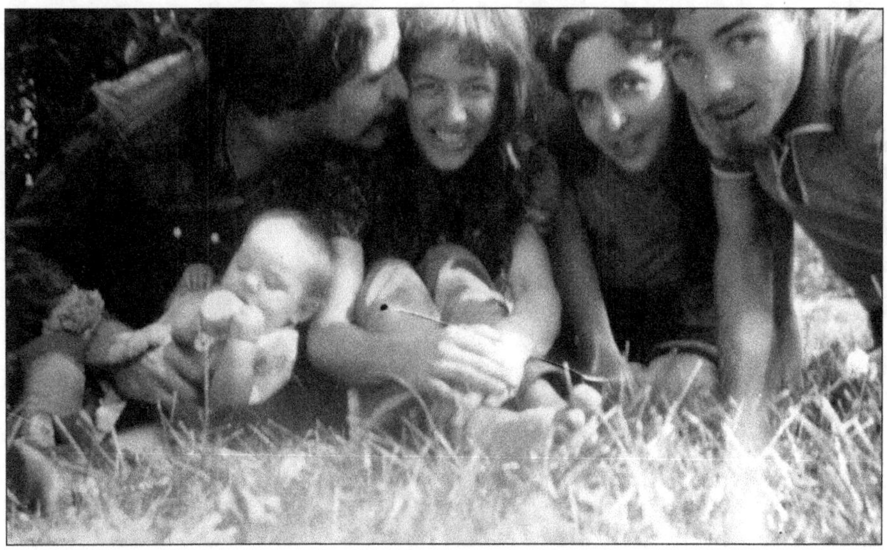

Stan, baby Myrrena, Jane, Carolee Schneemann, and Jim Tenney, Illinois.

We pretty much got along, except that we're not socially… I don't know. They were not all that polite. I would burst out with something that came to my mind about one of Carolee's paintings or whatnot. Then she made a painting of me, of course. That's still somewhere, I don't know who owns it now. But for a long time somebody owned it and had it behind the couch so that nobody could see that I was naked.

Were you reluctant to be naked for the painting?

I was naked for the painting, yes.

Were you reluctant?

No. I had accepted the burden of stripping for artists and so I stripped for Carolee and sat there naked and pregnant, and she was interested in the pregnancy.

Did you like the painting?

I think it's good. I think it's good. I wouldn't have it on my wall, but I think it's a good painting.

Do you recall in the film, there are images of you, of Stan, of Carolee, and of James. I assume that Stan shot all the footage of you and James, and you shot the footage of him.

Probably.

You don't recall shooting Carolee or shooting James?

I don't think so. Do call him Jim, will you for me? Call him Jim, for my sake.

OK—Jim. And the photography of you in this film by Stan is very different from the photography in Wedlock House. *In this film, you are so beautiful, you're smiling and there's a rosy glow that comes whenever you're on screen. You're just totally captivating.*

Well, there's a color film.

Yeah. But in your photography, Stan is much more severe; he's smoking, he looks miserable, he looks kind of aggressive.

I remember, yes, he was wanting to show irritation there, I don't know. I remember the visit pleasantly. I liked Jim and Carolee, each one, and they're very different people. And Stan was making a film, and he was acting, and I don't know if he was that good of an actor. But of course he was trying to say something there and make a dramatic scene.

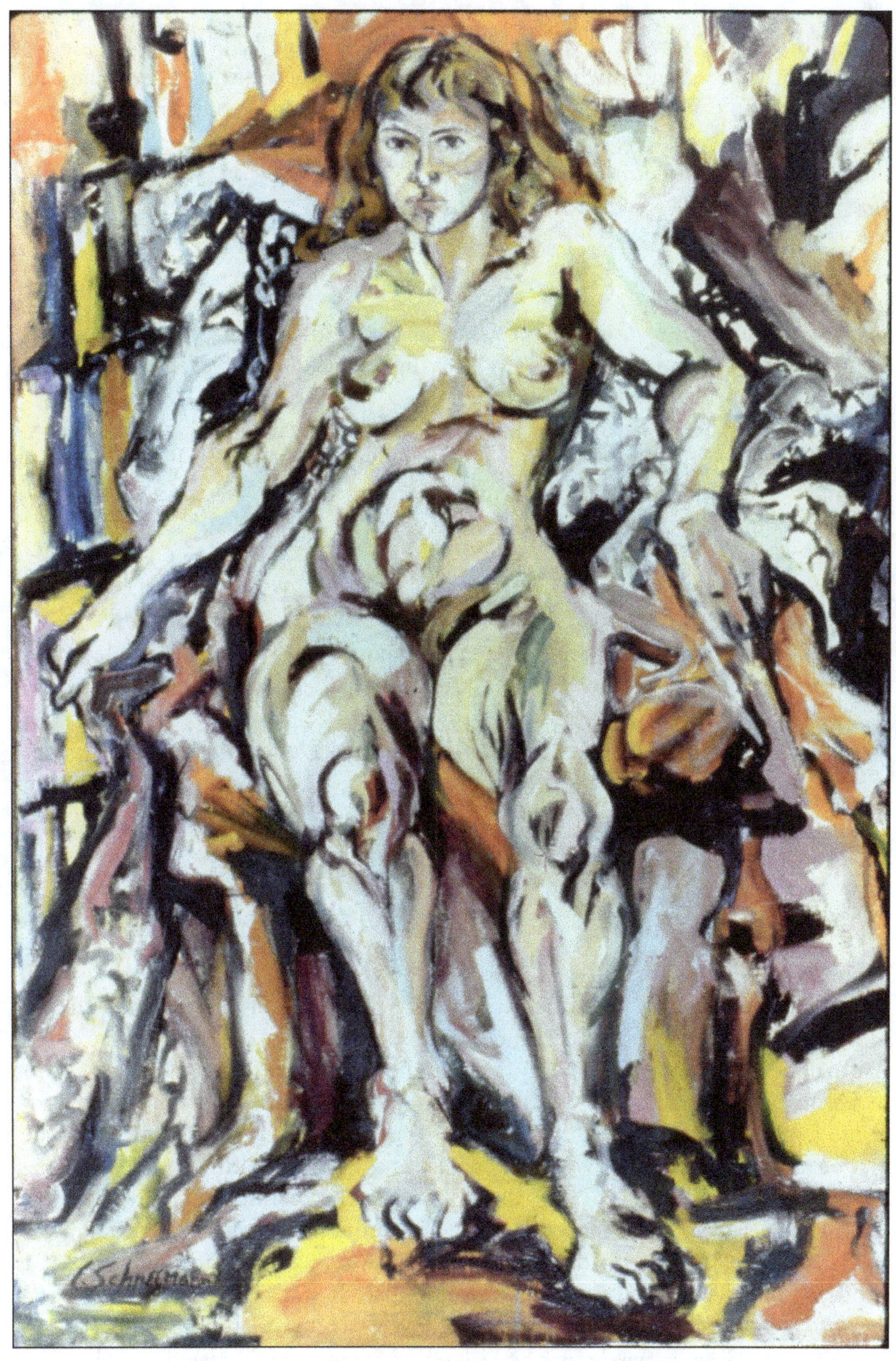

Portrait of Jane Brakhage, Carolee Schneemann, oil, 1958.

I'm surprised by how little there is of Carolee in it.

Well, I don't know what relationship Stan and Carolee had before we met, or before Jim came along.[*] I don't know. She was quite a beautiful woman, and maybe he didn't want me to compete with her or that sense of competition.

You are definitely the star of this film. There's no doubt about it that you are just glowing throughout. You should look at that one also.

Great. [*laughs*]

So your recollection of the sequence is Wedlock House, Cat's Cradle, *and then* Sirius, *and then* Window Water Baby Moving. *That's the correct sequence, right?*

I'm not sure where *Sirius* came in.[†] He died in January, or was it February? [*counts*] January, February, March, February. Well, it was either January or February. And Myrrena was born in November. So yes, *Window Water Baby Moving* would be before *Sirius Remembered*.

And November 1958 is when it was shot?

Yeah, '58, eleven months after we were married. We were married in December of '57 and had our first baby in November '58.

Window Water Baby Moving. *Do we have time? Do you want to talk about that? I'd love to if you've still got enough energy?*

I have energy if you have time.

Yes.

Yeah. It was so nice that we found Dr. Rose. He was a very nice guy. He was excited to be part of a film, and he was all go. Stan was worried that he wouldn't be allowed to be there, and Dr. Rose was totally open to it and excited. And then when I started having false labor, he'd come over and it was a lot of trouble. It was like a few miles from his office, and he'd come and look at me and he'd say, "False labor." He'd go away, and I think I did it twice or maybe three times so that when the actual labor came, Stan was saying, "Well, it's probably false labor." "No!" I said, "This is the real thing" because I could feel the difference, and finally I persuaded him and he called. The doctor was at the football game and had to be paged. Anyway, we were upstairs, there was another family that lived below us in the house. It was a two-family duplex so

---

[*] Brakhage met Schneemann through his high school friend, James Tenney. There could have been no previous relationship with her. (PAS)

[†] Sirius was their pet dog. After his death, his decomposing body became the subject of the film, *Sirius Remembered* (1959).

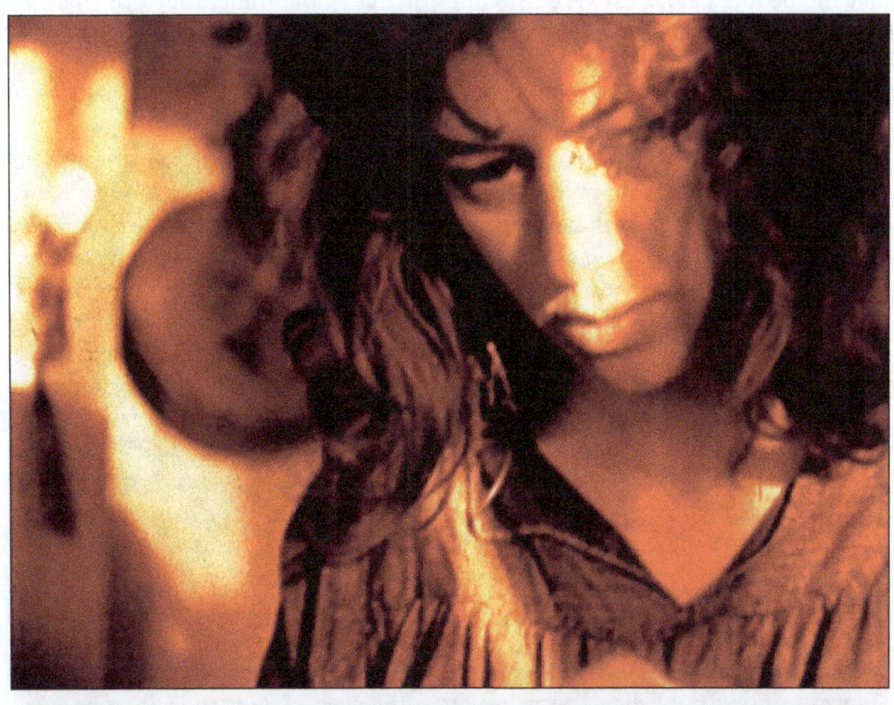

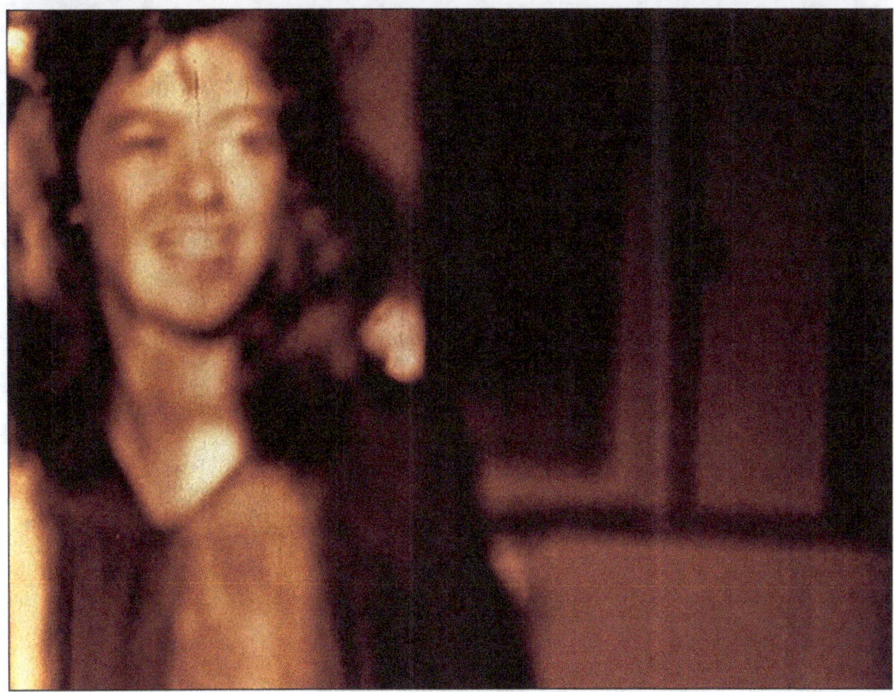

Jane in *Cat's Cradle*.

that the people below us were listening for the whole thing, they got the film in sound. They were worried and everything, but they had heard the official-looking steps going up and down the steps, so that was pretty fun. We heard about it afterwards; they were not friendly to us, but they did tell us that that it was a big deal for them.

It was a very happy thing, a happy occasion for both of us, as I think you can see in our faces. Yeah, I worked hard and did an excellent job having a baby. And I was just talking with her yesterday on the phone, she's 61 years old now, you know, going on 62. I was telling her, "One thing about you is you've always been determined and you do what you want to do, by God." I don't know if there was one shot when she was just emerging from the womb and kind of jumping out, and you can see just her upper arms moving like this. He had seen that she was crawling out on her fists, and he thought, "This is weird, this is symbolic, nobody's going to believe it." So he went in closer to cut off most of her arms, but she was crawling out of the womb. That's something that I've told her, "You just go on doing that. Whatever you want to do, you do that. You go, you do it." And so she's pleased with being there, the star of that film. I wrote a little story about it for P. Adams Sitney in his, what was the name of his magazine? *Film…*

Culture.[*]

Yeah, *Film Culture*. Yeah. So that was my first piece of writing that was published. He was my first publisher. It was heavily influenced by Gertrude Stein because we had been reading quite a lot of Gertrude Stein. We were also reading the entire *Remembrance of Things Past* by Marcel Proust. Stan was reading it to me. It took about a year and a half to finish that, but we were also looking at some Gertrude Stein in the meantime and getting involved with her and her ways of looking at things, in her rhythms. I liked her, she had kind of a girlish silliness that I found amusing so I had a lot of Gertrude Stein in that story.

Let's see, the doctor was very pleased with everything. Everything came out fine. There was no problem at all. I had lots of milk.

Do you recall anything of the discussion as to whether or not the birth should have been filmed? Did you decide that? Did Stan decide that?

Well, I think he said, "I'd like to film the birth," and I said, "Sure," because I had taken my clothes off. I mean, that was like a big thing that I did, you know, to present myself as part of the film work. From then on, I kept finding myself taking my clothes off. It's given me a little trouble and especially in ham radio. They had a weird idea about me as a porn actress.

Stan said that you hated hospitals and that's why you wanted to have the birth at home.

---

[*] Jane's essay, "The Birth Film," was published in *Film Culture*, 31 (Winter, 1963–64); it is reprinted below in Appendix 3.

Yeah, I do hate hospitals, I still do, and I wanted to try to do that. We achieved it with most of the films; all but with [our son] Rarc. With Rarc, our doctor was away so I had to use another doctor. We had to go to a hospital. Stan said, "Can I bring along my camera?" "Yes." "Can I bring along a tape recorder to play music?" "Yes." "Just you have to be at the hospital, that's all."

How did you find Dr. Rose?

I think we looked in the telephone book. We liked his name.

And then just called him up and asked him if he'd be willing to…

Yes, I think Stan called him and said, "My wife is about to have a baby. The only thing is that I really have to make a film. Can we do this at home?" Dr. Rose seemed to express that this was a dream come true, that he wanted to be privy to such a film and there it was.

Did he like the film?

I think so, I think he loved it. I think he had decided to love it before he looked at it. [*laughs*]

It was controversial, not only with Maya Deren. But many people found it profound.

I caused somebody to faint. People are somehow faint about birth; it's a trauma to them. I don't know why, but I felt good about it; Myrrena felt good about it; Stan felt good about it; Dr. Rose did; the nurses did. Yes, there were people that were opposed and horrified who thought that I should be ashamed.

You're in Princeton because Stan had found work there? Or did you go to Princeton, then he found work?

We were looking for work when we went from Jim and Carolee's place to New York. He was looking for a job and somehow somebody found there was a film company in Princeton that made TV commercials that was called On Film.* He was hired as an editor or something, but he very soon became what they called a Wild Man—that is, he would present a technique to do in an ad. The ad has to be quick and it has to grab people really quick. He invented the slow fade and he invented the quick cutting that TV commercials are still using even today, and a bunch of other things that he introduced there at On Film. He was very useful to the whole commercial community and then he went away and I guess

---

* On Film Inc. was a film production company known for its innovative creative productions and advertisements and also for its collectivist politics. Other filmmakers associated with the company include Willard van Dyke, Len Lye, Stan Vanderbeek, and Weegee.

that's all they needed. He did some other commercial work but none of it for commercials.

How long did you live in Princeton?

Six or eight months, I guess. Then we went to New York. Months passed, it would have been six months at least and then we came across country in the spring. We had acquired a cradle, which we carried in the back of a station wagon. I guess we had acquired the Brown Dog. If you want to leave Princeton now, I'm ready to go.

Shall we stop here?

It just seems like it's very short when we talk. So we didn't get very far.

We covered three massively important films.

Well, yes. OK, that's a way to look at it. I guess *Sirius Remembered* wasn't massively important.

It's very important, but it's not on the Criterion discs…

We could start with *Sirius*. OK, See ya!

Four

2021 February 2. Walks in the woods with Myrrena; Jim Davis; *Sirius Remembered*; return to Colorado; Silver Spruce; Crystal born; *Mothlight*; *Dog Star Man*; George Gamow; *The Dead*.

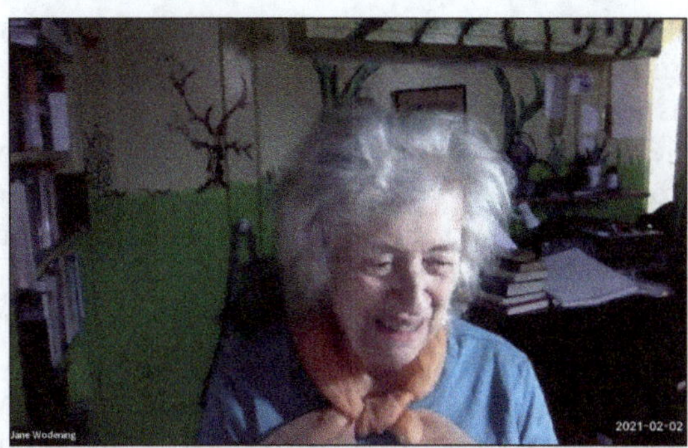

What does this say? This meeting is being recorded. Continue. OK.

I think we're going. OK, so you're reasonably well?

Reasonably well? Yes, and I have an appointment for a COVID shot.

Great! We left you last time in November '58 with the birth of Myrrena and the completion of Window Water Baby Moving. *I had a couple more questions about that if I may.*

Oh, sure.

How did you come across the name Myrrena?

All the names are Stan's doing. She was so vigorous in the womb, she was always kicking madly, and violently, and he could feel that sometimes. He was very impressed with her dancing and we started with "Ballerina," but that was just the beginning. And then there was "Myrrh." Now what he felt about myrrh, I don't know, but it was I guess a gift, a gift to the spirit or something like that. And so it's spelled with a remnant of Myrrh and adding ballerina.

He fabricated it?

It was handmade.

Could you give me some idea about the dailiness of your life in Princeton. Did you get up and fix breakfast for Stan and things like that? What did you do while he was at work?

I couldn't take a walk. I think I was feeding him breakfast, whether I made him a lunch... Probably he wanted to go and have a hamburger or something. He had developed his taste for food as a single child groping in the cupboard for something to eat or for some money to buy a hamburger or some candy. He loved pork and beans and he loved spaghetti and meatballs in the can. I think my childhood preferences were peanut butter sandwiches and things like that. But Carolee had taught me a few things about food, and I was taking that quite seriously. I was trying to cook with some sense of interest in whole grains and well-balanced meals and stuff. I think I gave him eggs and toast, and the toast would be like whole grain toast, so he went off with some kind of breakfast in him anyway and drove to Princeton where he had this job, and that was not far.

What I did in the daytime? What did I do? I had a baby. I could, of course, take the baby in a sling or something and go for a walk in the woods. We had a woods, a real woods, right behind the house, and it had a wild pig in it. A pig had gotten loose and had moved into the woods and was seldom seen, he kept away from people. It was a really nice little woods to go into and walk around a little bit. It wasn't that big, two blocks square or maybe four, I don't know. I got into crafts early on and I was starting to crochet at that time. I may have been reading books, although at that time it was important to note, as I said, that Stan was reading me the entire *Remembrance of Things Past* by Marcel Proust. Every evening he'd read a little section, and I remember it was about 800 pages in when he read, "You may call me Marcel," and I almost fainted. It was so thrilling, but I mean, that was a reward for reading that far, I'm sure.

And you had Sirius when you went to walk in the woods.

Yeah, I would take Sirius and the baby and we would go for a little walk in the woods. I wouldn't go far, but just to roam around in the woods helps me a lot, to get a hunk of nature.

Did you ever go to the movies? There must have been cinemas in Princeton.

There were movies, and I'm sure we went to them. Stan really liked... But no, I think we didn't go because Stan didn't want to admit that he really liked movies. He was really enamored of movies, but he didn't really admit it until, I think, some years later. I'll try to think when I can feel like it was part of our life. There was a man who lived in Princeton whom we did visit sometimes, not a lot, but sometimes. He was Jim Davis,* a filmmaker, and he was kind of elderly. He lived in an apartment upstairs on the second floor, and he couldn't come down.

---

* Jim Davis (1901–1974), painter and member of Princeton University's art department. Beginning in the mid-1940s, his more than two dozen films were largely abstract manipulations of refracted light. Brakhage was especially engaged by his *Death and Transfiguration* (1961).

I guess we would ring a bell by his box or something, push a button by his box, and then he would come to the window and toss a key down to us, and then we would go in and give him back his key. He was diabetic and was not allowed to have sherry, but he loved sherry more than anything. So he would feed us sherry and neither one of us got a desire to go on drinking sherry after that. But it was an elegant thing to do to go to visit Jim Davis and drink sherry.

He was a very nice gentleman to visit. It made a big difference in our sense of where we lived. Also the fact that Einstein had died just a few years before then, and the whole town was still thinking about him a lot. But I didn't go to town hardly at all. We would just drive to town, we had Finnegan at that time. Finnegan was a Willys station wagon, so it was kind of like a Jeep with a big backend, big space for I don't know what. That's what we had to drive and we had a gas-station man, a mechanic, and we would take Finnegan. I think we called him Finnegan because he kept dying—the car not the mechanic—the mechanic was Mr. Schwing. But the car kept dying and coming alive again and only Mr. Schwing could make it come alive so that was a problem. Several times he would come to our house and start the car so that Stan could go to work. Down the street was an apple orchard, the most delicious apples: Carson Road or Carter Road Apples, they were called then. I think they've changed their name, but evidently they don't travel well, so they're sold locally and known locally only. So I don't know. What else do you want to know?

Did Stan show his films to Jim Davis?

Yes. They looked at each other's films. We looked at Jim Davis's films and he looked at [Stan's]. I think there was a projector. We couldn't go anywhere, we couldn't see him anywhere but at his apartment, because coming down the steps and then going back up was a big deal for him.

Stan admired Jim Davis's films.

Yes, he did. And he admired Jim Davis too. Jim Davis was an elegant gentleman, and so it was so nice to be visiting an elegant gentleman with a baby. I guess we could leave the dog behind. So they looked at films together, they looked at each other's films and admired each other's films. It was a very pleasant relationship, but it was two different worlds meeting, and it was always like, "OK, how do you behave?" I didn't know at all how to behave. I just more or less kept quiet and kept my eyes and ears open and drank the sherry. It might've been the first alcohol I had ever had, I don't know. Goodness.

Did Stan ever talk about his days at work when he came home?

Not really, not much. But I did talk about that in last week's thing, about how he was admired: "What can we do with this incredible person that has these wild ideas?" He was a wild man, that's what they're called, the people that think up new ways of advertising. And he fed the business for many decades to come with his fast cutting and so on.

So Sirius died after Myrrena was born?

Yes. In January, I had this thing got into my head, "January mort." I was thinking, "Oh 'mort'—that's French for death." That was after Myrrena was born, and so I was thinking, "Well, who's going to die? I wonder? Could be anybody, but somebody will die in January." And sure enough, it was the dog, he got hit by a car. It was cold, the ground was frozen solid, and there was no way we could bury him, so we laid him on the top of the ground up there in the forest. Then Stan made *Sirius Remembered*, watching him rot and by spring, of course, we left. Neither one of us went to look for the bones years later. *Sirius* was a fine dog, but he was nervous, he was nervous and jittery. We got another dog, the Brown Dog. Brown Dog was our next dog, but he didn't stay with us very long.

Sirius Remembered *is on YouTube. By the way, did you look at* Wedlock House?

I'm very sorry, I was going to, and I didn't, and I'll try again this week.

I so much want you to see your photography.

Thank you.

Anyway, so Sirius Remembered *is on YouTube, so I watched it again since I spoke to you last. There are a dozen or so closeups on Sirius' eyes that reminded me of the exchanges of looks you first mentioned in Rembrandt and that are so important in* Cat's Cradle *and in* Wedlock House. *There are several of them in which his eye is very close up. His eye is very large.*

Yes, I have a memory of that. Yes, yes.

I assume you watched Stan editing the film.

Sometimes I didn't, quite often I wouldn't, I'd just not bother him. He would just go ahead and do it. No, I was not hovering over his editing that much. I mean, I would tell him and he would show it to me, and then I'd say this and that and the other, and then I'd go away and do the dishes or feed the baby or whatever. He would do with it as he chose, whatever he did was his business.

So that occupied the winter and the early spring of 1959. Then, you say some-where, that six months after Myrrena was born, you left Princeton.

Yeah, that would've been what, May? Something like that. She just wanted to sit up, and so she was feeling a little good about that.

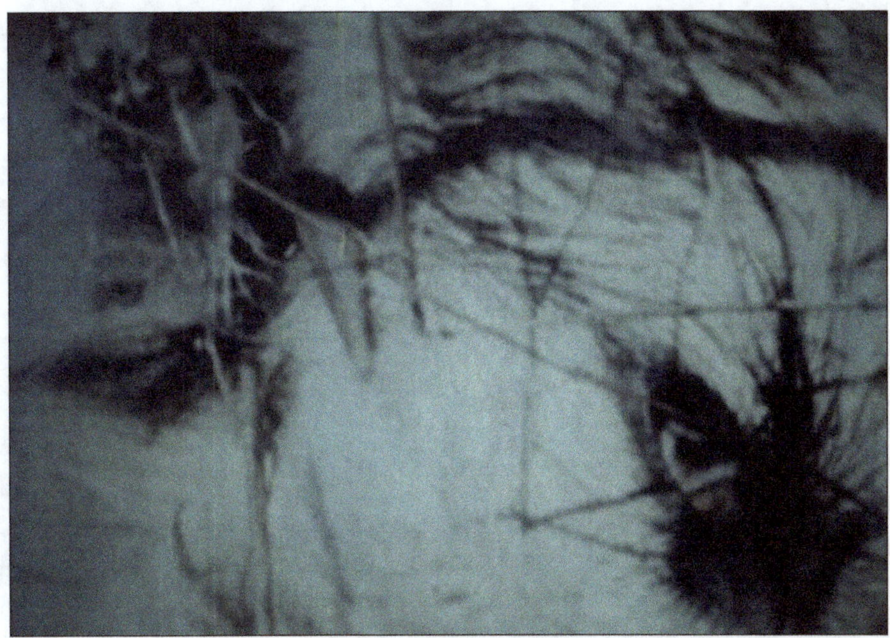

Sirius Remembered.

Do you recall why you left Princeton?

It may be that Stan was getting crabby at work. I wouldn't be surprised that he just got tired of working for them. And we had some money now, and he wanted to get away from 'em. They were commercial people, and so they were in a different world too. They were not in his world, but not in a good way. Jim Davis was, he was in a different world in a good way. So we left, went back to Colorado. We stopped in Illinois to visit my aunt Dor, and that was kind of an interesting occasion.

Her husband, Uncle Hap, had died, and so she was living alone in a house there. I can't remember where, somewhere in La Grange, Illinois or something like that. She loved to paint, she loved art. She just loved to paint. She painted big canvases of things that she loved, some landscapes and some people and whatnot. She did rather well, but not in a way that would be really important or anything. But she could spot an artist when she saw one, and she just thought Stan was just the most amazing, wonderful person. She was very welcoming and so we stayed there. Then the next day, I guess, the Brown Dog bit the neighbor's child. So we were told that we had to stay for a number of days, I think it was five days. We were planning to leave the next day, but whatever length of time it was to see if Brown Dog got sick with rabies. If he had rabies, then they would have to put the child through a routine of shots in the stomach and really an appalling thing. Well, of course, we'd have to kill the Brown Dog. And so we stayed and the child was fine, and we finally left. But we got several good days with Aunt Dor, and that was just delightful. She was a grand hostess as well. Everything was beautiful around her. At the same time, she had a—what do you call it?—a suitor who was a still-photographer of some merit. I know I wrote it down somewhere, his name, but it doesn't come to mind right now. He took some pictures of us, and they're stunning pictures of us at that time with the baby out on the lawn mainly. And geez, it's just on the tip of my tongue.

Do those photos still exist?

Some of them, yeah, they do, they're around. There's some in the scrapbooks over there in Yale,* and I think I might have one or something here in my little scrapbook. He came over one day and did some pictures, so that was great.

So then you got back in Finnegan and continued towards Colorado.

That's right. We got it started and we went just ourselves and the baby and the dog in the back, baby in the cradle. Actually, we had found an antique cradle, which I think Neowyn has now, she had the first baby.

When you went back, you went to stay with your parents?

First, we went to Silver Spruce, that would be in the spring. I don't know why. I think my parents went on a trip and left us with the house over the summer. Stan was starting to grow his hair, he just was growing his hair for a film. To anybody that asked, he said he was going to play Jesus in a movie or something. We were staying at Silver Spruce, we had that house. That summer, a really nice couple came and moved into Silver Spruce, and they had a little baby. Wait a minute, no… Crystal… I'm sorry, the Willoughbys haven't shown up yet. We'll have to go back a notch, we have to go back to Crystal being born in Silver Spruce and that wasn't until the following February. 16th February of 1960, Crystal was born. Yes, she was born in Silver Spruce. We were still there because when my parents went down and were trying to teach Navajo kids, I may have mentioned that my father was very happily teaching English to Navajo tubercular men that were in the sanitarium, and things like math and history and stuff of our culture. They seemed to like it so he was encouraged, and they went down and taught Navajo children, except that they had kind of a miserable year because Navajo children didn't come to school and because they were being taught American civilization. They were being taught our ways and that was trying to erase their

---

* Using material collected since 1958, in the early to mid-1960s, Jane made three scrapbooks consisting of collages of letters to her, Stan, and their family from other artists (many of them mentioned below, including Kenneth Anger, Wallace Berman, Robert Creeley, Guy Davenport, Ed Dorn, Robert Duncan, Robert Kelly, Michael McClure, and Jonas Mekas), photographs, newspaper clippings, leaves and flowers, fragmentary strips of Brakhage's films, and other miscellanea. The original volumes are now kept in the Beinecke Rare Book and Manuscript Library at Yale University. Digital copies may be found through the Yale Library catalogue. Facsimile reproductions of thirty-three pages were published by Granary Books in New York in 2021 as *Selections from the Jane Wodening and Stan Brakhage Scrapbooks, 1962–1966.*

ways, and that was not something anybody wanted. But we didn't know that until they came back all discouraged and miserable. But we were there in the house for better part of a year, I guess. And that was some of *Dog Star Man*, and *Mothlight*. Also Stan had a job, I think it was that time, working for the State of Colorado doing [films of] some historical legends, *Colorado Legends*, it was called. And there were maybe three or four of them that he did, and there were more that he could have done, but then he got tired of that and moved on, of course.*

Those were documentary films?

Well, they're not really documentary films because they're legends. Somebody, I think, more or less told him what to do and I think it was a silent; it wasn't that people would talk, but that there would be pictures of people, places and Colorado things like mountains. One of them I remember was about some early Spanish monastery that was here somewhere in Southern Colorado, I guess, so I had to make a… well, what did they wear? I mean, it is a robe. Anyway, a robe with a hood out of burlap. And Stan would wear it, and I would photograph him wearing that. But when he put it on, I screamed. I don't know why, but he was very impressed that I would scream at him. And it was like he was a monster. It was a noteworthy moment.

I'm imagining him in this burlap robe with his long hair.

Well, yeah. Yes, I think his hair was still long. We were still photographing [*Dog Star Man*], going up the hill behind the house there. There's a lot of shots of him going up the mountain, and I did handle quite a few of those. Then, if you remember, he got to the top, and I think there was a white tree up there, which is very proper—there should be a white tree at the top of every spiritual effort, I think. That was where we did most of that. Crystal was born in *Dog Star Man*. She's in there, Part Two, I think it is. It's kind of small part she plays. But anyway, she's happy to be part of *Dog Star Man*.

Did Stan grow his hair for Dog Star Man? *He told people it was because he had to play Jesus, but what was the real reason why he grew his hair?*

Well, I liked long hair. [*laughs*] But he was thinking about doing some film; he would be the actor and he would have long hair, and he would be therefore some kind of spiritual person doing some spiritual effort. It was kind of mulling in his head. I don't know how visual it was in his head at that time, or how maybe it was literary, but he knew he had to have long hair.

---

* Actually there were two, *Colorado Legends* (1961) and *The Ballad of the Colorado Ute* (1961). Stan Phillips, Brakhage's high school friend and frequent collaborator, produced the two Colorado legends films; in different filmographies he is credited for direction, photography or production. (PAS)

That was way before long hair became fashionable in the '60s.

It was hideously, hideously, unfashionable, it was just outrageously unfashionable. And he enjoyed that.

I could imagine him being attacked by people in Colorado for having long hair.

Well, no, we had the old West. In the old West, there were people with long hair, and we had that to remember. I mean, some of the great old westerners were long haired, and who wasn't in those days?

Of course. So let me get this clear. Around May '59 you returned to live in your parents' house in Silver Spruce. They've gone to teach the Navajo, and you stay there together with Myrrena. In February 1960, Crystal is born. At this time, Stan had already, vaguely at least, conceptualized Dog Star Man, *and you were both shooting some of the mountain footage in the mountain behind your parents' house in Silver Spruce.*

We had this Arriflex that we were borrowing. It's a kind of camera, and it's a kind that really likes to live on a tripod, we were doing some things on the tripod. It was just such a quality camera that Stan liked to use it if he could, even though he didn't like the tripod much. But he got to where he was using it with some assurance. I can't remember what all he did with it, but he did take it outside, but we couldn't take it up the mountain, I don't think. Maybe we did, yes, we took it up the mountain. He set it up and then he would come climbing up towards the Arriflex on the tripod.

That reminds me of something I wanted to ask about your photography of him. Did you look at the film frames I emailed to you last night?

I did. I did.

I have to say how impressed I was with the photography. It's fabulous imagery. But I was struck by the difference between Stan flailing away in the snow and falling over and the absolute stability of the camera person. That was you with the Arriflex on a tripod in the snow.

That was the stability of the tripod. Not so much me, at least I didn't shake the camera at all. Of course, Stan is famous for his shaky camera, so maybe what you like is a still camera, and that's me with a tripod.

You are pretty sure that all the mountain scenes in Dog Star Man *were shot with the Arriflex, and he didn't have a handheld Bolex up there as well for some of them?*

It's up to if they were shaking or if they were still, that's all I can say. You can tell.

But do you recall whether you and Stan possessed a Bolex at that time?

Yeah, we had a Bolex that was our camera,* but the Arriflex was borrowed, and I can't remember from whom, the university, I think, or from the State of Colorado perhaps. Yeah, it was borrowed for the *Colorado Legends* films, I'm sure. But they were kind enough to let us keep it for a while and work as much as we needed with it on *Dog Star Man.*

The Colorado Legends *people loaned you the Arriflex?*

I'm not sure about that, but it seems reasonable. I can't think who else would.

Can you remember anything about your conversations during the gestation of Dog Star Man, *when Stan was coming to think about it? Or do you know to what degree it was conceptualized before he began shooting or how the whole thing came about?*

Well, I think again, he got pictures and that was the world that he worked with, so that he didn't have a tremendous concept that was all worked out with it, he didn't have an outline planned, but he had a legend in his head that he was building, and it was involved with a white tree. It was really important that there be a white tree and that he would climb towards it. And so he would have to climb the mountain, which wasn't that big of a mountain really behind the house. I knew it well, it was the one that I had wandered on for years living there.

So in some sense, Stan was making a Colorado Legend *of his own.*

Yes. He was making one that was not necessarily Colorado, but a legend made in Colorado. Yes, of climbing the mountain to the top to the white tree. Of course, the white tree is supposed to be alive, but this one was of course dead because we don't have at that altitude any aspens or birch or whatever that I can think of, at least there wasn't on that mound.

Somewhere in the literature it says that when you and Stan were living with your parents, Stan felt a little bit distressed because he had really no way of contributing to the house. So your parents told him to gather and chop wood, and that was part of the origin of Dog Star Man. *Does that seem likely?*

I have no memory of it. I can imagine my parents wanting wood chopped because it was going to be cold or something, and they had that wonderful fireplace Daddy had made and that I had given them the andirons for when I came home from college one time. But anyway, I don't have any memory of that and

---

* Brakhage could not afford a Bolex at that time, although he did acquire one in the '70s. His personal 16mm camera was a Bell and Howell Filmo (without a reflex viewer); DJ seems to have prompted Jane Wodening into thinking—perhaps generically—that the camera was a Bolex, the preferred tool of most American avant-garde filmmakers. (PAS)

the thought is horrifying. I'd rather take his place and chop wood myself than watch him do it because he just wasn't muscular, he was not a biceps type.

Those photographs you took of him with the long hair and the beard struggling in the snow with that two-headed ax over his shoulder, he looks so magnificently virile.

Yeah, yeah, yeah, he did. [*laughs joyously*] I thought so too. I thought he looked great and I was horrified when he finally cut his hair. It was great loss to me. And he never grew it back.

Even in the '60s when it was fashionable again?

No, no, not then. He didn't grow it back. And he had a great head of hair, I mean really strong and thick and good.

And Crystal is born during the making of Dog Star Man *in February 1960. Crystal is born and you are seen… Are you pregnant with Crystal in some of those scenes?*

Oh yeah. Recall, I might have spent seven years pregnant or nursing. I was something the whole time.

As soon as you'd given birth to Myrrena, you became pregnant again with Crystal within a few months.

Well, not really. I mean, it was how many months between, let's see, March, April, May. So in May when we started across country, I suppose when we just arrived in Silver Spruce, I had just barely conceived.

Were you happy living in that house with one baby and another baby on the way? The house of your childhood? Were you happy there?

Well, yeah, it was really the nicest place we ever lived in, I think. I don't know about niceness being important to me, but yeah, I knew the place and they had allowed me to pick out the curtains and so on, but I didn't know. I felt like I don't want to hurt this place for my parents to come back and find that it was damaged by us. I was kind of particular and careful and so on about that, and of course it was OK. It was fine. I knew the mountain and I knew the place and I knew the neighbors, and that was all to the good.

You were glad to be home?

I wouldn't say that. No, I wouldn't say that, no. I had suffered loneliness there, and they didn't know what to do about that or anything.

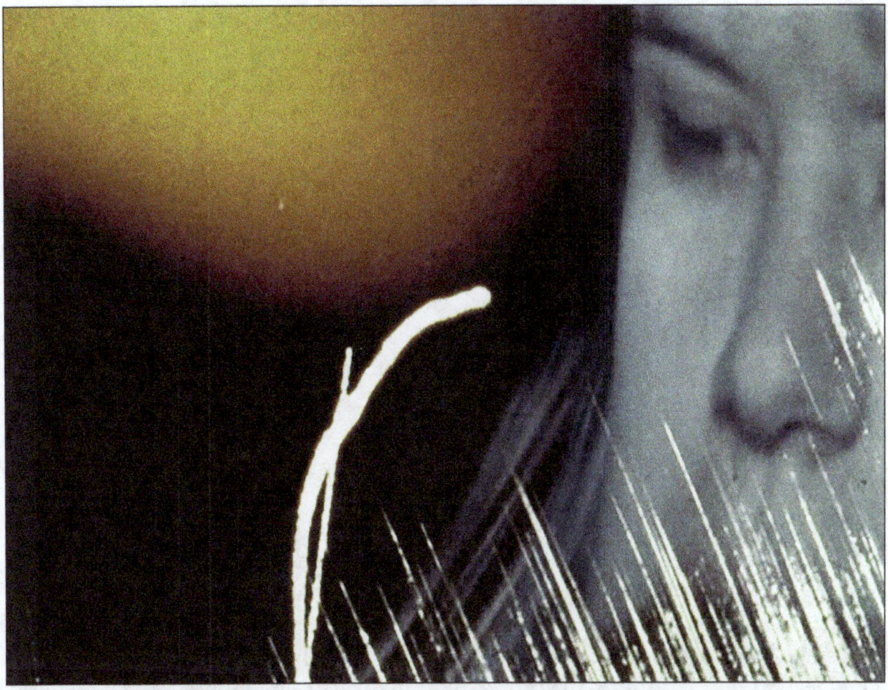

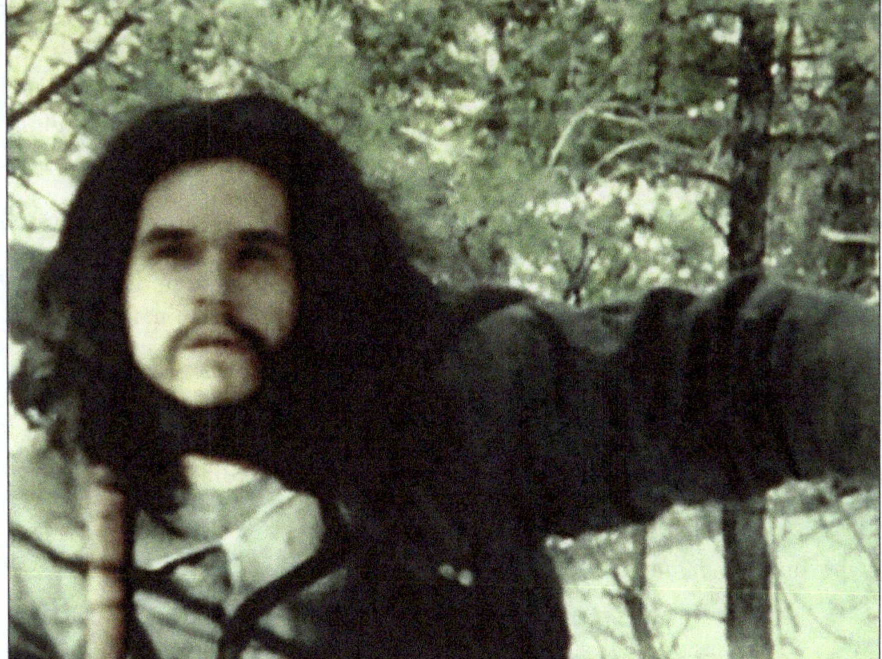

Jane and Stan in *Dog Star Man, Part Three.*

Did Stan renew his acquaintance with his old filmmaking pals?

A small extent, yeah. They were in Denver, of course, which is quite aways from Silver Spruce, and I don't think we went to Denver much, going to Denver was a big deal. We didn't ignore them completely, but I can't remember an image of any of them. I can't remember if we saw any of them in the house.

They didn't come to the house.

I don't believe they came to the house. So if we saw them, we would've had to take the trip to Denver. I don't think that happened, at least not much. I don't have a good memory of that. Yeah, that's right, that's interesting.

Were you perhaps less unhappy than you had been in your late teenage years by this time?

The house was… Yes, you're trying to get an image of us living there, and I think we were both too conscious of it belonging to my parents, and it was constricting for each of us to be thinking of it that way.

I was really trying to get at your state of mind. We missed talking about the film, The Dead, *but in P. Adams Sitney's account of* Sirius Remembered *and* The Dead *in* Metaphors on Vision *there are several quotations indicating that Stan was still suicidal or at least prone to thinking about that. And the two films were in some sense part of this preoccupation and the possible imminence of his death. And you said also that you were almost suicidal when you met Stan. I wonder if after this first year or so of marriage, one or both of you was a little bit more optimistic and less distraught.*

We had reasons for living. We had numerous reasons for living now, and so we weren't that concerned about it. And yes, *Sirius Remembered* was a stark statement as to what death is. And especially, we couldn't bury the poor guy, and I don't know how people have done this through the ages, but I think they usually found caves or something to bury people in, to get them out of sight. But this dog was right there in sight.

Yes. We were feeling better, and also we were eating better—or Stan was, somewhat—and we had work to do. We had lots of work to do, we were busy, so it was good. We knew where we were going. We were going along with *Dog Star Man* and the *Colorado Legends* and *Mothlight,* don't forget.

Was Mothlight *made in Silver Spruce or when you moved up to the mountains yourselves?*

It was made in Silver Spruce. I was cleaning in the fall. My parents had these wide kind of glass things under the ceiling lights. There were two ceiling lights with these big moth-catchers underneath. I got on a ladder and I took down the one big glass thing and showed it to Stan: "Look!" There were like a hundred or fifty, or, I don't know, two hundred, there were a lot of dead moths in there. He said, "Wait, wait, don't take it away." And that was the beginning of *Mothlight*. He immediately saw, OK, that's just the size of the 16-millimeter film frame. That was something he could do, and he had a roll of this sticky stuff, he had a large quantity of this, and he had gotten it probably in case something came along that he could stick onto a film.* Then the thought of having the whole film be stuck with moth wings, each one getting a frame. Then other things too, like flowers and bugs and stuff. There were two of them, so then after he was oohing and aahing over this one fabulous load of dead moth jewels, I brought the other one. So that was the beginning of *Mothlight*, and I think it's partly because of that roll of 16-millimeter of sticky stuff. That was the essential, and he was so happy doing that. He just loved doing that, just sticking those little dead moths onto the tape. He had an ability to do things concisely, I mean, tiny, tiny stuff.

So that was manufactured in your parents' house in Silver Spruce?

Yes, I guess. Manufactured is a word that I don't think Stan would use, but created, I suppose it was something that he would prefer.

Created, absolutely. At the same time, you were shooting Dog Star Man. *Could you talk a little bit about the dailiness of the* Dog Star Man *shooting? Did you regularly get out and do some photography two or three days a week or something like that?*

[*laughs*] There was no regularity. It was all, "OK, we haven't done anything for ten days." I'm just thinking, "Well, I wonder what we're going to do next. It's been like a week and a half." He'd been busy, of course, with the *Colorado Legends* or with *Mothlight* or who knows what. Then he'd leap up and say, "OK, we're going to do this." Or maybe he would just go into his place where he was working. I'm trying to think what all he did with the Arriflex, but obviously we went up the mountain with it. Or maybe he'd say, "Let's go around and take some pictures of some other mountains." Of course, Crystal's birth was just a shooting day.

Could we talk about that a little bit? This was the second time that you'd had a birth photographed. Did you have to have a doctor come into your parents' house and be with you while this was happening? She was born in that house, I assume.

I don't think so. No, she wasn't. She was born in Community Hospital. I'd forgotten that. I thought it was just Rarc, but no, she was born in Community Hospital. We called the doctor. It was early in the morning, so I guess we woke him up and he said, "OK, just come down to the hospital and I'll meet you there."

---

* Mylar transparent 16mm film editing tape, with sprocket holes and glue on one side. (PAS)

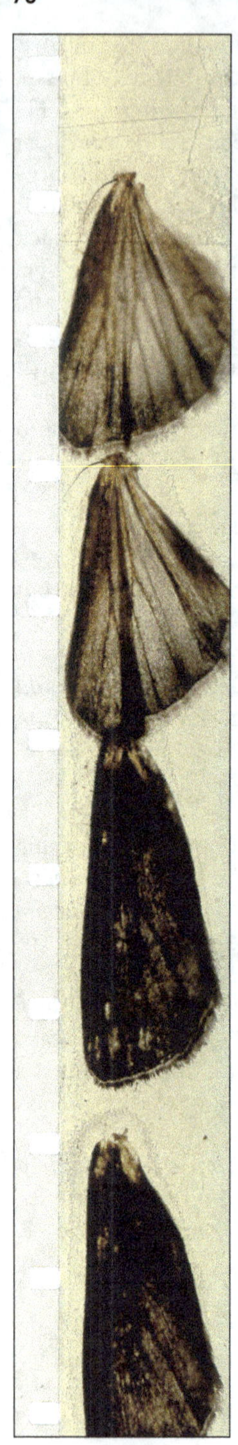

Mothlight.

So we went down to the hospital and he wasn't there, he was having breakfast. Stan thought, well, it took me how many hours to have Myrrena. Crystal was a different situation, so that I was on one of these movable tables, this roller table that you carry patients down the hall in and a nurse managed to catch Crystal as she came out. And Stan was there photographing urgently, and it was a really easy birth except for all fuss about the doctor not being there. The nurses were upset that the doctor wasn't there and he couldn't, I don't know, do all the proper doctor things. I think they waited and didn't cut the cord until he showed up, but he was called, told that he had to rush to the hospital. But I was happy.

Crystal wasn't born in the corridor, they got you into a proper room?

Oh, yes. It was not a proper room, it was in-between rooms. It was not in the corridor quite, no, it was in the delivery section or whatever. So it was not like an outrageous, spectacular thing happening in the corridor. It was perfectly acceptable where it was.

And there were no objections to Stan's filming?

No. That was set up beforehand. Yeah.

This eventually became Thigh Line Lyre Triangular, *I guess?*

No, no. Oh no. It all went into *Dog Star Man*. Wasn't it in Part Two?

So Crystal is born in Dog Star Man *Part Two. That's a whole area of* Dog Star Man *that you made together. Any other recollections of the filming of* Dog Star Man? *You mentioned going out and shooting other mountains and there are long shots, very beautiful shots of snow-covered mountains, snow-covered trees. Any other recollections of shooting* Dog Star Man?

I would be driving the car and he would be shooting out the window with the Bolex.* If I looked at the film, I would be reminded of things, but I'm not remembering

---

* Actually, a Bell and Howell Filmo. (PAS)

all of it at once. So yes, I remember going out and looking at other mountains. I remember what all happened in *Dog Star Man* besides the climbing of the mountain. There were things in the house. Boy, I just don't know.

There's a lot of photography of you. And then of course there is all the imagery of sun sparks that he got from the university.

Oh, yes, the stock footage, the wonderful really big sun flare. Yes, I remember that and also I think we were still adding to *Dog Star Man* when we were in Crisman, when Neowyn was born. He was doing another job then. *Dog Star Man* took years to collect the footage for. I don't know why he didn't put *Mothlight* in there, but he didn't. He was working for George Gamow making a couple of George's books, science-for-children: *Mr. Tomkins Inside Himself,* where Mr. Tomkins and another scientist were swimming together up the bloodstream and talking about the blood cells.* It was kind of silly, but it included some wonderful bats' wings where you could see the blood surging up the artery or vein—vein, I guess.

Can you tell anything about the production of that?

That occurred during the birth of Neowyn. It is all about *Dog Star Man* because some of that microscopy that went into *Dog Star Man* was made at that time, that would have been in 1961.

If you wouldn't mind, would you talk about the commercial project, Mr. Tomkins Inside Himself.

That was 1961 also. That was how come we got that fabulous footage. I haven't been thinking about that. Let's see. George Gamow was quite a guy. He said, "Maybe you'd like to do a couple of films?" I think there were two, but I can't think of the other title.† So Stan tried to make something cute and charming for children. George liked Stan and called him "his own Cossack" since Stan looked just like a Cossack. That was the tribe that Stalin was killing just because they were Cossacks. Another problem with George was that he really drank a lot of vodka. He was Russian, so anybody who drank with him had to match ounce to ounce what he drank. Of course, if you drink with an alcoholic, you get very ill. I don't know how Stan survived. I guess he just wanted to go on living because he had to drive home from visiting George and talking about the film. Stan was not a very good drinker, he was staggering. I should have gone with him and driven the car.

Where did Gamow live?

---

* Born in Russia, Gamow was a distinguished physicist and biologist. He was on the faculty of the University of Colorado at Boulder from 1956 until his death in 1968.

† Brakhage made no other film with Gamow other than *Mr. Tomkins Inside Himself.* (PAS)

Gamow was in Boulder and at that time we were up in Crisman which is about as far away as Silver Spruce, maybe five miles from Boulder.

Was he a faculty member of UC-Boulder?

Yes, he was. He was a well-known scientist, part of the group that were building the bomb together, down in New Mexico.

And he commissioned Stan to make a film of his book, Mr. Tomkins?

Mr. Tomkins Inside Himself, I believe. He had written other books that were for grown-ups, for laymen talking about science and chemistry and radiation. I think one of them was the history of science, I'm not sure. He had a heavy Russian accent but his books were in good English. He was a character on the campus. If he hadn't been so famous, he would have been fired early on for his drinking. But he became a much-loved character on the campus. He had a son, Igor. Igor and his wife, Elfriede, worked on the microscopy, the bat wing photography, and all the stuff like that.

Who did the adaptation of the book? Did Gamow give Stan the book, and say, "Here, make a film about it"?[*]

I think so. The person who played Mr. Tomkins was a really fine artist who was one of the art teachers at CU.[†]

Did Stan enjoy working on that film?

Well, it was work. He did what he could, I think he just did it from the book. It has sound. I can't remember who played the scientist. Would that be Igor? Perhaps. Igor was also a scientist, and so was Elfriede, although she ended up selling silks in a shop for many years. We got really fond of George and his second wife, Barbara, not the mother of Igor. They were a delight to visit also. If I came along, then George was not so pushy with the vodka. So I would come to protect Stan. He needed me more to drive home than when he went alone. Things happen like that.

I only prepared as far as Dog Star Man. *I'd like for us to talk more about it next week and your move to the mountains, if that's OK with you.*

Yeah, have we gone for an hour and a half already?

---

[*] There was no book at the time. The film was an original idea of Gamow's. In 1967 Gamow and Martynas Ycas wrote a book version of the film. (PAS)

[†] It was Don Weygandt. Robert Benson played Dr. Streets, Elfriede Gamow played a nurse. Igor Gamow is credited as a producer. (PAS) The painter Donald L. Weygandt was a professor at the University of Colorado at Boulder around 1962–63.

We have not talked about The Dead. *As I understand it, Stan had got a commercial assignment to go to Paris. You didn't go to Paris with him on that trip.*

Right, I didn't, and I can't remember when it was. I guess it was when we were in Silver Spruce. I don't know much about it. I didn't know there was such an amazing graveyard as that. And he was very impressed with it as itself. When we were in California in 1962, Lawrence Ferlinghetti, the poet, fell in love with it. He wanted to make a poem that would go with it, a poem that would be a soundtrack. He would come over and Stan would run the film on the projector. Ferlinghetti would sit there and read. "Oh the *dead*, the *dead*, the *DEAD...*" He'd go on a ways, and say, "Well, I'm not done yet." I don't know that he got very far with that poem, but it was kind of wonderful to have him come over and talk about *The Dead* with us, talk about death.

Stan was willing to have the poem as a soundtrack at some point?

I think he was not too enthralled with the notion, but he couldn't say no to Ferlinghetti, but he witched it to not happen.[*]

Good, well I think you've done a magnificent job. We'll pick up with Dog Star Man *and the move to the cabin in the mountains.*

No, no, we don't go there yet. [*laughs*]

When do you move up there?

At the end of the summer. We have to go to Lafayette first and spend the summer in Lafayette. That was a miserable occasion, but we did it.

---

[*] This editor vividly recalls Brakhage's account in 1963 of this incident, in which he claimed he adamantly refused to allow Ferlinghetti to put the poem on the film. He also said he had no respect for Ferlinghetti as a poet. (PAS)

Five

2021 February 10. Crisman; Stan's clothes; Bearthm born; P. Adams visits; closed-eye vision; quarrels; sewing; Ken and Flo Jacobs; *Thigh Line Lyre Triangular*; *Blue Moses.*

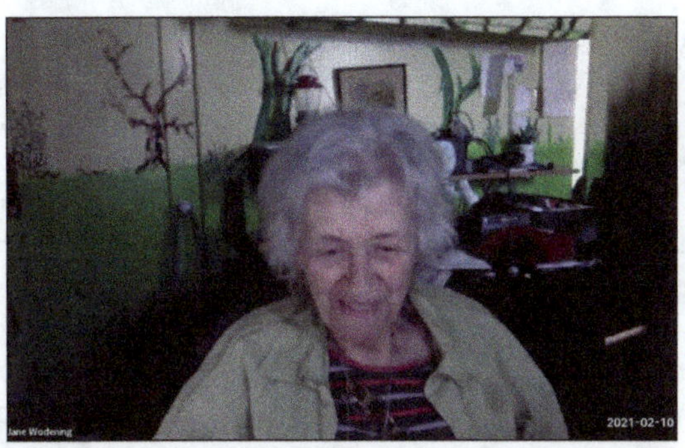

OK. I've done the phone, I've done the email, I've done the recording, and I've done the transcript so we're ready to go. How are you?

I'm great, except I can't see you because there's something here. Should I click "Continue?" Yeah, that worked.

I can see you. Are you well?

Yes, I took my shot on this Saturday and I'm well.

Excellent! I have a lot of questions and I'm afraid that I might lead you in a direction you don't want to go. Are there other things you would like to talk about first, or shall I just dive in with my questions?

Well, if you just dive in with your questions, we will skip the Lafayette summer, which is perfectly all right. The only thing I wanted to do with Lafayette summer, essentially, was to give you the image of Stan and me sitting in folding chairs on the front porch of this crumbling building which was our home, with two babies crawling around in there. We were reading sci-fi. We had a huge amount of sci-fi, there were four stacks, one on either side of each of us and we had them organized according to whether he had read it and whether I had read it, and whether neither had read it or whether both had read it. That's the image of that summer. Also, there was a glorious, glorious lunar eclipse and I remember it fondly. So now we can skip Lafayette summer, if you like, and go to Crisman. That's where

Neowyn was born, and we lived there for two years, which was a record at that time for how long we lived in a place.

Why did you go to Crisman?

To get away. Stan was having bad asthma in the Lafayette house.

The sense I'm getting is that you're still using your parents' home as a base and then periodically moving out to other places.

That was the end of using my parents' house as a base. We went to Lafayette for the summer and we read sci-fi and did very little else. We had visitors. Jim and Carolee came and visited at one time, and there were others, I can't remember who. And then we moved to Crisman, which was a little neighborhood about four miles up the canyon or five. And we liked that house. That house was a happy house, it really was. That was the house where I had the first idea that I would try to understand everything, and that was my reasoning behind writing this book that I'm writing about the history of the earth. That's when that book began. We had friends there, people that were interested in the arts, and yet they lived in the mountains. There's quite a few of those, that's a common thing to live in the mountains and love the arts—to keep away from civilization except for the arts. We even had guests there. Jim and Carolee came and a bunch of other people. Nancy came and there was Ester and Sue Hoover and lots of people came there to visit us.

Were Nancy, Ester and Sue personal friends of yours?

I suppose so. Nancy liked Stan too and me; she was the one who, when she left some years later to spend some years in Europe, she got her friend Betsy to be forward and try to befriend me, to replace her because she said that "poor Jane, she has no friends of her own." And so Betsy became the third of the three of us. Anyway, we're still all three alive and bemoaning being old.

The three of you are still alive?

All three, yeah, Nancy and Betsy and I. We talk on the phone. We can't see each other because I never lived in Boulder. The other two live in Boulder, actually Betsy is in a little suburb of Boulder.

Could you give me last names for Nancy, Ester, and Sue?

Ester Clevenger, she was a painter. She died shortly after Stan did. She was a good artist and she loved animals and worked with cattle and raised the value of the cattle that she worked with always. But they were sold anyway and were killed. As she pointed out, their lives were short but at least they were happy. Nancy Stetson and Betsy Hassrick. Betsy was a potter; she quit doing pottery and then turned to collage because the clay was too difficult or I don't know. I have some of her pieces of clay and some of her collage work too, but I have one piece of Ester's that I value a lot. It was the one time that she tried to do a mosaic with paper: little, tiny paper pieces that she stuck on with glue. By the time she finished with it, she swore never to do it again and she never did. Nancy is not an artist. What is she? I can't remember the title of what she is interested in. She's interested in interesting ways of handling health and wellness, even including waves and light and various things. Whatever ways the three of us have to keep alive, we have all succeeded until this point. They're both about my age, just a little younger, both of them.

So these are fifty-year-long friendships.

Yeah. Susan went away, she went east, and I've been actually in touch with her on the phone since then, off and on, every, I don't know; every six months or so we call each other up, but Ester died, as I say, shortly after Stan did. And yeah, it was nice to have friends that were mine pretty much, although I wondered if they would've noticed me if Stan wasn't there.

You've said so many things that are of interest. Can I go back over some of them? You said you wanted me to have a picture of you, I believe it was at the sci-fi reading at Lafayette. When you say a picture, are you referring...

I want you to just see that: Stan and me sitting on folding chairs on the front porch with four piles of sci-fi and all organized as to whether who had read it and then whether they hadn't.

Do you remember anything about your tastes and interests in sci-fi?

We were reading them all. We were reading everyone, and we did like some over others. I think Isaac Asimov was both of our favorites; Ray Bradbury was another, but I guess that wasn't exactly sci-fi. I don't know if he was in those piles of books, but I can't remember other names.

When you said that...

That was the period where everything that went into my brain went deep into the subconscious and vanished, dribbled away or something.

When you said that about the photo, it reminded me of the photograph that we talked about a couple of weeks ago of you, Stan, Jim and Carolee on a lawn, very low down, and I noticed from one of my books that that picture was taken by Carolee on a timer.

Yeah, time-lapse camera.

You mentioned your desire to understand everything and that you're now writing a book about everything.

Well, it is just the history of the earth. It doesn't include all the physics that is so exciting to me. I was thinking, should I start at the Big Bang or should I start at the birth of the sun? And I decided that since I was over eighty, I should start at the birth of the sun and see if I could do the prequel if I still was alive at the end of the book.

That's so wonderful. [laughs] *I'm sorry.*

[*laughs*] Oh, don't, be sorry. I love it when people laugh at my jokes. I don't know why you apologize.

I think it was fabulous. Your mention of these friends of yours doing crafts reminded me that when we were talking about Princeton, you talked about crochet. I let that drop and we never picked up about whether you followed that interest in crochet and other crafts.

No, I could show you a shawl I made for my old age, but that's all I have left from the crocheting period. It was enjoyable, it was also something that I could do when people were talking because I, of course, never joined the conversation.

Did you crochet anything for Stan?

No, no, they were for me. I made quite a few wonderful dramatic shirts for Stan. There was an interesting little story about that. Stan had a suit, he had bought a suit, and he thought, "OK, this'll be my suit. I now have a suit for my adult years." And he was riding in the train wearing the suit, and the two women behind him were whispering about him and saying, "Well, that suit is elegant, but it's shabby." So he came home and he said, "I can't wear my suit anymore. It's elegant, but it's shabby." And I said, "Well, I'll make you a shirt out of this tablecloth." And I did, that's the golden shirt that I'm sure you've seen him wearing sometime or other, it was quite glorious. And there was another leather one that I made, and I can't remember what all else. But then somebody must have spoken ill of those things, and he stopped wearing them suddenly one day, and went to casual sportswear, which was a lot cheaper than an elegant suit.

Did you make clothes for the children?

No, not much. No. Well, I did, yeah. I found myself buying them clothes because they grew so fast so that you'd have to hand them down, and that was kind of tacky, because the third girl would get really kind of worn-out things.

That must have been tough on Neowyn because as the third in line, she always got stuff third hand.

That's right.

I remember hand-me-down clothes very well in my own life. OK, so I think we've come to the place where I can pick up with some questions, if that's OK with you.

Those questions. Yeah, sure. Let's hit 'em.

You talked about the origin of the name Myrrena. Crystal, I guess, is pretty much self-evident. Any recollections on the origins of the name Neowyn?

It may be that Stan forgot, I doubt it, but there was a character in a Tolkien book, a beautiful Elf maiden who was maybe a princess or something. Anyway, he put the N in front to call her the new Eowyn but he never mentioned that. We had just been reading Tolkien for the first time through, and what he did say was, it's "New Harvest." "Wyn" is a harvest in what? Old English or I don't know what. And Neo, of course, is new. I can't remember what the other meaning of Wyn is. It might be the New Field, the new place to plant.

Neowyn is an established name, I looked it up. It means a person capable of great sympathy.

Oh, that's just wonderful. I'm going to tell her that. Where'd you get it?

On the web? I've just put in "Neowyn, meaning." It means sympathy, ability to help each other. It can often be accompanied by artistic skills, but the danger is that the person is, may well involve herself in other people too much to the detriment of her own development.

Oh, my God.

Maybe too generous, too kind.

Oh my God. I hope I can remember all that.

I'll send you the link to Neowyn.

Oh, that would be great. I'll send it to her then, and that'll work.

Your talking about Tolkien reminded me of the period when Stan read Proust to you and then read Tale of Genji. *Could you talk a little bit about Stan's reading? You indicated he read to you for a short time each night, twenty minutes, half an hour. Was he a good reader?*

He really liked to read aloud, but he did prefer a bigger audience than just me. So that when the kids were grown enough, he could read to all five of them, the whole Tolkien series. I was doing this rug, I was needlepointing or whatever it was. I set them up with a rug too that was going to be easy for them, and even the boys who were quite young could do the outer edge. And that took a couple of years, I think. That was his goodbye song, but it was grand. But yeah, the *Tale of Genji*, he would read to me, but he didn't read that to the kids. This was before the kids seemed to be old enough. But he kind of slowed down on the reading aloud, I think.

Did he read dramatically? Did he impersonate the voices?

Yeah, he impersonated the voices. Yeah, he did very well. Rarc learned how to read partly from his father, but then he had five kids himself, three girls first and then two boys, surprisingly.

The same as you and Stan.

He read to them constantly, all through their childhood.

When you had three girls in a row, did Stan wonder if he was going to have a son, was having a son important to him?

When Bearthm emerged, Stan had something akin to sibling rivalry. He was jealous of him, he didn't like it that somebody else loved me, that another guy loved me, and then I loved him. It was OK for me to love girls, but not the boy. Rarc was, I don't know… Bearthm became handsome and strong and capable in a lot of ways, whereas Rarc was kind of clumsy, and he had dyslexia[*] so bad he couldn't run until second or third grade. I think that Stan was more sympathetic to Rarc, but he just couldn't stand Bear. I mean, he did, of course; he stood him and he fathered him, and he tried to be good and everything, but it was hard for him. One time we were walking along and I was holding the baby and looking at him, baby Bear was in my arms and looking at me, and Stan said, "What is he saying?" And I said, "Me Oedipus, you Jocasta." Stan didn't like that at all. He didn't like it at all, he hated it. He remembered it all his life. He was upset because his first thought was that Oedipus killed his father.

While we are here, do you have any comments on the names Bearthm and Rarc?

Bearthm was, according to Michael McClure, I believe, "splendor, brightness" in Old English or something like that.[†] I accepted it because I could give him the nickname "Bear," and because he would like that, because he was a strong baby.

Rarc?

---

[*] Jane probably meant dyspraxia, which does cause difficulties with motor skills.
[†] Two letters were transposed; in Anglo Saxon "bearhtm" does mean brightness or glittering.

We had just seen the movie of Thor Heyerdahl crossing the Atlantic in a grass boat called Ra.* Stan wanted Ra in reference to the sun god Egypt had temporarily or briefly, I don't know how brief it was. Stan felt like it'd be nice to honor the sun, and he named Rarc, the ark of the sun. So it was meaning sunshine, sunlight, the arc of the sun, Ra—arc. That's how he put things together, and this is true of everywhere, all his titles and stuff he created.

Great. I'll go on with my questions as long as that's OK with you. Over the weekend, I reread Metaphors on Vision *in its entirety for the first time in many years. I assume you've seen the new version with P. Adams' notes?*

Goodness sakes, David…

It was a very chastening experience. It made me realize how ignorant I am. It's an amazing work of scholarship by P. Adams, and the text by Brakhage is so overwhelming that I can't really assimilate it fully. But I'd like to talk about some of the issues it raises. I wonder if you have any recollections of the period when Stan was writing it, and perhaps also of the period in Denver when P. Adams Sitney was interviewing Stan. Do you have any recollections of that?

Was that when he came to Denver where we were living in the Theater Innovations?

In my notes, all I have is P. Adams Sitney in Denver, 1963. That's just before the wonderful interview in which Stan produces the chronology of his films and comments on them. There are just some magnificent passages.

That would've been the Hooker Street house, then, when P. Adams visited us. He must have interviewed him then, but he will remember. He is awaiting us now, ready to pounce.

I know he's going to be embarrassed by the next question, but let's go anyway. Can you recall your first meeting with P. Adams and how you got along with him?

He was a nice guy to me. He was nineteen years old when he first came to Lump Gulch. For some reason, he came for Christmas,† which was really odd because we were very offbeat in our celebration of Christmas. We had a dead tree because we didn't want to kill any of the trees out there, even though there were thousands around our house, millions, I guess, but each one was somebody. So we took a dead tree and decorated it, not with Christmas decorations that you buy

---

* This is impossible. Heyerdahl built Ra 1 in 1968; Ra 2 in 1970. The film *Ra* was released in 1972, when Rarc Brakhage was seven. Directed by Lennart Ehrenborg and Thor Heyerdahl, *Ra* (aka *The Ra Expeditions*), 1972, documented Heyerdahl's attempts to cross the Atlantic in papyrus boats in 1969 and 1970. (PAS)
† Again, in 1964. (PAS)

at the store, but with cloth. I was even then collecting cloth to make things with. I don't know what, but anyway, I had some pretty cloth. And then a lot of people sent us presents for the children because I think that was their first Christmas there. P. Adams was there, and he was a nineteen-year-old with a beard, and that was strange enough, but that he was precocious was upsetting. But I put up with it because I realized that he didn't know anything about winter in Colorado, and certainly I had things to show him. I don't know if he liked dogs then, but he does now.

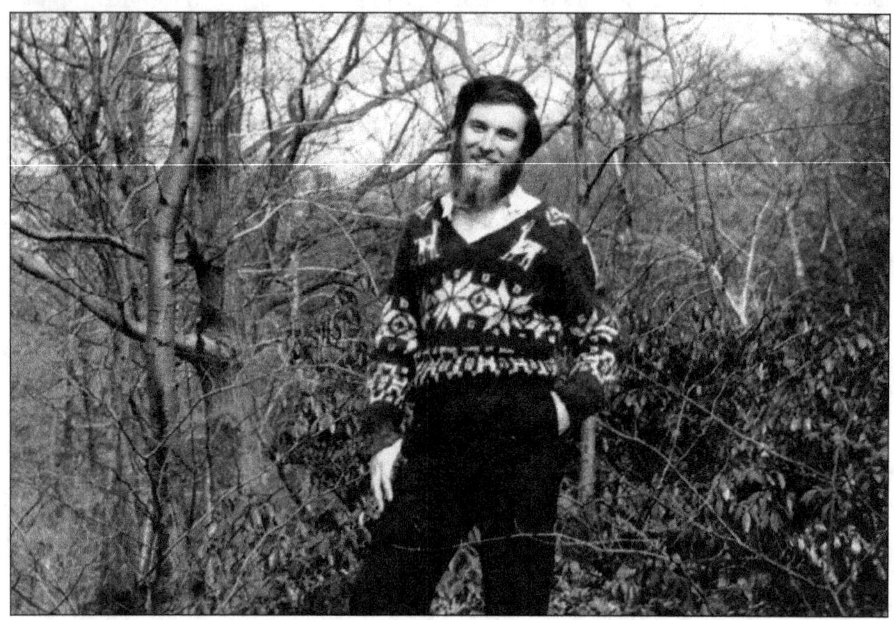

P. Adams Sitney, circa 1964

Interesting things happened then on that occasion. That's when a dog came and scratched on the door. It was a strange dog so I went out; I got my coat on and I went out on the porch and said, "What?" And he turned his back and he started running in his certain direction, so I followed him. And I said, "Come on, P. Adams, this might be interesting." He ran until he got past some trees, and there were six or eight horses in the deep snow. The new snow was coming down. It was really quite a blizzard that was coming down, only it wasn't blowing much. It was just thick, thick snow and maybe a foot and a half or two feet of snow at that time. Then the dog stopped and looked up at me and as if to say, "See, do it, you know." And I realized that these horses were not able to dig down to the grass, and nobody was there to feed them. I didn't have my goats yet, so I didn't have hay. I had nothing, but I did have some milk, and I had a loaf of bread. So I cut up the loaf of bread in a big bowl and poured the milk in there and went out with this bowl and tried to feed each horse. Of course, the horses have hierarchy too, they're horse number one, two, three, four, and nobody. So that nobody, I don't know, I tried to pass him a piece of bread or something, but the two or three big top ones got most of it. They drank it, they ate it, they consumed it immediately, and I felt like, well, that's not enough, but that's what I've got. And I put some dog food out for the dog on the porch, and he ate it. In the morning, everybody was gone and the snow had covered over the footprints. Now, that was a thing that happened; I don't know what P. Adams thought, but it was definitely foreign to his East Coast upbringing.

Stan had met P. Adams several years before this point. But this was the first time that you met P. Adams?

Yeah, yeah. There was another moment when I was nursing the baby, which must have been Rarc, in the living room, and he walks through. I was wearing shorts, it was summertime then, I was wearing shorts, and I had long hair so I could nurse the baby and cover my bare breast, and it was all right. I thought, anyway, he could walk through and he said, "Do you have anything on at all?" [*laughs*] "Yes, I felt like he and I were friends, I've always thought that he and I were friends, although we've hardly seen each other since Stan dumped him.[*]

So the summer meeting was the first meeting, and the Christmas meeting was the second meeting, is that right?

I don't know, but there were two distinct meetings, one meeting in summer and one meeting in winter. I'm sure P. Adams will know the dates on them.[†]

Even though P. Adams was so young and, as you say, so incredibly precocious, he was also something of an ambassador from the East Coast intelligentsia. Did that have any resonance for you or for Stan, that the East Coast intelligentsia were coming to Colorado to seek Stan out?

Well, I think Stan was pleased at a new audience. Yeah, the intelligentsia was a good thing to have because they would take notes.

Yeah, fabulous notes. Stan says at the very beginning that you agreed to dedicate Metaphors on Vision *to P. Adams.*

I didn't have anything to do with it, I don't think. Oh, he might have said, "What do you think if I dedicate it to P. Adams?" "Oh, yeah, fine," like that. It wasn't that I was working with him. It wasn't *we* who were dedicating, it was he.[‡]

---

[*] P. Adams Sitney suspended all personal contact with Brakhage in 1969 after what he regarded as bullying and severe disagreements, especially over the latter's role in the selection of films for the Anthology Film Archives' collection, "Essential Cinema." Sitney only agreed to resume relations in the late 1990s after Brakhage's cancer was found to be terminal.

[†] Sitney visited the Brakhages three times: August 1962 in Denver; Christmas 1964 in Rollinsville, when the horses were stranded in the snow; and September or October 1968. The breastfeeding incident must have occurred in December 1964. (PAS).

[‡] In essence, JW's recollection is correct. However, she sat in on the word-by-word editing of *Metaphors on Vision*, often making suggestions, and more often arguing forcibly against any of

Right. Amongst the texts assembled there, there's a description of something that Stan calls The Dailiness Film. *It was written as a grant application for the Ford Foundation, and I just love that whole sketch of consciousness emerging from dreams in the morning, and then the parallel that he proposed between a day in the life of you two and the whole history of the cosmos. It reminds me a little bit of what you just said about* The History of Everything. *The history of everything in Stan's vision was implicit in the history of the life of a man and a woman who loved each other and had a family. Anyway, I just thought it was an amazing text.*

Yeah. That was all that was made. I don't think we got the Ford Foundation grant, and we didn't do the film. I think it was in his mind often, but then he kind of went to town. I don't know, it just seemed like he gave it up.

As I recall from the book, Stan says words to the effect, "This is basically the last time in which I allowed myself to translate everything into the words so thoroughly. And from this point on, I basically stopped writing scenarios, because words were ultimately a detriment."

They take away from making the film. It's like, OK, that's done, so why do it again?

But around the same time or a little bit earlier, there was a film that I'd forgotten about—in fact, I've never seen it—called Films by Stan Brakhage: An Avant-Garde Home Movie, *1961. He said he'd been given two reels of film that had been exposed to fire, and that freed him to do whatever he wanted to. It sounds very much like drafts for a dailiness film. As I recall, it's about you and him together in the house. Do you remember that film?*

No. I'm sorry, I don't. I think it was very short.

Two rolls max.

Two rolls. Well, that's what, five minutes or something. But if he used it all, and probably if it was through a fire, he had to cut out the outside leader or whatever. I don't know, I remember the title. But I think, I don't know *Films by Stan Brakhage: An Avant-garde Home Movie.* Yeah, *An Avant-garde Home Movie.* The title sounds longer than the film itself. I don't know. I suppose one could dig for it and see if it shows up.

In Metaphors, *there's also the description of the end of* Anticipation of the Night *that has become pretty much canonical, but which you disputed in your account of it. When we talked about* Anticipation of the Night *about three weeks ago, you*

Sitney's cuts or revisions. On the final night of editing (at the home of JW's parents, for once), SB took JW into a room out of Sitney's hearing for about ten minutes. They presented the dedication immediately after that, so that he thought it was a mutual decision. (PAS) *said you were a little bit miffed because Stan went off with Bob Benson to film the end of it. But in the text, Stan says that after he'd finished shooting* Anticipation of the Night, *he handed the camera to Jane and then stepped off the chair nearly killing himself. So he indicates that you were present for that almost-suicide.*

Well, I mean, it's not for me to say, but I would believe me way over what Stan said. [*laughs*]

Me too. So you're pretty sure you were not there for that?

I'm positive. I remember him telling me that Bobby had caught him.

I sent you a couple of texts. You said you couldn't read them as transcripts. He pays you this extraordinary compliment of being able to see closed-eye vision and open-eye vision simultaneously. Perhaps I could read it for the record, I think it's so beautiful.

Yeah, I remember it. Yeah, I did read it when you sent it to me the second time, but if you want it allowed into the video, that's fine.

"My wife, thru the needling eye of extreme concentration, has been able to retain the fabric of shut eye patterns with her lids wide open and thread her sight through both sensory worlds at once, moving towards the sense of their interrelatedness." *Would you be willing to comment on how that appears to you or on when you developed this extraordinary ability which is so important in Stan's conception of what he was doing?*

We were at a period where I was feeling like playing around, but obviously he was trying to find something. So we were playing around in that kind of area, and I could do that. I tried doing it yesterday. It doesn't happen facing a bright screen, but I think if I were facing some kind of moderate light, I could do it because I could see what was going on inside my eyes. I get a shot in one eye every couple of months, and you can see the stuff bubbling into the eye. I can see it anyway, it comes in like an invader, but kind of cloud-like. Still, I can see inside my eyes and outside at the same time.

The issue of closed-eye vision is so fundamentally important to Stan and at this moment he indicates that you were way ahead of him in this kind of vision. You had pioneered something absolutely fundamental to his art before him.

Well, I hadn't gone and made it happen. It was just something I could do, it was easy. So he was asking me, "What do you see?" I say, "Well, there's this kind of a bubble here and then a black spot beside it, and those are covering the image of

---

* Stan Brakhage, *Metaphors on Vision*, ed. P. Adams Sitney (New York: Anthology Film Archives, 2017), p.119.

the coffee cup." I didn't see much use to it, but he did. It was fun playing with it, but it was confusing.

But there's one thing that bothers me. I don't know, I think this may be the only time in his life that he called me, "my wife." Who was he talking to? Was that in conversation with P. Adams?

*It's in a text he wrote called "My Eye."** It's in* Metaphors on Vision *and I don't know offhand anything more about it.*

It's not in an interview with P. Adams or somebody else?

That is correct.

Yeah. OK. Well, I don't know what to think then. I mean, if he was talking to P. Adams, he would surely have said "Jane." If he was talking to anybody that knew me, he would surely have said "Jane." But if he was talking to the world, then perhaps he would call me "my wife." But anyway, that's the only time I've ever seen it.

In fact, he calls you "my wife" many times in that text and in other texts in Metaphors on Vision.

OK, so that was his title for the day, I mean, for that project.

A couple of pages later, he talks again about his attempt "to communicate with my wife" and he describes a quarrel between you in which he perceived you as having a dog's head. I'll read it again: "I saw my wife's head reshape itself through the emergence of animal forces, most particularly and recurrently the head of a dog, an animal she has always felt related to."†

I think that's very suitable; as a matter of fact, it's very perceptive of him. I was really raised by dogs and I think a lot of my social problems was that I responded more in relation to dogs than to people, even talking with people. And I remember him saying that I had the head of a dog. I worried because, although that's relevant and true, it sounds like he's gone crazy and might do some damage to me.

Stan also describes what he believes to be your perception of the same quarrel, "her seeing me in that silence and thru her limiting anger." He continues, that you saw him "as if through heat waves, which distorted my form in terms of size more than in terms of a change of shape, my becoming larger than ordinarily perceived, my concentrated visage, or rather something simply referred to as 'you,' filling my wife's field of vision, then diminishing to a size more normal yet presenting

------

* *Metaphors on Vision*, pp.118-122.
† *Metaphors on Vision*, p.121.

an aspect abnormally wavering as if unbounded and again able to assume giant proportions." So he says that in this quarrel you saw him as this huge entity, not as an animal, but nevertheless filling your entire frame of vision.*

It was like he was coming at me, but it was an enlargement of him. [*shouting "Arggh," Jane approaches the camera so that her face fills the frame.*]

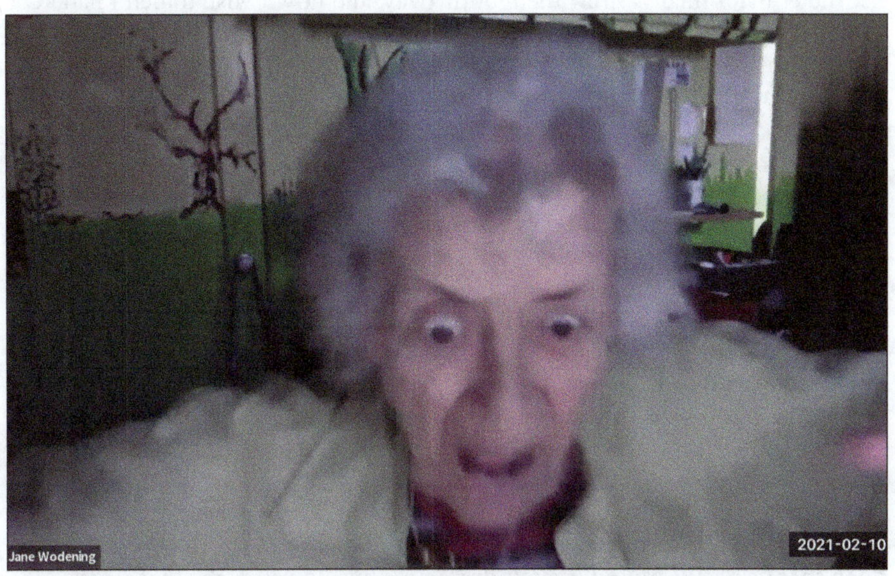

"It was like he was coming at me, but it was an enlargement of him."

So you do distinctly remember the quarrel?

I remember those parts of it. I don't remember what we were fighting over. We fought a lot. That one seemed dangerous.

And then he goes on to say that this vision of him that you had was in fact film-specific or related to film because it's as if you saw him "photographed thru a zoom lens and rippled glass." That's Stan's interpretation of this vision.

That would be how he would translate it, I guess. That wouldn't be how I would have perceived it. He was just scary.

I was struck in that first quotation that Stan used the metaphor of sewing in respect to your ability to see simultaneously in the two registers: "My wife, thru the needling eye of extreme concentration, has been able to retain the fabric of shut eye patterns with her lids wide open." That reminds me of all the times we've talked about your interestest in sewing and in cloth. I meant to ask you why you began to save pieces of cloth and what your relationship to fabric was.

---

* *Metaphors on Vision*, p 119.

I don't know, I've always enjoyed working with cloth. I didn't have a sewing machine for many years actually, and I'll tell you about the time I did get one to make my clown costume. That was sometime later.

The main thing about cloth was, yes, I like to make things out of cloth. I like to play with cloth. I actually made two ragdolls, one for Myrrena and one for Crystal, but not only did neither of those babies like the ragdoll, nobody else did either. I finally threw them both away, and now I wish to hell I had kept them because I think they were good, they were good pieces. Yes, I like to work with craft materials and make things, and I'm even considering making another ragdoll. Maybe I'll do that.

That'd be fabulous.

But for whom? For me, I guess, or for the world. Yeah. I like to work with cloth, and I used to have a pretty fine stitch, so I could really sew things together so that they would hang together and be good and strong. I don't know what else to say about fabric except it attracts me. I got into making quilts much later on. It was years after Stan left me, but I made forty quilts and then I was making little appliques that were just a picture made out of sewing, out of appliqueing little pieces of a clown onto something and then surrounding that with clouds or a dog or something, a train, whatever that I found pictures of. So cloth is good, yeah. There are other things I work with too.

Ken Jacobs told me about when Stan came to New York with you, he wore a big cloak that he threw around himself dramatically. Did you make that cloak?

Yes, I did. I did. I made that cloak, but that vanished with the shirts at somebody's comment, I'm sure, about how dramatically he was dressed and how silly that was or whatever.

*While we're on the topic of Ken Jacobs, do you recall any meetings with Ken and his wife, Flo?**

Oh, yes. Oh, yes. By the time Stan left me, I felt like they were dear friends to me. They were the first people I went to when I drove to New York on my driveabout.† They represent New York. He particularly is always presenting New York. The one time I went there by myself during driveabout, he talked about Brooklyn Bridge and how I should know all about the history of it. He just went on and on about the history of it, how people died building it and what a strong, local patriotic feeling there was about the Brooklyn Bridge. And then loving Chinatown as he does and Flo going along with it with all her love. She's

---

* Ken Jacobs (1933–2025), renowned filmmaker and a great friend of the Brakhages. Initially a painter, his wife Florence or "Flo" (1941–2025) played an essential role in his filmmaking.
† After her divorce, Jane drove alone around the U.S. in a year-long journey of self-discovery, which she understood to be analogous to Australian Aboriginal "walkabouts." Her book, *Driveabout*, is an account of this.

just a lovely lady. The two of them were something special to visit, and I was really glad that I knew them well enough to do so.

You visited them after you and Stan had separated in New York. You went to stay with them?

Yeah, yeah. And I remember those visits better, maybe because more recent. I went there and had the honor of being allowed into their loft, into which few people were allowed. Usually they'd go out and meet people on the street. It's a six-flight walk-up, and they're still walking up, and I believe both of 'em are older than I am, at least I know Ken is.

Ken made a film about the Brooklyn Bridge called The Sky Socialist *and a rag doll appears in that film.*

Ohhhh! Ken! [*laughs gleefully*]

Their friend, Joyce Weiland, is an important filmmaker who never had a child. Ken thought that was a terrible misfortune, and so in the film, she holds a little box with a rag doll in it to symbolize the child that she never had.*

Oh my God. She's got to keep it in a box.

Yeah.

That's interesting. As yet unborn.

Yeah, it's a difficult moment for me. Any other recollections of Ken and Flo? You went upstairs to Ken's amazing loft.

Oh, yes. You can see that loft after it's been cleaned up in Azazel's film of them.† Before it was cleaned up, the shelves were considerably taller. There was just more stuff there, and it went up mainly. That was a grand place to be because it was really away from New York City.

Going back to the sewing metaphor, in the quotation that I read, Stan picks up that metaphor to describe himself. He says, "I am not seamstress enough," as if implying that your seamstress ability has a terrific potency which he's trying to emulate or looking forward to emulating.

---

* Joyce Weiland, Canadian feminist artist and filmmaker who lived in New York for most of the 1960s. Her best-known film is *Rat Life and Diet in North America* (1968). Between 1956 and 1976, she was married to filmmaker Michael Snow.
† Azazel Jacobs, *Momma's Man* (2008).

I could not decipher the value of being able to do that. But I think he was trying to say that I had this peculiar talent and that he wished he had it, and he called that "seamstress."

It's very clear in the text that this is an ability that you have and he wished to acquire for himself. A bit later on, he talks about the fact that he had that ability to see with both registers simultaneously but only at very extreme moments. You had this ability all the time; he had the ability only rarely, as when a child was born. That is the reason for the compositional procedures of Thigh Line Lyre Triangular.

I did look at that and *Blue Moses* and *Wedlock House*, all of them on YouTube which is just infuriating. They don't have to make 'em so bad.

Would you like to talk about Thigh Line Lyre Triangular, *the film in which he tried to superimpose closed-eye vision on open-eye-vision?*

It seemed to me that the closed-eye-vision superseded the open-eye-vision, although there were a few shots, the birth was kind of seen, and he was trying to do that. He was trying to wipe out all, but when Crystal was born that he painted black around her head, and that was, he said, to erase the hand of the nurse who was holding her head. I was guiding her out into the world.

Do you recall seeing Thigh Line Lyre Triangular *for the first time?*

I think it had a lot more childbirth and less painted stuff, so I don't know. He was saying that he could see the inside vision or whatever you want to call it— hypnogogic—only when a child was born, but later he was using that over a lot of things. He was just using it over everything that he saw. So he must have worked up a skill at it later on, or he just imagined a skill at it, one of the two, and either way, it would work on film.

Any more about Thigh Line Lyre Triangular? *I always thought it was an amazing, amazing film. I liked it very much.*

What amazed you?

The density of the perception, the optical density of it.

Yeah.

Recently I've only been able to see it on YouTube and in that version the birth is definitely subordinated to the work on the film.

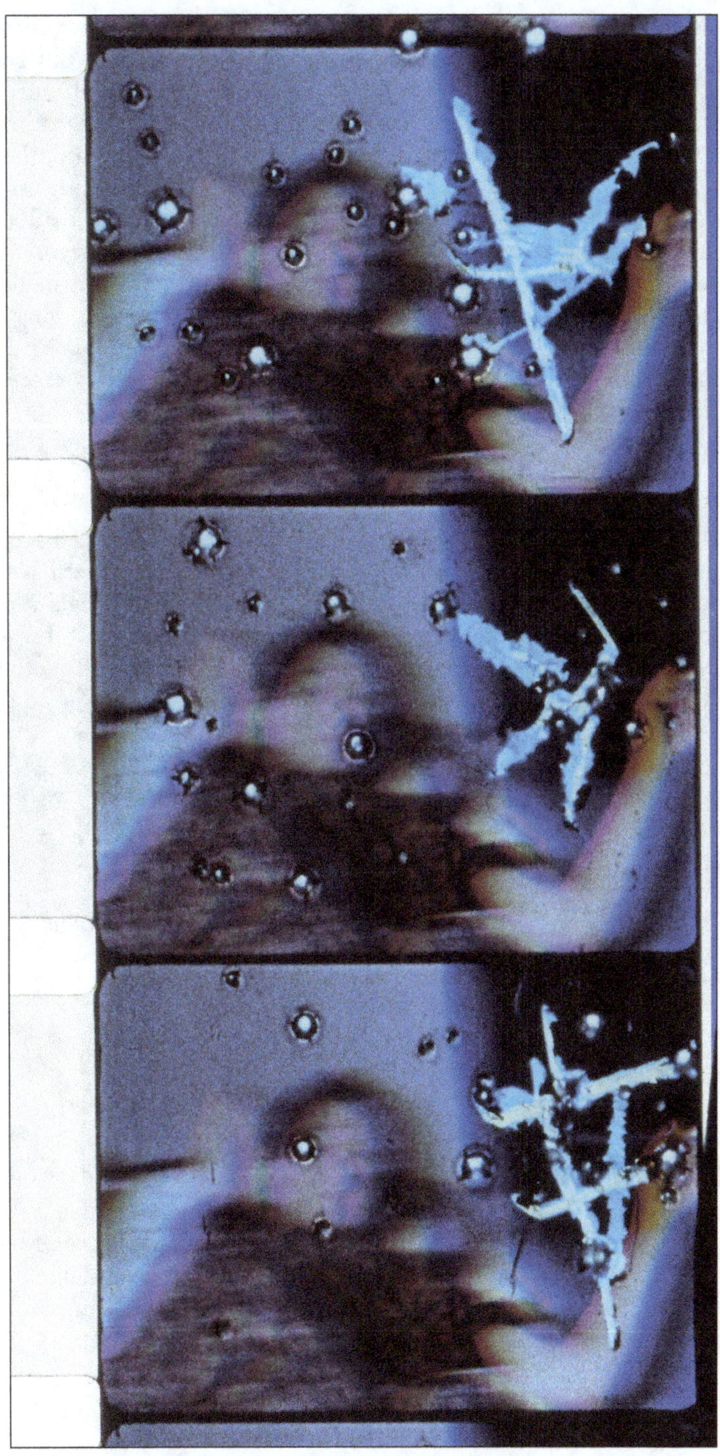

Jane in *Thigh Line Lyre Triangular.*

Subordinated, that's what it is, yeah. As for my viewpoint of the occasion, I was having a baby, I was making it available for him to make a film, but I was not making a film really. I was having a baby and it was a beautiful, beautiful June day, and the sun was shining, and I had a picture window to look through at our own front yard, and it was an easy birth. The nurses were kind, the doctor was there, and he was nice. I was looking forward to wearing a slim costume of some sort and afterwards when I tried to put it on, I realized that I still couldn't get into it, but I could eventually. So it was a very happy birth because it was at home and it was pleasant, and I could have a cup of tea right after the baby was born. Being at home and doing something at home, that really is a thing to do at home. Of all the things that you do, you should probably have a baby at home. Although, of course, I'd be told, "Well, I wouldn't have lived if… etcetera." So there's that too.

The film we've missed is Blue Moses.

Yeah, *Blue Moses.* I saw that yesterday also on YouTube, and I was disappointed because it didn't have my line in it. [*laughs*] I mean, I could almost have recited the whole thing with him. It was something that he went through again and again and again, and I was enjoying it. It had a power or a rhythm to it, but the line that I liked, of course, was the one referring to me. "'Someone's been running here.' She said, 'You can see a space between, I mean, the tracks.'" And that was left out.

As I recall, there are several versions of Blue Moses *on YouTube, but they're all silent except for a fragment, which is with sound. It's only about two minutes long.*

I don't know how long the original was, but it was full of Bobby Benson talking.

Was that made in Colorado?

Crisman.

Do you recall anything about the creation of it?

Yes, I do. It was great fun. Stan was writing the script and he said, "I want Bobby to do this for us, and he'll have to come here, of course." I guess he sent the script to Bobby and he memorized it and came and then recited it in several segments across one day; he came early and left late. He was very professional in his actorship even then. He had an idea of being Blue Moses and what being Blue Moses would be like.

He seems to be enjoying himself very much in the film.

He was enjoying it. I was enjoying it. Stan was enjoying it. We had a good day. It was a very nice day.

We've been going for an hour and three quarters. Maybe we could leave it here and pick up next week. Just to recap, you haven't sent me your elaborated version of last week's text.

No, I haven't. I've got to go through it one more time. P. Adams said to go real slow.

Next week we can perhaps clear up with Dog Star Man *and then go forward.*

The Songs weren't started until we got to Lump Gulch, and we have got places to go and films to make in between. I was going to explain to you that after the fifth baby was born, I don't know dates at all because I can't say, "Well, I know I was three months pregnant, therefore it was…"

Don't let me pressure you, and if you want to postpone it for a week…

Well, we could skip a week if we get really desperate, but I don't feel we're really desperate yet.

Well, have a terrific weekend, and thank you so much for everything that you're giving us.

Thank you, David. It's really fun. It's really fun and it's good for me.

Six

2021 February 24. Western Cine; San Francisco; poets: Chris Maclaine; James Broughton's wedding; theater in Denver; *Fire of Waters*; Custer, South Dakota; Sidney Peterson; Lakota Sioux.

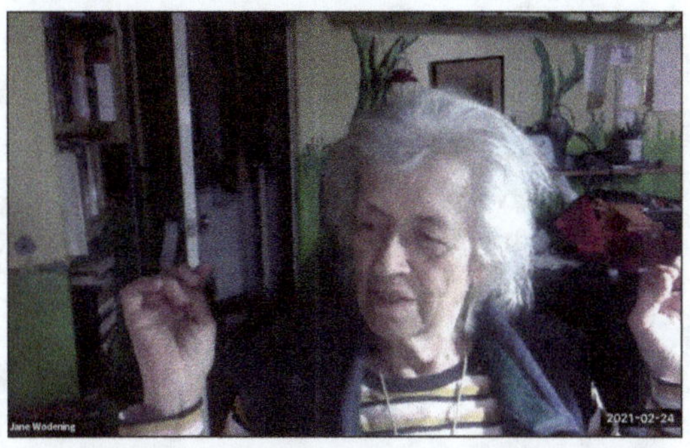

Good to see you. I note that it says recording is on, so we're not going to blow it this time. * *Have you been well?*

I have, as a matter of fact. I really felt that this week without working on the interview has been very refreshing and I needed a rest.

I thought we might begin with Colorado Legends *and the film about the two miners that P. Adams discovered. In your note, you said that you had no part in this project, but you do remember two people, Herman Herschel and George Nyberg. I wonder if you might fill in details of them.*

They were people from Western Cine Lab, the lab that Stan always used, and they were also involved with film in their ways. They didn't seem to have anything to do with Stan's films, so I was quite surprised to see that they had made a film together. It must have been that Stan got paid or he probably wouldn't have done it. But I'm not sure of that either, because he really did like John Newell, the top guy in Western Cine. John Newell was a very good fellow, he was so good that he would allow moths [in the original strip of *Mothlight*] to go through his tank of chemicals and trusted Stan to have them perfectly sealed. It was lumpy but it worked OK as far as I know. Anyway, Herman Herschel and George Nyberg were peripheral technical people [at Western Cine].

---

* Since I had failed to set the Zoom controls correctly for the previous week's interview, it was not recorded. This interview attempted to cover the same material.

From previous conversations, I had the sense that two or three films were made in a series called Colorado Legends.

Well, yes, there was the one that I mentioned with the monks, and then there was another one with the Indians. I don't know if that was made or not, I don't remember any images from it, so maybe there's only one left, the one with the Spanish missions coming to Colorado.* I only remember the image of Stan wearing the costume and me screaming. That was the high point in that production, from my viewpoint.

The people at Western Cine have been very reluctant to talk about their relationship with Stan.

There's nobody left at Western Cine [who knew Brakhage]. John died and he was the one that you should have talked with. His son took up the lab for a while and was running it for quite a few years, and he finally quit. The son was sympathetic to a point, but we didn't go with him. I don't know why.

Do you remember when Stan began his relationship with Western Cine, or did that predate your meeting him?

I believe he was already established with Western Cine, and that would have to be if he was making a film with them. That film was probably just about done when I met him, I guess, it might've been in the editing stage.† But yes, he was with John Newell and John was a very positive and friendly influence. We didn't socialize with him, but he was on our side. So it's interesting that Stan made up this story about having trouble getting the lab to print *Window Water Baby Moving*, but I don't know. Anyway, it was good drama, I guess.‡

You said that Stan made up a story about printing Window Water Baby Moving?

Well, just that the lab objected, but I don't think it did. Supposedly he had to get a letter from the doctor, sort of like the teacher demanding a letter from the parent. It's the kind of tale that I feel like, "Should I break it up or should I leave it?" because it made a better story than not having it. [It resembles] my story about going to Princeton and finding Dr. Rose in the telephone book and liked his name and made an appointment to go and talk with him. The first thing anybody said was Stan: "We want to make a film and we would much prefer a

---

* There was one other, *The Legend of the Colorado Ute*. (PAS)

† JW's uncertainty here arises from her not realizing that Brakhage's high school friend and frequent collaborator, Stan Phillips, was one of the founders of Western Cine. He produced the two *Colorado Legend* films. (PAS)

‡ In 1959, film labs were very skittish about printing film containing nudity. The lab, not the filmmaker, could be prosecuted. Roth v. United States (1957) upheld the "community standards" basis for prosecution until Miller v. California (1973) overturned it. There is often a nucleus of truth in the dramatic stories Brakhage habitually concocted. (PAS)

home delivery." Dr. Rose was extremely favorable from the get-go, but Stan had this whole complex thing about how I demanded to have the baby at home, and I demanded that he'd be there. I was fine with that. It wasn't a story at all there, no drama to it.

I'm sorry that we were never able to talk to the people at Western Cine because their support was very important for Stan's whole life.

It was hugely important, and everybody was envious of Stan in having a lab that not only was supportive but knew him by name and liked his films. That was just an enormous help. John Newell gets kudos for that, and I suppose Herman Herschel and George Nyberg.

Can we go back to where we were last week? We'd done Crisman, you'd gone there in…

I would like to know what this document was that you sent to me about Crisman with all these inaccuracies.

Those were my notes to ask you questions about. And the ones that are printed in black are P. Adams' addition to the chronology.

Well, I have to correct all those inaccuracies about Crisman, every little bit is wrong.

OK.

Crisman is not a town, it's an ex-ghost town. It is a ghost town that was actually little cabins or whatnot that were taken and fixed up by people, each by a different person and probably a subdivider got hold of it and sold each house separately so that each person could make a home out of it. Our house was bought by a man called Homer Hill and his wife, and they made a nice little house out of it, just kind of fixing it up and made a nice big picture window, which was an important part of my life. It had no shop, no gas station, and certainly no hospital. It was just a few houses that were like a suburb of Boulder up Four Mile Canyon. So that's the image of Crisman. It was in a little gully and below it downstream were signs of a ruined mill that was rather more ruined to be much use to anybody. But it was kind of fun to walk down there and look at the ruins. And that was the place where I said, "Someone's been running here. You'll notice the space between the tracks" that was quoted in *Blue Moses.*

Blue Moses *was shot in Crisman?*

Yes. *Thigh Line Lyre Triangular* was also shot in Crisman in the front room. So I had a nice view out that picture window of the hill across the way and the stream between our cabin and the hill. There's a broad meadow there and, of course, the classic white picket fence.

So Neowyn was born in your own house, not in a Crisman hospital?

That is correct.

Incidentally, you never give the dates of your children's birth. Are you deliberately keeping that from us, or could we put those in?

I just feel like it's one of the, what, three or four things that people get people's identities with and they could try every day and finally end up with it; but I don't know, maybe that's a foolish thing.

No problem. We talked about Neowyn's name a couple of weeks ago. You said last time that the house in Crisman was a happy house. You and Stan liked it there, Jim and Carolee visited there.

Many other people visited there. There were the three ladies that I mentioned: Inger, Sue Hoover and Nancy Stetson. There was also Robert and Bobbie Creeley* and their three kids, and George and Barbara Gamow and also Igor and Elfriede Gamow. There were numerous filmmakers and artists and oh, Aldine Weygandt came and I remember a tea party with Aldine, when she brought almonds. And as she was putting the bowl down, she said, "Every day that you have almonds, you won't catch cancer that day," and so I've been eating almonds ever since, pretty much daily. Aldine was the wife of the actor who played Mr. Tompkins in *Mr. Tompkins Inside Himself.*

I think last time you talked about how Robert Creeley's children and your children played together?

Yeah. They became friends through childhood and sadly it stopped happening after a while. That was too bad. Anyway, they were friends and also David† and Tina Meltzer's kids, three girls they had. They were family friends with our kids, and that was awfully nice.

Most of this time Stan was shooting or editing Dog Star Man *as well as* Blue Moses. *Were there commercial jobs while you were living in Crisman?*

Yes. There was the *Mr. Tompkins* series. I am trying to think of other sources of money. We were selling and renting films and so we were making some money that way, but that was not a living. So he always had to back it up with some-

---

* Robert Creeley (1926–2005), poet associated with Black Mountain. Bobbie Louise Hawkins was at that time his wife; he dedicated his most celebrated book, *For Love,* to her.
† David Meltzer (1937–2016), poet, especially associated with the San Francisco Beat movement.

thing. He had put his foot down and said that his wife was not going to have to work for a living! And I was happy with that because I had a lot of things to do at home. [*laughs*] So I took advantage of it and enjoyed a peaceful married life, except that Stan was not peaceful. He was not a peaceful influence.

Do you want to talk about that?

No, not particularly. We fought a lot.

P. Adams said that during the time at Crisman, Stan was getting shows in New York at the Provincetown Playhouse, went to Maya Deren's funeral, and received the Fourth Independent Film Award from Film Culture. *Do you have any recollections of those things?*

Well, P. Adams says that I was there for some of that, and I was trying to remember an award that Stan got, and I mentioned it to P. Adams just before the interview today. And maybe he's going to try and look it up, but I don't know how he can.* I remember going to that and meeting Robert Rodale, who was the son of the guy who really invented health food or made it very popular amongst Americans.

Did you go to New York for Maya Deren's funeral?

No, I don't remember Maya Deren's funeral, but I did go to the Maya Deren Award. I don't know if Maya Deren's funeral, that award, and seeing P. Adams Sitney were all in one trip.

P. Adams didn't tell me you were there, he just said that Stan attended Maya Deren's funeral, and I wondered if you'd gone with him.

No, I don't believe I did. I have no memory of it. We need P. Adams to straighten these things out.

But you do remember a trip to New York during the time you were living at Crisman?

Well, it might have been, but only because of the dress I think I was wearing. I have a memory of the dress but I can't be sure. But that was a dress that, as I told P. Adams this morning in an email, that I had used to catch a bat in Princeton. The bat had come into the house and the dress was a sack so that I could just pull it off and fling it up to the ceiling, and the bat flew into it and got tangled up in it. So I picked the whole mass up, tossed it out the window, and went and

---

* JW did not visit New York City during the time she was living in Crisman. She attended the ceremony a year later when Brakhage won the Maya Deren Award of the American Film Institute. (PAS)

got another thing to wear, and gave the bat also time to find his way out of the dress and then go.

But that was a few years earlier, when you were living in Princeton.

That's right.

OK, I think we've got everything we can about Crisman, unless there's something you would like to add.

No, I can't think of anything at the moment, but if things like that bat show up when we've moved somewhere else, I hope we can tuck it into the right place.

So now we're in autumn 1962 and you moved to San Francisco.

We went to San Francisco and we rented an apartment on Mission Street that had a rose in the front yard. I saw that the rose needed to be pruned, so I pruned it, and in response, the rose bloomed in January, which of course, in San Francisco, I guess that's all right. But I was thrilled.

It was a fairly nice apartment?

It was nice, but it was on Mission Street, which was the slum street. I thought it was nice, but I didn't get to know the neighbors, so I really don't know.

But you had a really interesting social life in this period.

Fantastic! Fantastic! That's when the poets started showing up. I don't know how this happened, but they would visit a lot. Michael McClure[*] and his wife, Joanna, I think was the one that got the closest with Stan. We visited with them often. I don't remember going to their place, so maybe they just came to ours. Lawrence Ferlinghetti would come, and he was trying to put a soundtrack on Stan's film *The Dead*, which was all made, but that was kind of charming. Stan got tired of it and said he didn't want a soundtrack on *The Dead* anyway. That was too bad in a way, because I liked Ferlinghetti as far as he went; he was not really sociable, but he seemed quite charming anyway. Other people, of course: Chris Maclaine,[†] he would come and talk about being a Methodist, meaning that he was on methadone, or was it methedrine? It was methedrine. He really was good at playing the bagpipes; I think he must've stayed overnight one night and at six o'clock the next morning, he was playing his bagpipes in our bay window. I felt it would be rude to the neighbors for him to be doing that, which I'm sure

---

[*] Michael McClure (1932–2020), poet and playwright who initially became famous as one of the five poets who read at the Six Gallery reading in 1955. His play *The Beard*, about a meeting of Jean Harlow with Billy the Kid became a *cause célèbre*.

[†] Christopher Maclaine (1923–1975), San Francisco-based Beat filmmaker, best known for *The End* (1953).

is why he did it. But he was quite fun. And James Broughton,* of course, and his fiancée, Suzanna Hart.

I'd like to talk about that in a moment, but Michael McClure must have been a very striking figure.

I think he was always a striking figure. He had this incredible grace, and I remember him walking. I gave him one of the roses, which was a beautiful color of kind of orangey crimson. He held it out in front of him and walked and was like being pulled down the street. It was quite charming because it seemed to refer to what is the 20th-century or 19th-century German group of writers who were all writing mystical stuff, what was it?† Aren't you a professor? [*laughs*] I'll think of it or maybe P. Adams will be shouting it to us.

You enjoyed this social life?

I loved it because it was so nice. Those people could talk. Poets are so good at talking, and somehow filmmakers talked a lot also, I'm not sure why. But the poets spoke always poetically, it was a great thing to listen to them talk. They had perspectives on things, they were always saying two or three things at once, you know.

You hadn't begun writing by this point?

No, no, no, no, no.

I think last time you mentioned that Philip Whalen‡ was also a visitor.

Phil Whalen! He was wonderful, I liked him a lot. He was not forward, not in the spotlight. He was quiet, but when he spoke, it was pithy and good. He was always taking off his shoes when he came into the apartment, which was not called upon by me. It was just his habit because he was a monk and he was always taking off his shoes wherever he went in the monastery.

I don't recall Stan ever mentioning him.

He was not that much of a talker.

---

* James Broughton (1913–1999), poet and poetic filmmaker prominent in the San Francisco Beat scene. In 1962, he married Suzanna Hart. Brakhage's footage of the wedding and events by the ocean comprise most of James Broughton's film, *Nuptiae* (1969).
† Possibly the George Circle, a group led by the poet Stefan George that criticized bourgeois materialism and embraced a mystical vision of cultural renewal.
‡ Philip Whalen (1923–2002), poet who also read at the Six Gallery reading. A Zen Buddhist, he received the transmission and became a monk.

Did you also say last time that Alan Watts came?*

I'm not sure if he came to the apartment, but we did meet him and got to know him a bit at Jimmy Broughton's wedding.

Could we talk about the wedding?

OK. We drove up there. I had been instructed to bring white doves and actually found a pair of white doves in the Japanese market that were supposed to go into somebody's soup I think but instead went into this wedding. They were turned loose at the proper moment. I've always wondered what happened to them, if they survived, and how they may have affected the genetic doves in the area. So we drove up there, it was way north, I'm not sure where it was. On the Pacific Coast, maybe a hundred miles north, so it took us a while to get there. We rode the train to get to San Francisco and we rode the train back. I don't know how we had a car, but we did; huh! The mysteries pile up. Anyway, we got there and it was a few days…

A three-day ceremony?

Yeah, it was a complicated thing. There was buildup, and then there was the wedding, and then there was other stuff and vows and whatnot. Each of them had his and her own guide or whatever. Alan Watts was Broughton's and Suzanne had another well-known person who was also into Buddhism, I'm not sure. Anyway, they were both guiding them separately, and it was kind of nice to have them there. Alan Watts was there with his wife or girlfriend, I believe her name was Jano, and we got to talk with them some. I think Stan had a good conversation with Alan Watts. I don't remember any really good exchange with me, but I was enjoying being there with all these people and listening to them talk.

So there were rituals here and there across the three days. We participated in them, and at one point we released the white doves up a chute. In the midst of three or four houses, there was a chute that led to the sky and so they were released in there. The problem was there was a tree partway up, so they didn't go straight up to the sky. [*laughs*] On the way home, we did stop at a beach and found this huge pile of abalone shells there. I ran off with a big bag of 'em, actually, and later put them in a footlocker and sent them home by slow truck. Boy, it was a slow truck, it was weeks and weeks before it showed up at Silver Spruce. I had just about forgotten about them, but they arrived, and I could tell a story about that with the Willoughbys when we get to the Willoughbys.

I understand that Stan was shooting film, documenting the wedding.

---

* Alan Watts (1915–1973), British writer (naturalized into the US) who lived in San Francisco, promulgating and popularizing several Asian religious traditions, especially Buddhism. His *The Way of Zen* (1957) was especially popular.

That's probably so, he would do that. I don't remember a film being made. It may be that Broughton just took the footage and he could make whatever he wanted out of it. Stan was cameraman for the wedding.

Still in San Francisco: P. Adams mentioned some films that have been lost: Silent Sound Stars Subotnick and Sender *and* Oh Life—A Woe Story—The A-Test News. *Do those ring a bell with you?*[*]

All three of them ring a bell.

Can you say anything about them?

Not much. *The A-Test News* had to do with stock footage of the atomic bomb. Raymond Sender and Morton Subotnick[†] are two composers. I know that Morton's a composer, I'm not sure about Sender, but I don't know anything more about that.

Somewhere, Stan mentions an event that took place in 1962, it might be one of his yarns. He said that the Ford Foundation arranged for a visit from a Polish film critic; he visited you and you had no food. You went out and borrowed some eggs and made an omelet, and you and Stan and the Polish film critic shared the omelet.[‡]

I am sorry, I don't remember. It's all quite possible, every detail, although I don't know who I'd go out and borrow eggs from. In '62 it would probably be San Francisco. We went to San Francisco with a little money, we had a few months' money in our pocket if we didn't spend much and got a cheap place to live. Mission Street was cheap, but we wouldn't have been out of eggs in California because we would've gone home on the train before that. We would've saved however much it cost two people and three children to get home on the train. So that might've happened in Crisman, that's possible. Let's see if I can remember it happening. I don't remember borrowing eggs from anyone. We never got on with our neighbors because I didn't go out and meet them and say, "I'm your new neighbor and dah, dah." Generally, we'd huddle in the house and hide so we didn't have a good relationship with them. But I suppose there were times in Lump Gulch when we were down to nothing. We can talk about that later on. Maybe that's where the Polish gentleman goes; it would be in Lump Gulch rather than anywhere else.

---

[*] JW thinks that *Oh Life—A Woe Story—The A-Test News* are two films. It was always one collage film from television and stock footage. It was never lost. (PAS) *Silent Sound Stars Subotnick and Sender* is lost.

[†] The composer Morton Subotnick was a pioneer in synthesized electronic music. A member of the Gadflies, he was a close friend of Brakhage's for many years.

[‡] The Polish critic was probably the film historian and director of the Łódź Film School, Jerzy Toeplitz. (PAS)

And it's just a mistake on the date.

The date, yes. Stan was not really good on dates. You point in the direction of them, I guess.

After being in San Francisco for a few months, in 1963 you went back to Silver Spruce because Bearthm was about to be born?

Yes. Bearthm was born in late February. So we had to have left at least by the first of February or sometime in January, although the rose was still blooming. I have this phrase in my head, "Roses in January," as if that was a definition of San Francisco.

And you returned to your parents' house in Silver Spruce?

Yes, as a place from which Bearthm could be easily managed, although Stan and Dr. Lockwood worked up a paranoia against me saying that they'd better induce labor on this one, because I might just go off in the woods and have the baby by myself. I'm sorry I allowed it, because it was not the happiest birth. I remember saying to myself, "Oh, I don't enjoy this"—which was the first time I even had that thought about having a baby. But he was born and he was fine, and then we moved to Hooker Street.

Did you meet the Willoughbys before Hooker Street?

1963, summer. Yes, we must have spent the summer there. I think the folks went off and did a little RV traveling or something, so that I was able to go in the mornings to visit with the baby. She would be nursing her baby, who was younger by a couple of months, and I'd be nursing mine. We'd be smoking cigarettes and drinking coffee and feeling as innocent and good as anyone could be.

So then you moved to this house on Hooker Street in Denver. It was loaned you by Taggart Deike?

He lent it to us. It was a rich or well-to-do upper-middle-class neighborhood. It had been very well built, made of brick and had a nice porch and everything, all the houses around it did. I'm saying all this in reply to Stan's downgrading the neighborhood as being creepy. It was a nice neighborhood, although it was kind of old buildings, but he said he was creeped by it. *Fire of Waters* was made from footage shot there.

Stan said there seemed to be an awful foreboding about that neighborhood. The houses looked like inverted bomb craters with a sense of imminent disaster.

That's what I was referring to. I didn't agree with that impression at all. It seemed like a safe neighborhood. There was a sense of the houses being old, but he had lived in an old big house when he was a kid, and it was one of his happy times in childhood. So I don't know what the problem was about having a house like that.

The basement had been transformed into a really nice little theater by some-body before Taggart showed up, I'm sure. We used it like crazy: we had people over once a week to do a show, with a few people in the audience. We would say to all our friends, "Come over and see what we've got." I particularly remember Robert Lee Tipps, a pianist, he played Eric Satie stuff, but he played other things too. I think Jim Tenney also played Charles Ives' Symphony No 2.* I crept under the piano to hear it better, but that was not at that place. I have a feeling that Jim might have played something there.

Stan and I did some interesting pieces from Gertrude Stein. There were read-ings of other things, or enactments of them. Was there a Chekhov? I don't think a whole play was done. I would like to have seen a Beckett play. I didn't see one there but I saw one in New York some other time. We had theatrical events in the theater. Sometimes there wasn't much of an audience, but always we were glad to have the show going, even if there wasn't much of an audience because people were busy or whatnot. We certainly brought the theater to life as best we could for the time we were there, which might have been six weeks or shorter. P. Adams came during that time and stayed for a few days interviewing Stan.† He says that I disagreed with all of his recommendations. That would be just like me, I guess.

Then the next thing that P. Adams says is that you visited Jack Collum in Seymour, Connecticut.

From Hooker Street? We left in the second or third week of September. I think we went straight to Custer, South Dakota. Now it may have been that on our trip to New York after we left South Dakota—that would be after Kennedy's death—I remember visiting, not Jack, but Tom and Gloria [Bartek], and their two kids, Aaron and Ethan. Ethan was born in 1957 or '58. I think he's a little older than Myrrena, but not by much.

Maybe we can return to that. But in late September 1963, you moved to Custer, South Dakota and you enjoyed that very much.

We enjoyed that. We worked for Chuck and Jane Nauman who were very nice people. Jane was a fabulous cook, she taught me how to make pickled buffalo tongue. It was excellent stuff. I sent P. Adams a huge container, I have always had the image that he opened it and smelled it and thought "this is not for me" and threw it all away. All my work over the hot stove was a failure.

Yes, what else happened in Custer? In America Center, where we lived, there were a few cabins that were usually just for summer people and we went in the

---

* It's more likely that Tenney played Ives' *Concord Sonata*, which he performed at Sprague Hall in New Haven in 1966. (PAS).

† Actually, they were editing the final draft of *Metaphors on Vision*. (PAS)

winter. We moved into a summer cabin, the neighborhood was empty. Custer was a little town, so if we wanted to do any big shopping, we'd go to Rapid City. The main thing I remember was the discovery of Korczac Ziolkowski who lived in the area.* He was a sculptor of some gigantic degree. He had worked for Gutzon Borglum on the Mount Rushmore faces, then he stayed in the area to make a mountain into a picture of Crazy Horse. He was just getting going on that, he was cutting it out, but he had made a little image of what he was aiming for, a gorgeous thing on a table. I was very pleased with what he was doing. He was a stompin', yellin' artist, just like that one in [Joyce Cary's] *The Horse's Mouth* only more so: "I can take a mountain and turn it into a sculpture of a great man in history and his horse." I remember he and Stan got into shouting arguments about aesthetics. He was a big strong guy, kind of overly fat, but very powerful. He bragged about how, when he was driving up the mountain one time, his car rolled over. He landed on his head; he got out of the car; he was fine; he had a headache but he was OK. Anyway, he was one tough guy. I couldn't—I don't think even Stan could—find anything really wrong with him, he was fascinating. He had ten kids who were being trained to grow up and continue the work because he didn't think he would finish it in his lifetime. He certainly didn't. At least one of his sons is continuing to work. It's going along; it's hard and slow, but it's going along. It may take another generation or two to finish the job, but it's a family project. That was fun.

Another strange thing happened. As we had seen that pile of abalone out on the beach in California, we saw a pile of fool's gold. Fool's gold is a beautiful thing, we took some hunks. Christmas was coming up and we wanted to send presents to people like Sidney Peterson.† He was another one we met in California and he's really important to me.

We failed to talk about Sidney Peterson when you were in San Francisco in '62.

That's correct. I don't know what else to say about him except that we met him at parties. I don't know if he came to the apartment or not. He talked with Stan, and he talked with me, and he talked to the both of us. He told of his history, he was doing work with Hollywood, at times, but he had dreams and he had made some films that Stan liked. I found him one of the wittiest people I've ever met. He just was so elegant and witty and marvelous. Then his films were strange— crazy things went on. He would talk about how he'd like to make a film about "throwing in the towel." Throwing in the towel is a gesture that has nothing to do with towels or with throwing them, so he'd like to do it as a statement of

---

* Korczak Ziolkowski (1908–1982), a sculptor who was asked by Chief Henry Standing Bear of the Lakota to carve a monument to Native American heroes. He began a sculpture of Chief Crazy Horse in the Black Hills that was to be 563 feet high, big enough to contain all the presidents' heads of Mt. Rushmore. The work continues today.
† Sidney Peterson (1905–2000), filmmaker and educator who began the filmmaking courses at California School of Fine Arts (later renamed the San Francisco Art Institute). His own surrealistic comedies, especially *Mr. Frenhofer and the Minotaur* (1949) and *The Lead Shoes* (1949) were very influential on the 1950s avant-garde.

"OK, I'm not going to do that anymore." But he never did. *The Lead Shoes* was strange. He did write a funny book, you had to get the joke to get the whole story. I think it might have been called *The Fly and the Ointment*. It was a fly in a painting by somebody like Breughel. It was so realistic that it came out and flew around in the museum. Then it was the fly on the wall, you know, when you listen to people, eavesdrop on a really important or embarrassing conversation. There were all the references to flies possible. He had this dry wit that you maybe not laugh about it at the time, but you laugh about it thirty years later, which I do. [*laughs*] I was very fond of him because of his grace and his kindness and his gentleness. He was a lovely, lovely man. I did see him later in New York in the old-folks home, with Marie Nesthus* years later in my travels. That was a wonderful thing.

What kind of work was Stan doing for Nauman Films?

I think he was photographing Indians in their lives. I'm not sure, I did not go with him in that work. I stayed home and minded the babies. I don't know what I was into craft-wise, but I'm sure I was into something, something that probably could be rolled up and tucked away somewhere. He was doing something for Nauman Films, but it wasn't essentially for the State of South Dakota, and I don't think it was necessarily for the Indian nation, which was the Lakota Sioux, I believe. I got to know them many years later too and I went to many sweat lodges and a few sun dances and really got involved with their ways. I liked them very much.

You say that when you were living in Custer, you got very involved with the Indians?

No, not until many, many years later, but that was the same tribe.

Did you have any connection with Sioux when you and Stan were living in Custer?

No. But there was one day when Jane [Nauman] had some of them over for lunch and I was invited too. Chuck and Stan were off doing something, so she thought, "Well, we can have a few of the ladies together and talk." I didn't make any distinct friends, but I heard stories from them, mainly about crafts using porcupine quills in decorating clothing and different powders to use to soften leather or to make it possible to draw on it. They were talking crafts and I was listening, of course, all ears. I noticed that Jane, who had been giving us buffalo meat, could now give buffalo meat to the Indians who are the ones that like it. But there were hamburgers. I said, "Why did you do that?" and she said, "Oh, you know the Indians don't like buffalo meat so much now; what they

---

* Marie Nesthus (b. 1942), archivist and programmer at the Donnell Media Center at the New York Public Library. She has written extensively on Brakhage.

like is hamburgers, they like fast food. So what I give them is the closest thing to McDonald's as I can, so that they'll like it and feel at home with it." So that was sad. I think that was the only touch I had with the Indians, that luncheon with them. I was very pleased with the talk we had with them about crafts.

Did Stan enjoy working with Chuck Nauman?

Yeah, he didn't have much trouble with Chuck. Chuck was very understanding of Stan. He would explain to Stan what was actually needed: a picture of this or that and do it, as you feel like. Be sure and get what it looks like so don't do the abstracting stuff.

So you stayed in Custer from late September 1963 until you moved to New York in July 1964?

That's right. I was pregnant with Rarc. That was the incident of the six-flight walk-up that somebody offered us so that we could stay in New York City.

I think we've done enough for today, but next time we might talk about when you visited Robert Kelly and met Guy Davenport. When did you begin making the Scrapbook?

On the occasion of settling down in Lump Gulch.

So we can talk about the Scrapbook *next time.*

If we can get to Lump Gulch! [*laughs*]

OK, this has been wonderful.

Always a pleasure, David.

Seven

2021 March 3. Ed and Jenny Dorn; Lucia Berlin; drugs; psychoanalysis; Robert Kelly; "The Birth Film"; jazz; Jonas and Adolfas Mekas; Film-Makers' Co-op; move to Lump Gulch; John Cage; birds and flowers; hippies; Kenneth Anger.

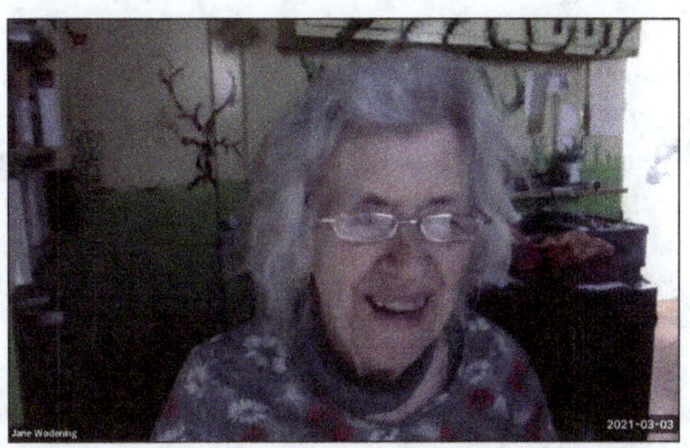

Hi, Jane.

How are you, David?

Can you hear me?

Yep. You don't have to shout!

OK, how are you?

I'm OK. I just hung up on P. Adams.

Were you arguing with him?

No, no. [*laughs*] It was time to talk to you. I warned him I was going to do it, but he kept on talking anyway. He was talking when I hung up.

He's so gifted in so many ways.

Yes, he is.

I have things to catch up on from last time, but if you've got stuff you want to talk about, then I'll follow your lead.

I haven't got a thing to talk about, I don't think. Oh yes, next week I can't come, I'm having a shot in my eye for macular degeneration, which is an old-age thing. Something to look forward to. My mother had it, it is genetic, so you may not get it.

OK. Was Ed Dorn one of the poets you met in San Francisco?

No, he wasn't there at the time.

Should we just get on record when you first met Ed Dorn and your general feelings about him?

Stan and Myrrena went up. Stan decided to take one child on every good trip, where he had a family to go to, especially if they had kids. So he took Myrrena on the first trip to Pocatello where Dorn was living with his first wife, Helene. I got to know Helene in my driveabout when I went to Gloucester many years later. They had a wonderful time. I think Stan had met him before with Creeley at some occasion where I wasn't at. They had a nice family occasion and Myrrena was enjoying their kids; one of them named Peter was interested in dinosaurs. Myrrena had a great time and they became family friends without me ever having seen them. He didn't come to Boulder until after he had gone to England and exchanged Helene for Jenny, so they were being frowned upon by everyone. They lived in the Boulder Chautauqua,† and they would come and visit. I remember them talking about ice-skating on the lake in Rollinsville. We got to know them then, when Ed and Jenny were just first married and having a lot of trouble with people frowning on him for breaking up with Helene, leaving her in the lurch in England.

The thing I was particularly impressed with was that when he spoke, he was always speaking in two or three lines at once. He was stating something practical and interweaving it with some fabulous social philosophy, and then maybe something else too. Very often he would talk like that and it made my jaw drop. I couldn't reply to him or even smile at his witticisms because it was too many things to listen to at once. So I was really impressed with him. Later on, he wanted to put a book together of my writing and Lucia Berlin's.‡ She died a few years ago. She's from California, you should know her. She wrote short stories, very dynamic and very funny, and yet very down-home. I think it was the down-home quality in one of her longer stories about the laundromat that he

---

* Edward Dorn (1929–1999), poet associated with Black Mountain and Charles Olson. He and his second wife, Jennifer Dunbar Dorn, were close friends with Stan and Jane Brakhage. His most celebrated work is the long poem, *Gunslinger* (1974). He taught at the University of Colorado at Boulder from 1977 until his death.

† Located in Boulder, the Colorado Chautauqua began in 1898 and has operated continuously since the Chautauqua Movement peaked in the 1920s.

‡ Lucia Berlin (1936–2004), short story writer who received posthumous acclaim for her selected stories, *A Manual for Cleaning Women* (2015). Ed Dorn, an early admirer, brought her to teach writing at the University of Colorado at Boulder, where Jane took one of her classes. Berlin wrote a preface to Wodening's book, *Book of Gargoyles*.

wanted and one of my longer stories, two that would be about the same length.
[They were] to be in the one book, facing opposite directions so that she would
just read on the right-hand side and then you could turn over the book and read
on the right-hand side and it'd be the other story. But it never happened. I've
always thought that it should have, but I think it's past the time for that. Ed was
very encouraging to me with my writing. He seemed to feel it was good stuff and
well done, and so did Lucia. Jenny became a very good hostess and very involved
with the people; she knew everyone and so she became a hub to visit. It was
much easier to visit Ed and Jenny than Stan and me, partly because the ride up
the mountain was something. But anyway, yes, as soon as we met him, Ed Dorn
was a real good, strong influence.

I'd like to come back to your writing, but just one question: would your contribution to the book have been something like the Lump Gulch Tales?

I think he was thinking about a biography I wrote of a chicken. I've written
two chicken biographies, actually, and this one was a hen who lived on the front
porch and loved Beethoven more than anything.[*]

Has that story been published? It's not in Lump Gulch Tales.

No, it's not in *Lump Gulch Tales.* It's in two places, *Mountain Woman Tales* and
The Lady Orangutan and Other Stories, where I've brought together a lot of
the stories I've written into a book, fifty-seven stories, it's a lot. And there's a
chapter on Lucia in my book *Driveabout.*

*When Stan told me about Dorn and Jenny's visit to your place, he emphasized
their sneaking off to smoke dope. Stan thought this was silly and that, if they
wanted to smoke dope, they could have smoked in front of him.*

Well, they wanted to sneak off and smoke dope out of the house so that they
wouldn't fill the house with dope smoke and affect us and the children and
whatnot. So I think that was very gracious of them.

*Would you talk about your and Stan's attitude towards drugs in this period. By
now we're in the late '60s, drugs are ubiquitous, and Stan is speaking vehemently
against them.*

The drugs didn't really become ubiquitous until we moved to Lump Gulch and
then kind of immediately they were there, or maybe they had been for a couple
of years, and we hadn't noticed because we were amongst people who were not
involved with it. But when we got to Lump Gulch, we became a place to visit
much more than we had been when we were living on the road. We had kind
of a place, especially after we added onto the house and made it bigger, and that

---

[*] "Biography of a Hen," *The Lady Orangutan and Other Stories*, pp.137-145.

would've been in the early '70s. We decided early on that we were just not going to participate in any of the drugs because of the same reason that Stan didn't want to go to a shrink: because he was afraid it would mess with his genius. He said it would mess with his angels.* He had a sense that he had a balance and he had to toe the line in a way. But there were many things that he was allowed to do that I would've preferred that he didn't. In my case, I just didn't want it for very much the same kind of thing. I didn't know what I would turn into. I think I felt like it would make me stupid, and I really struggled to be smart, but it's always a struggle. Anyway I didn't want any dope, although one time somebody brought some brownies and they even mentioned Alice B. Toklas, but I didn't catch on until I had eaten one or maybe two. They were absolutely delicious chocolate brownies, and then I just slept through the whole party and was no fun hostess at all. [*laughs*] And so that was my one real event and it was just pot.

But the stronger drugs: we met a lot of people who were taking acid, that was something that they were kind of religious about. They'd say, "You must take acid, it opens up your mind" and whatnot. A lot of people actually inadvertently killed themselves on acid. There was one guy that stepped off a cliff and another guy that had a car accident. The one that stepped off a cliff, his parents came to visit and hoped that we would tell them what the problem was. But we didn't, I don't know why. In retrospect I feel ashamed that we didn't tell them that he was taking acid and that he just did something really stupid. But their daughter had also died and probably had the same thing. And so they had no kids, they lost both their kids to acid. They seemed like, "What did we do wrong?" "Why have we been given this awful thing?" And I've felt bad about them all ever since then. They were just very square, very moderate-in-every-way-people but their children leaped into the immoderate and lost their lives.

And of course, Chris MacLaine finally took so much methedrine that he became a catatonic. I don't know if that follows, but anyway, he did become a catatonic. He may have been having fun being a catatonic, you just can't express yourself because things go so fast. But things were going fast with the methedrine also, so he jumped into a zone where he didn't have to take the drug anymore. A lot of casualties there and Stan and me just watching and not criticizing, just like, "Cool it at our place, OK? We've got kids, cool it." That was all we did, that was the attitude we took. But yes, we were both trying to maintain our own identities. It was so nice that we were together in this. But if he had taken drugs, I would not have joined him.

Could you talk about Stan and psychoanalysis. Did you discuss it often? I'm especially interested since Stan thought so highly of Freud.

Yes, he adored Freud. He gobbled up his books and all of his people and all their stories and their needs and how he affected them. He was just very interested in it and he had strong opinions about his students. Who was the guy that got into symbols?

---

* He was quoting Rilke's response about psychoanalysis to Lou Andreas Salome. (PAS)

Jung?

Yeah, Jung. I guess he fought with Jung, but Jung was like a fantastic world of thought also. But he stuck with Freud; if there were sides to take, he would take Freud's side. Of course, symbols were very interesting to Stan. But to the question of getting a shrink, what would he get a shrink for? To clean up his act in some way? That would disturb his system of working and thinking? No, those things that Freud did changed people. They took away their angst. It was terrible. What would he do without his angst?

But nevertheless, you and he did discuss the possibility of psychoanalysis at certain points?

No, no, no, no. He would bring it up and say that he would never dream of doing it because he didn't want to change. He wanted to be Freud, not to be changed by him.

Through my mistake, we missed your account of your visit with the Kellys. I wonder if you'd sketch your meeting with Robert and Joby Kelly. Did you enjoy the meeting?*

I did very much. It was such a sight. The two of them were both of them extraordinarily fat, side by side on a couch. I liked her very much. She was much more quiet. Kelly had this great booming voice. One reason that many opera stars are fat is because if you add fat to the voice, it enlarges it, it makes it resonant in some wonderful way, and he had this wonderful booming voice that came out of this large container. [*laughs*] She was quiet and she was listening and she was smart. We went out to lunch, I guess we went to a quick hamburger joint. Stan and I got something and he asked for four hamburgers with nothing on them. They looked so little in front of him, so tiny, they looked like four little cookies. He was working hard to lose weight; it looked that way because of the great size of him and the littleness of a hamburger with nothing on it, nothing, not even mustard. I don't think he just liked the bread and the meat together. But he was so amazingly smart and he was a killer at talk. It was really hard for Stan to rise up and face him and with Kelly, there was always a battle going on. When two artists converse very often it's a battle over aesthetics or how to think about things. I wish I could have remembered the conversations. Oh, there's your crazy machine!

Well, then I saw Kelly after he had lost about 150, 200 pounds or maybe more years later in New York. He didn't recognize me, and I didn't recognize

---

* Robert Kelly (b. 1935), a poet who shared Brakhage's preoccupation with immediate perception. Starting in 1961, he taught at Bard College for many years and corresponded with and wrote about Brakhage, most notably in "On the Art of Vision," *Film Culture*, 37 (Summer 1965); rpt. P. Adams Sitney, ed., *Film Culture Reader* (New York: Praeger, 1970), pp.258-59. His lines, "man lives in a fire of water and will live eternally in the fire of water," inspired Brakhage's film, *Fire of Waters* (1965). His wife, Joby, also taught at Bard.

him, but somebody said, "Well, you just were looking eye-to-eye with Kelly." He had also grown a beard and looked very, very different, a totally different person. He had a wonderful way. I loved his poetry, some of it was very magical, and Stan loved it too, so they admired each other, and that was good. But it was always a fight in a way, just because that's what they were. They were fighters.

I'd like to ask a bit more about your writing. Last time when we were talking about the Denver and Custer periods, I asked you if you were writing at this point, and you said you weren't. But in winter of 1964, you published "The Birth Film" in Film Culture.[*]

I didn't publish it in *Film Culture.*

Well, I have it here in this copy of Film Culture.

Oh, "The Birth Film," yes, "The Birth Film." I thought you said, *The Bird Journal.* "The Birth Film" was published in *Film Culture* shortly after Myrrena was born, isn't that right?

Myrrena was born in '58, and this essay was published in the winter 1963-64 edition.

"The Birth Film," yes. I don't know if P. Adams asked Stan for me to write that, but anyway, Stan did ask me to write it and said we could put it in *Film Culture.* If I could make something, I was pleased to do it. I felt like I had a viewpoint that was really special. And with the film going on at the same time, that was a crazy combination. I'd been obviously reading a lot of Gertrude Stein, and I kind of leaned on her rather more than I should have, but it was a nice piece I thought, and it had a feeling in it.

So you wrote it in Princeton?

I believe so. I believe I wrote it right there as soon as possible, within a couple of weeks or something. I feel like Stan was talking with someone—that would have been P. Adams,[†] I guess—and thought, "Well, a story could be made from that side and it would enlarge the field in a way."

You've not told me much about your writing, and I'm surprised that a work as sophisticated as this could have just appeared. I think it's beautifully written, and I'd like to talk a little bit about it if you're willing.

OK.

---

[*] *Film Culture*, 31 (Winter 1963-64); see Appendix 3.
[†] Inaccurate. (PAS)

The first sentence—and this is just a shot in the dark—"Being an artist's wife is strange, and when the artist uses moving pictures to express himself, it is very strange indeed." Would you care to elaborate on that, or is that self-sufficient?

Well, I think it's self-sufficient, yeah.

OK. But then the subsequent account is really marvelous. You go fairly straightforwardly through the early contractions, then there's this wonderful sentence, "…a strange sinking into a beautiful and frightening world then rising again a moment of bliss, then normalcy." You imply that this cycle of sinking into a beautiful and frightening world, then back into bliss and then normalcy, was something of an ongoing process.

That was the early contractions. I had actually studied up and taken the Lamaze classes very seriously. I was really capable of breathing in a way so that I didn't have so much pain. Besides, I have a high pain threshold, so I didn't consider the birth painful, but that was only partly because I was following along. I went into the contractions with a need to join them as kind of a great moment, this great thing that's happening. So that it was a period of bliss where other people would've said, "It hurts," but it didn't hurt me. I've always been able to hypnotize animals, I can just hold a sick puppy and let somebody give him a shot and shave his hair or whatever. And I can hypnotize myself sometimes, so the contraction was a period of bliss. That was the early contractions where you'd go into it and then you'd be released, you'd become something else. You'd be taken over by this contraction, and then you'd be released to normalcy or something like normal normalcy that would go away again in a few minutes.

After these early contractions, Stan reads Proust to you till 2:00 or 3:00 am and eventually the water breaks and Stan starts filming and you tell him you love him. Then there's this amazing paragraph, it's 450 words without a full stop, and it's just wonderful, ecstatic writing. Do you remember it? Shall I read a bit?

Please do, go ahead, yes.

OK. "I ask the nurse if she could deliver the baby all right without the doctor, and she says he'll come, and I'm doing fine, and I roar and roar louder and louder and pant and pant and pant faster and faster, and Stan talks to the nurse and films and films and, finally, the doctor comes and already there's a bit of hair born, and I go and lie on the delivery table and then the doctor says I can push, which I've been wanting to do all along, but I've been panting so as to wait for the doctor and everything to be ready because, when you pant, it comes slower so anyway I'm pushing and Stan's filming" …I'll go right to the end… "The head is born—the anterior shoulder—posterior shoulder—and then there is the baby held by her heels, and she's crying and I'm saying, "Baby, baby," over and over, and Stan is laughing and covered with sweat, and the placenta is born, and the doctor and the nurse do this and that to the baby, while I take some pictures of Stan because he is so beautiful, and then they all have a drink, but I'm quite drunk, and I eat a sandwich, and the baby is in the cradle and asleep, and then we were left alone and happiness everywhere." It's just a magnificent paragraph, five hundred words without a stop.

You counted the words?

I did, yes, it's so amazing.

[*laughs*] Well, thank you. I have always loved long sentences, and I've been scolded about them actually a lot of times, and very often I succumbed and cut them shorter. But yes, that one, I think, I was allowed because there was nobody that wanted to edit it. But yeah, I love long sentences. And when I discovered Henry…

Henry James?

James, yes, James, of course. Are you related?

[*laughs*] *No, I'm afraid not.*

Well, not that you know of! When I discovered Henry and what he would do with long sentences… and he was just really capable! I have actually written one story that's a half a page long and has only one period in it, at the end. But it is not like this at all, it's a story.[*]

What I'm trying to get at is your sophistication as a writer.

I've always liked to read a lot.

OK, I won't push you anymore.

I listen to music. I really love rhythm, and it seeps into everything I do, and reading is a musical event in a way to me, although the fact is I can't carry a tune. The only time I could carry a tune was when I was playing the recorder, and so I learned to carry a tune, even I could sing in tune at that time. But now that I'm not playing the recorder, I can't sing in tune. Rhythm is still the center, rhythm is everything; it's the maypole I dance around.

I have to tell you, it's just started raining here, and it's so beautiful.

Congratulations!

---

[*] *What the Ambulance Driver Said (a story with sentence diagram)* (New York: Granary Books, 1998).

It's only rained two days this entire winter, now it's raining quite heavily. Anyway, back to rhythm. Were you ever interested in jazz?

I have listened at great length at times to jazz, and it's not my rhythm. The only one I do like is Louis Armstrong, but I just like him personally. Although really jazz is not something you quite compose in—it's a community effort—there is one, Thelonious Monk. I listened to him a few times, and I think he's what I would call a real composer, a real artist, but I don't know what jazz is. Jazz is a whole different thing because it's a community thing. Maybe it's more like theater that way, but theater is all memorized, but there's a lot of scope always. Anyway, I haven't understood jazz, the main reason is that I'm a morning person and I can't stay up that late, it's just really hard to stay up that late.

In all his writings, I've never seen Stan mention jazz at all. Do you remember him ever saying anything positive about jazz?

Nothing, either positive or negative, nothing at all. I think people have asked him and he said, "I don't support jazz." He was saying something negative I suppose, but not from any knowledge.

You lived in Custer from September 1963 and then sometime in '64 you went to New York. In your annotations to P. Adams' transcription of last week's talk you wrote, "I was pregnant with Rarc. This was the six-flight walkup that somebody offered us because someone was on vacation so we could stay in the city. That's when we first met Jonas and Adolfas." Could you talk about that meeting?

I would say we went to a meeting that was actually a *meeting*, and it was for the formation of the Film-Makers' Coop, I think, and that was when I met Jonas and his brother.* Adolfas didn't hang around much after a while. He went off and was having his own life, I think.

He taught filmmaking at Bard College, where Robert Kelly was teaching.

OK. Interesting! Well, so the Co-op was being built and there was talk about what would be the proper attitude about the filmmakers and so on. I don't know if Stan contributed a lot. I didn't contribute anything except I was there and the kids were there. The kids were always pretty well behaved, except very often they would wet the bed they were sleeping on. [*laughs*] I remember they wet Guy Davenport's bed one time, and he didn't know about it until he got into bed, after we'd gone. [*laughs*] Anyway, Jonas seemed… talk about strange! He

---

* Jonas Mekas (1922–2019), Lithuanian-born filmmaker and poet. Active in New York from the mid-'50s till his death, he co-founded Anthology Film Archives, The Film-Makers' Cooperative, and the journal *Film Culture*. His brother, Adolfas (1925–2011), also a filmmaker, assisted in several of these projects.

was fresh from some unknown country in Europe, one of those strange little countries that you don't hear about much.

Lithuania.

Yeah, yeah, right. But it was strange. He seemed to know what to do and he was gung ho to do it, and he wanted permission from people; it seemed like his ideas and other people's ideas. I don't remember if Leslie Trumbull[*] was there or not at that time, but while he was there, which was for many, many years, always I took him as the major mechanism of the Co-op.

Not Jonas?

Jonas was, of course, the head honcho guy, but Leslie was always there to talk with him, and he would do things. So yeah, we went to this meeting and it was a strange room and a strange building, and I guess Stan presented that we needed a place to stay. Then this person said, "Well, a friend of mine has gone away for a couple of months, so you could use their six-flight walkup to live in." And I was about six months pregnant at that time, no, not six more, like four-and-a-half. So I did go and buy groceries and haul 'em up the steps. But I want everybody to be terribly impressed by Flo Jacobs and her living six flights up at eighty years old. Ken Jacobs and his wife Flo always have lived in a six-flight walkup. Flo had it back in whenever they met, she had that loft as a painter, and it was probably cheaper for being up six flights so they could afford it. So he moved in and the rest is history. I just was saying, you should be impressed that they walk up and down those steps even now in their eighties, because I had trouble carrying groceries up and pregnant and hauling four kids along with me. That was really complex.

Do you remember where the apartment was?

No. It was surely in the Lower East side.

Do you remember your response to New York? Did you like it?

I had been to New York before with my brother, and so I had a fondness for New York. I really had a fondness for it. I considered it a friend, although it was a troublesome to get around and dangerous, of course. But I was always careful about danger and I'm very fond of New York. New York is great because it has a pulse, it's aglow with energy. It's just an amazing compact of energy. You can hear the humming of the subway and the smell of it would come up through those incredible grates that were all along the sidewalk. You'd get the smells of the different shops as you were walking by, each one had the door open and emanated its own smell. Of course, the dogs had taught me to struggle to get the

---

[*] Leslie Trumbull (1933–2017), filmmaker who devoted his life to working at the Film-Makers' Co-op and Anthology Film Archives.

smells and I had learned my lesson well, so I was smelling what was going on inside. I guess it was around Christmas, and there were chestnuts cooking, especially down around the Metropolitan Museum, and it was great to walk in New York City. It's a great place to walk, you can just walk and it's many worlds. So I suppose that's why I walk down Colfax instead of sneaking through the residential streets nearby here in Denver. So I have a good impression of New York. Also, the museums: so much to see in the museums and everything has been seriously collected, or at least a lot of things have that I went to.

On your last night in New York, Stan's 16-millimeter equipment was stolen. Do you have a recollection of that?

I guess we had our car parked out on the street, and he had left the Bell and Howell in the car, and that was his only camera. And so he had to buy the Bolex right away because he couldn't do without a camera. I don't know if he even reported it. He just went and he got some help. Somebody said, "Where is the best place to buy a used a 16-millimeter camera?" And he went there and there was this nice Bolex and he bought it.* And so we went to Princeton with a camera. He couldn't stand to be without one.

OK, shall we go to Lump Gulch now and pick up where we left off. You moved to Lump Gulch in July 1964.

The first day of July 1964 we arrived; it was evening and all we had was canned goods. We hadn't stopped at a grocery store, we hadn't done anything. I think we might've had a loaf of bread, but no butter. We had I think two big cans of pork and beans and we had a big frying pan. It was a big cast-iron frying pan, and we had a fireplace. So I just pulled together some wood and some newspaper and built a fire and made some coals because everybody was hungry and they wanted to be fed. There was no gas in the stove. The fireplace was the only source of not only heat, but of light. I think we might've had candles, but we certainly had flashlights. So that was our first meal, and somehow we all remember it fondly, the big pot of canned pork and beans and some bread. We were all together and we had found this charming place that was made of logs, and it was very beautiful. And we were buying it, or my parents were buying it for us, and we paid them back year after year for a while.

Can you talk at all about the decision to move to Lump Gulch?

I don't know if my parents brought it up, but they had actually looked around and they had actually found this one. I had said, "Well, we don't want to go

---

* This "recollection" is confused. The car break-in occurred in 1964. Editing equipment was stolen, which Brakhage replaced with an entire set of 8mm film-making tools in Boulder. He did not own a Bolex until later. The Bell and Howell camera may have been stolen along with the editing equipment, but Brakhage did not indicate that in a letter he sent to several friends May 8, 1964. (PAS)

above the narrows," thinking that Stan would want to be closer to Boulder. But the price differential was just amazing between below the narrows and beyond Rollinsville. Beyond Rollinsville, it was an $8,000 house and below the narrows, it was $150,000 or something. So we kept looking and finally we realized that that one was the one to buy. So we settled on that, and it was kind of a long commute, but it turned out really all right. So many people took that commute as like, "OK, you have to drive for an hour." Maybe it wasn't an hour, maybe it was 45 minutes, but Mom and Daddy were really sick of us growing up in their house. They didn't want that anymore, so they were willing to put the money down and buy it and let us pay them back slowly. So that's what we did. It was a great relief to all of us, all of us, including Mom and Daddy.

You must have been very happy to be moving so far into the mountains.

Yeah, yeah. I was really excited about that. I didn't know it was 9,000 feet; what I was accustomed to was about 7,000 feet or less, 6,000, and the difference of flora and fauna between those two levels of altitude was amazing. We were then entering a totally different world with different creatures living amongst them. There were some other houses in the Gulch, it had been a little town called Gilpin.

What was the question? What was my reaction to living there? I was pleased, and then I realized, well, I could have animals. By God, I could have animals. Boy, I followed that one up. Living there, I could have animals, and it was a great thing for me to get to know many different kinds of animals beyond dogs. I had met horses of course, and done a little bit of riding, but nothing much. I'd pay a dollar an hour, that was how long ago it was. But yes, it opened a big world for me, and I was very grateful to my parents for wanting to get rid of us and sending us up there.

So you began to keep more animals yourself, but also began to have relations with other wild animals in the forests?

I guess there were some, but not much. It was really the domestic animals that I really got to know. I did write *The Bird Journal* starting in 1960. *The Bird Journal* was a journal of the birds that would come to my feeder and other ways that I would feed them. I started holding out sunflower seeds for them to come to my hand or suet, actually. I found that suet was quite fascinating because they'd have to sit on the suet and hammer it so that I'd be holding the suet in my hand, and they'd be sitting on the suet and hammering my hand. I could feel it, and it was quite wonderful. [*laughs*]

Could you describe how you managed to persuade the birds to come from the feeder to your hand?

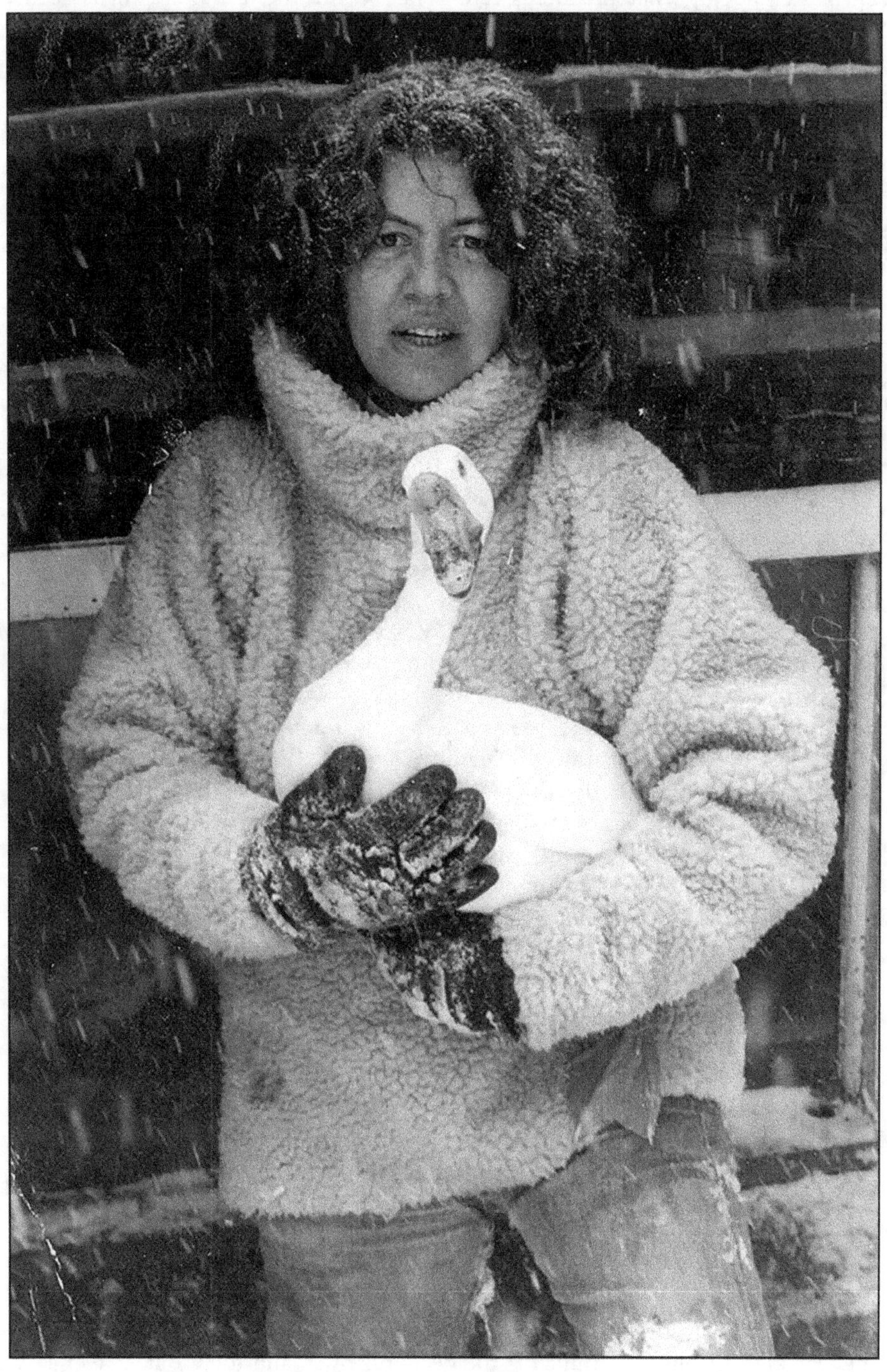

Jane with Goose, c. 1970s.

The difference of what was being fed. What was in the feeder was little seeds, millet and wheat; I can't remember what all was in the feeder, but there were lots of very nutritional seeds in there. But there was something absolutely wonderful about suet. It was a totally different hunger for suet. Suet was more passionate; it was like hot fudge sundaes. It was a different feeling than sitting down at dinner. It was like, "Yes, I've got to have it! I want it!"

How did you teach them that you had suet in your hand, and it was a good thing for them to sample?

They could smell it, I'm sure.

You just went out there one day with your hand out?

No, you don't start there! First, you have it on a tree, and they go to it on the tree, and then you stand by the tree, and you do that for a few weeks or something. You stand by the tree, and then you have some suet in your hand by the same tree, and they come to the suet in your hand, especially if there's two places. If there's one still on the tree and you have one in your hand, then they can see that the big guy's got the one on the tree, and so they'll come to your hand if they're the little guy. And then the big guys see that the little guy is getting away with something, so everybody starts coming to my hand. Then I go off to some other place, and they look at me and they think, "I wonder if she's got suet in her hand," and so they follow me, they come to me. [*laughs*]
    I asked Neowyn one time, "What do you think the birds call me?" And she said, "They call you 'The Feeding Woman.'" And I believe that's true, because years later, I was feeding them, and there was the name that they called me. It was a high and loud chirp, a single chirp—these were the chickadees—so I knew that was my name. Then I was walking down the road to town and I heard my name being called two miles away from my house. So I knew that it wasn't me that they were talking about, but it was food. They were calling me "food," yes, "food." [*laughs*]

When you have that kind of regular contact, do you ever get to the point where you can recognize specific birds?

Sometimes, sometimes. If they had some little thing like a black hair, a black feather where it should be gray, or something to give me some help, then I could do it. Or also, by the way they acted. There was one actually, when I was leaving the cabin in the Fourth of July Canyon—that would've been in 1998, so we're way ahead of time. But we're talking about birds and when I left there were several birds, and there was one particular one that was a new one. She came to me, and I saw that she was learning; she was clumsy and I recognized her because she was kind of big and chunky. I did recognize her, and for the next 10 years, I would come back and always have sunflower seeds in my pocket, always. I'd bring them out and I'd hear her calling before I even got there. She would be calling "Jane," that is to say "food," and I'd pull it out [*laughs*] and there would be that particular chickadee for the next ten years. So I knew that chickadees could live ten years, that's how I found that out. That was ten years of finding out a boring piece of information about chickadees.

Were there other birds or was it mainly chickadees?

Oh, there were other birds. You want to go to Fourth of July Canyon? This is leaping ahead 25 years, but we could do it.

Let's stick with Lump Gulch for the time being. What other animals did you befriend? ·

You're talking about wild animals, but it was other birds mainly, although there were ground squirrels.

Porcupines?

I didn't get along well with porcupines because I had dogs. Dogs have a real problem with porcupines, and I've had some hard times with porcupine quills. I did have a nice conversation with a porcupine once. I was walking through the woods—this was in Lump Gulch—and found the tracks of a porcupine around a tree. I looked up the tree and there was the porcupine. I just stood and looked at him and he looked at me, and we just stayed that way for a few minutes. I felt like I had communed with a porcupine, I liked him, I liked him very much. He was stodgy. He had his system that worked, and he didn't want to use it on me or anybody really, but he would if he felt the need to defend himself. So that's it for the quills, but within that, there was a person who was, as I say, quiet, slow-moving, careful and capable. He liked bark, so he was OK, eating bark. He had places where he kept his food and he had places to go to find more food. He was kind of an orderly individual person; he had it figured out, so I liked him. I thought, "Well, that's probably a lot of what a porcupine is." But I felt related to that because I've always felt like, well, you want to go slow; "Slow and careful wins the day," or the tortoise beat the hare, or stuff like that.

That was just enchanting. Thank you. I love that.

Glad it was enchanting. [*laughs*] I didn't think of it as enchanting.

I love the story of "Mrs. Shuster and the Porcupine" in Lump Gulch Tales, *so that's why I mentioned porcupines. What about flora? Did you have any interest in flowers and trees, or was it just animals?*

I memorized all the wildflowers, and I got to know them and their medicinal uses. I was particularly interested if they were edible, but it seemed as though there was not enough edible vegetation to survive, even at 9,000 feet, let alone the

10,000 feet I later went to. But the flowers I was charmed with; I would go and visit them and I had all their names figured out. I would take people on walks in Lump Gulch often across all those years. I don't know how many hundreds of people have gone on a walk with me in Lump Gulch, and I hope they've all remembered it, and I hope they've remembered it kindly. I would go and if there was nothing else to talk about, I would go naming the flowers as we went along. When it was John Cage,[*] he always really loved, not the flowers so much as the mushrooms. He'd come to go for a walk if he'd come to Colorado. He wanted to come up to Lump Gulch and go for a walk. But a lot of times it was so dry that we just didn't have mushrooms up there, just like LA Is it still raining?

No, it stopped. So Cage visited you in Lump Gulch?

A few times, yeah. Cage and that little guy who played the piano, David…

Tudor?

Yes, that was it. I would have wished that Merce Cunningham would come, but I only saw him in New York.

Did Cage stay overnight with you in the cabin or just come up for the day?

He would stay in a hotel in Boulder.

When you were getting to know the animals and the flowers, did you have conversations with other people who lived in Lump Gulch, the kind of people that you write about. Or were you self-taught?

Oh, I had books, and my father was interested so he and I talked. But mainly I had these books and I'd go out. I remember Billy Fisher and Bobby Benson and Windy [Newcomb], some of all that gang, were there. I was getting thirsty and I thought, "Well, we're not going to have coffee. We're going to have tea." And I said, "Let's all go out and pick tea." So we went out and we picked chamomile. I don't know why I wanted to give people chamomile, maybe because they were getting very nervous because it was very calming, especially the Rocky Mountain Chamomile, which is very small and not much noticed, not a very pretty plant. Anyway, so we went out and picked enough chamomile to make a big pot of tea. They were all impressed and remembered it all their lives, I believe. So I had to remember it too, because they kept mentioning it.

    I used the plants if they were usable to me. I used the red clover, I used the rose hips. I remember in the middle of winter one time there was a big blizzard, all the kids were coming down with a cold, and there was no way we could even

---

[*] John Cage (1912–1992), composer, music theorist and mycologist, best known for use of chance operations in composition. After first meeting him, Brakhage wrote to P. Adams Sitney that "Cage has laid down the greatest aesthetic net of this century"; cit., P. Adams Sitney, ed., *Film Culture Reader* (New York: Praeger, 1970), p.242.

drive to Rollinsville. So I went out with my big boots to where I knew there was a big rosebush under the snow. I dug down and picked a big handful of rose hips, brought them home and put them in the blender, and made some pink lemonade out of rose hips. It was amazing how well it cured that cold, it just went away. Those would be wild roses up there. So yes, I was very involved with plants also, and I got more involved with naming them because of their usefulness, I guess, or maybe because people asked. But the trees I would like personally; some of them I would go to visit and just sit with 'em or look at 'em or just sit under them for a while. I really liked them personally, just to be with. So there were a lot of things to go out into the neighborhood for.

You mentioned that a lot of the people who lived in Lump Gulch commuted to Boulder, presumably to work. I guess by that point, the demographics of Lump Gulch were no longer the old timey folks that you write about in Lump Gulch Tales. *How did you get along with the other people in Lump Gulch?*

Well, they were all different, and some of them were related to or descended from—or remembered—the 1930s. This was the '60s, so they would've had to have lived there for more than thirty years to tell me about those people, Henry Nicham and the various people that lived there. Jim, what was his name? And there was the one that told me the story about the ambulance driver. That story was one sentence, the one I just mentioned. It was a one sentence story that was half a page long, and I will send you a copy of that. It is actually a wall-hanging.

Did you encounter any social resistance? Were people suspicious of you artist/ hippie types, or was it easy to mix in socially?

It was hard. It was really nice when I went around and asked for stories because, even if they didn't like the gossip about Stan or about our guests, they were happy to tell a story. They were happy to tell me their memories of people in the '30s and how they struggled. That was a good thing, it was very warming to me, how they would open up and tell me stories. I got that whole book full of stories from them, from people that I didn't know if they liked me or not but assumed they didn't. But also I had not reached out towards before. So this time I was reaching out and they gave, every one of 'em, gave me stories. One of the stories they wouldn't let me publish because it was too intimate, they didn't want that as a family memory. It was about how their grandmother got married; it was not a love match, she just had to marry this guy. Not that she was pregnant, but that it was the proper thing to do.

When did you collect these stories?

I think it was about '82.

Not in the '60s?

Oh, no, no, no. We're going way ahead again.

So you'd been there for twenty years before you began to reach out to them?

Well, oh yes. You were asking about what people thought. Actually, yeah, later on, particularly when we were getting a lot of hippies… I guess the hippies were visiting after we added on—no, there were people there before. I wanted to tell you about being poor for the first three years, but these questions seem to be relevant to the whole period. But yeah, there was a time—I think it was after Kenneth Anger visited—that Smitty, the Sheriff, would stop by for a cup of coffee often, and be just aimable and friendly, and "How are things," and "Is anything going on?" "No, nothing much." I think he was checking up on us, although I was hoping that he liked us, that was what I hoped. But evidently, he had a guard on us later on that was watching from across the way with binoculars, watching visitors coming because somebody who lived in Lump Gulch was dealing dope. And of course, they assumed it was us. No question. I mean, the other people were square. So they were watching to see about us dealing dope, and obviously we weren't. But I'm trying to think where that was in relation to Lump Gulch. If you could find out when Kenneth Anger* visited us… because Smitty came when Kenneth was at the house. And instead of sitting down at the table and me giving him a cup of coffee, he said, trying to sound official, "We're looking for one Kenneth Anger." So I said, "Just a second, Smitty." And I went in the back room where Kenneth was and I just looked at him questioningly and said, "What do you want to do about this?" He had heard Smitty, so he actually came out and then was sent home to California. He had been escaping being a witness to something or other that was going on back there. After that, we were for sure bad sorts. So I don't know.

Do you remember any other gossip that was circulating about Stan and your guests?

Just mainly that they were wild hippies and druggies. The guy and his family that had been camping over at the county line lake, he came over to visit and stayed for supper, he and his wife. That was the Pig Farm, the Pig for President campaign.† That was a guy from the Pig for President group. What was the name of the pig?

Pigasus.

---

* Kenneth Anger (1927–2023), filmmaker, especially concerned with gay and occult themes.
† A long-lived Los Angeles commune, the Hog Farm was founded by peace activist Hugh Romney (aka Wavy Gravy). In 1968 many of its members set off on a cross-country caravan, intending to nominate a pig, Pigasus, for president at the National Democratic convention in Chicago. David Lebrun, a member of the Hog Farm, photographed the trip and digitally restored the footage to make *The Hog Farm Movie* (2019). Jane stayed at Lebrun's house when she visited Los Angeles in 2020.

You remember the pig! Well, I didn't meet the pig, but I did meet some of his friends, and they were very nice people, and they had two kids. I met him again when I was down there in Los Angeles last spring.

David Lebrun.

Yes. I was living in his house, actually, and reminded him that, although he didn't remember it, his wife inadvertently left a bowl behind at our house, and there was no way I could reach him because he was just camping out. Anyway, so I had the bowl, and I think my daughter Neowyn has it now.

There were no unpleasant confrontations between your family and the other inhabitants of Lump Gulch?

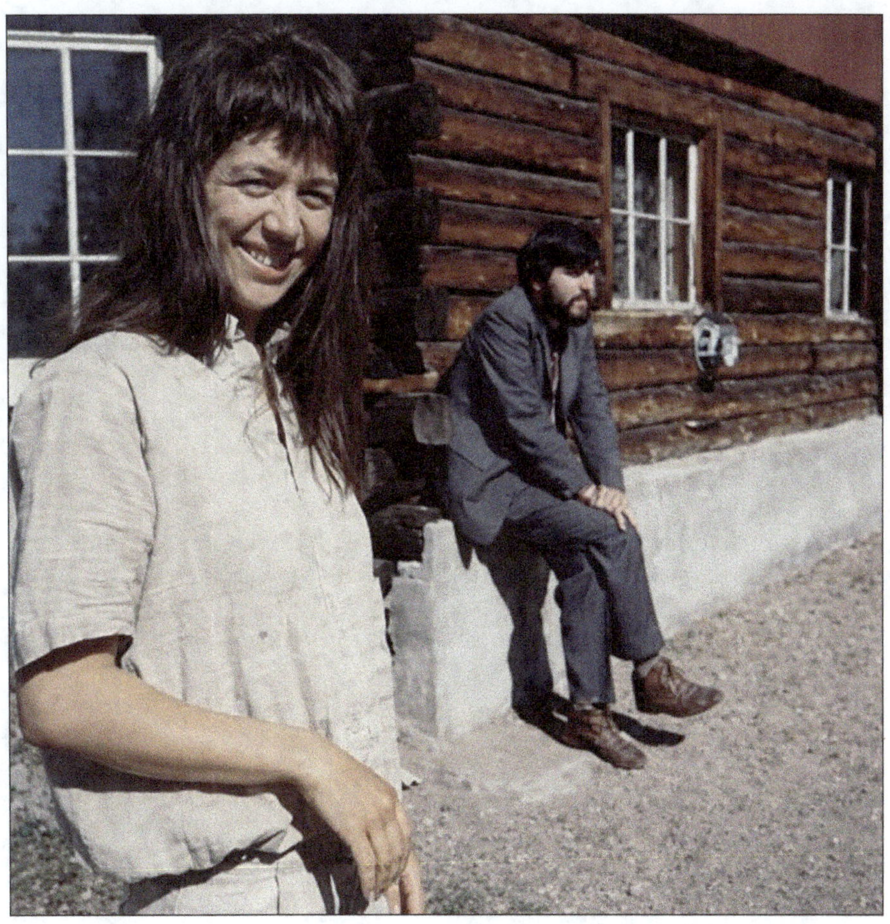

Jane and Stan at Their Cabin in Lump Gulch.

No, I don't think so. We did actually hire one of our neighbors to add onto the house, and so he became a friend, an associate, and he asked me one time, "Where is Stan at this time?" And I said, "He's out making money to pay you." I guess that was a suspicious thing that he would go away and come back; they didn't understand anything that we were doing, and we didn't explain it. I should have said more than "out making money," that could be thought of in a bad way, I guess.

But the fact that Stan was a celebrated filmmaker was known in Lump Gulch?

I think so, yeah.

But there was no attempt to capitalize on Stan's celebrity or have a little article in the local paper about this wonderful filmmaker who lives among us.

No, no. There was no paper that was anywhere near local to Rollinsville. There could have been something in the Nederland paper. Our kids went to the Nederland schools, and they were weird also. They were strange, and so they were not popular kids in school. I think they just wanted to keep quiet about it and not do much at all about us, not brag about us. If they bragged about us, there might be a kickback.

Do you want to talk about being poor for the first three years now, or shall we save that to start out next time?

Let's start it out next time. We should stop. I mean, yeah, being poor. Got some good stories in it.

Great. So we're not going to meet next week, but we will plan to meet the week after at the same time.

Yeah, yeah. We can catch up on other things. We have this ongoing interview, which is really a wonderful new habit, and I'll miss it when it stops. [*laughs*]

I feel very privileged to be able to talk to you, it's a great pleasure. Thank you.

Yeah, thank you. Bye, David.

Bye.

Eight

2021 March 17. Stan's jobs; Rarc born; Scrapbooks; the meaning of Art; gardening; dogs; goats.

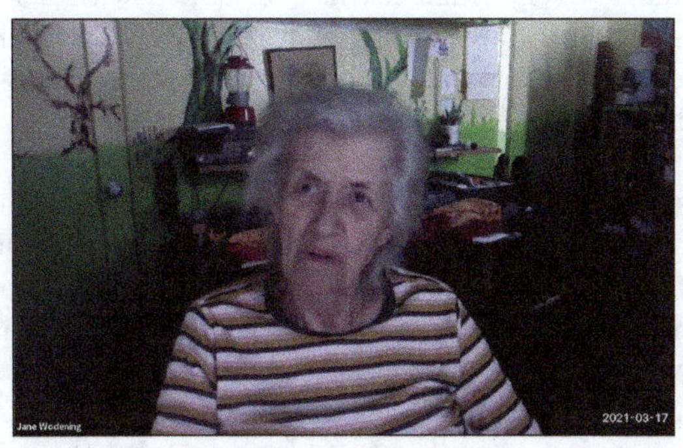

Hi, Jane, can you see and hear me?

Hi, David. Yes, except for this thing that's in front of you that says this meeting is being recorded. How are you?

Very well thanks, how are you?

I'm good. I have had two shots. You got a shot?

Yes, my wife and I have had both of them.

Oh, that's great. I felt ecstatic at the thought of it, I don't know why.

Alright! Last time you ended by saying you wished that we had talked about your being poor for three years. Would that be a good place to start today?

Well, I guess so. Oh gosh, I should have been thinking about that, us being poor.

Had you been thinking about something else that you want to start out with?

No, no. I've been thinking of something totally else and getting some work done on the book and visiting friends, and actually my friend Mary died. So I've been mourning about that and I haven't thought about you much at all.

So anyway: poverty, let's see. We came to that house and finally we had a house. We didn't have to pay rent, and we were a long ways from any job possibilities. Stan tried to fill in by setting up lecture tours. He'd call up a string of places in the West and try to get some lectures there so that he'd get paid. He never did a lecture without being paid. He couldn't do that that often, but that was something to do. I didn't have my job—that was just a dollar an hour job, no, it was piece work; anyway, it wasn't much pay. And besides, I was pregnant for the first bit. It was interesting you know; we got to Gilpin County and Gilpin County saw that new people had come to this particular house and that the woman was very pregnant. And so a county nurse came to visit and I thought, "Well, that's a very small town." We talked with her and we talked about our doctor down in Boulder, and so she figured we were really all right. But it was very nice to have such a small community that they would know to send the nurse over to visit.

We had our four kids and I was pregnant with the last one. I don't know how many times Stan went on lecture tours. Of course it was a good thing to do, but it was also not so great if he set them up. It was better if the other people set them up and then there'd be a much bigger crowd and it would be a better show, so he was kind of hesitant about doing that. So then, what to do to make money? He asked the lab, Western Cine, "Do you need me down there?" "No." "Know anybody that needs me?" "No." So it was hard.

All the years of driving around, we had been learning frugality so we were both very, very tight and frugal. I remember we got down one time to grapefruit and chicken bouillon cubes. [*laughs*] It could be considered a square meal in a way, but kind of short. But that's what we had and the kids put up with it. They knew not to howl about it, they just waited for something good to happen. One time—it was Crystal's birthday—and we didn't have any flour or anything to make a cake out of. We didn't have anything to give her as a present, and we didn't know what to do. We went to the post office as usual, our big trip to town, three miles. And there was a letter from… I was going to try and think of that guy's name; he had a funny name and he was a well-known writer of children's stories.[*] He said in the letter, "A dream instructs me to send you $50, which I do with pleasure." I got it memorized. [*laughs*] There was a $50 check, so we went right next door to the post office, into the grocery store, and bought a cake mix and some other edibles and spent the whole fifty bucks on food and had a celebration. The kids were very happy that we had plenty of food, including a lovely cake with frosting, and I think we had ice cream too. The horrible part was that Stan said, "OK, I've got to do this." So he wrote back and begged for more. That just irritated me. Then we never heard from him again.

That went on for the three years. He'd go and get some money and come back, and then that would get gone and we wouldn't still have any resources. But finally he got a letter from the Art Institute of Chicago, and they said, "We would like you to come and teach every two weeks." So it wouldn't be like day-to-day teaching, it would be a visiting thing because he would be gone every two weeks.

---

[*] Daniel Pinkwater (b 1941), artist, writer and broadcaster.

I was very aware that he got a mistress there early on, and other women too. I haven't mentioned his womanizing, but the Chicago Art Institute was definitely a place where he enlarged on that. I was miserable all the time. I tried to be cheerful, I had kids to raise, I tried to make life fun for them, and I succeeded in a lot of ways. But it was a constant burden during the whole thirty years actually, starting before Myrrena was born and going on. It was a definite constant background.

Very early on, as soon as we got there, I realized that a twenty- or eighteen-foot-long kitchen needed a ten-foot table. And so did seven people actually. I knew that we couldn't buy a ten-foot table, but I went and bought two split spruce trees and made a table of three of the halves with one half for a bench in the back. It took me six months. I turned everything over so that the table would be flat being on the floor, and I decided to chisel spaces. I brought out some maybe two-foot-long pieces of firewood that we didn't want to cut up because it's a hard job to saw wood full of knots. I put these six pieces, I guess… Did I have two sets of legs or three, maybe it was only two sets, so it was only four pieces and crossed them near each end, so you could put your knees under. Then I chiseled spaces for those logs to go, and I think I drilled a hole through each. As I say, it took six months because I was chiseling and I was just chisel, chisel, chisel, and finally I got it right, and I was constantly measuring. So that was my first project in that house, and it was a great joy, even though it was really hard. My father had taught me things when he was building cabinets when I was a kid, and I kind of understood about how to be a carpenter in a way. He taught me how to chisel too. We discussed it beforehand: how do I make a table? And that was the way he came up with, and it really worked well. One day, some people came over and I asked them to turn it over because it was too heavy for me, and certainly Stan never was the kind of guy that could do anything like that. I think it was Angelo di Benedetto and a couple other people came and just turned that table right over. And then I said, "Oh my God, I forgot to measure whether it was level." And I got out the level, and since I had been measuring and measuring and measuring, it was level. So that was taken care of, thank God.

Fabulous.

And that was after six months, it was like a new house. We had our kitchen table, and as soon as Stan went to work for the Chicago Art Institute, I brought out my scrapbook-making things and with Stan's first salary I bought this big hunking scrapbook. I don't know if you've gone to Yale, but anyway, it's at Yale, all three of them actually. I finally made three and pulled out that box of all the letters and pictures and notes and whatnot—things that I was saving—and started putting them into the scrapbook one at a time. And I set up another smaller scrapbook for the kids and gave them some pictures and a lot of crayons and paper to make pictures and illustrations with, and they were happy. So we would be happy working on the scrapbooks while Stan was gone in Chicago.

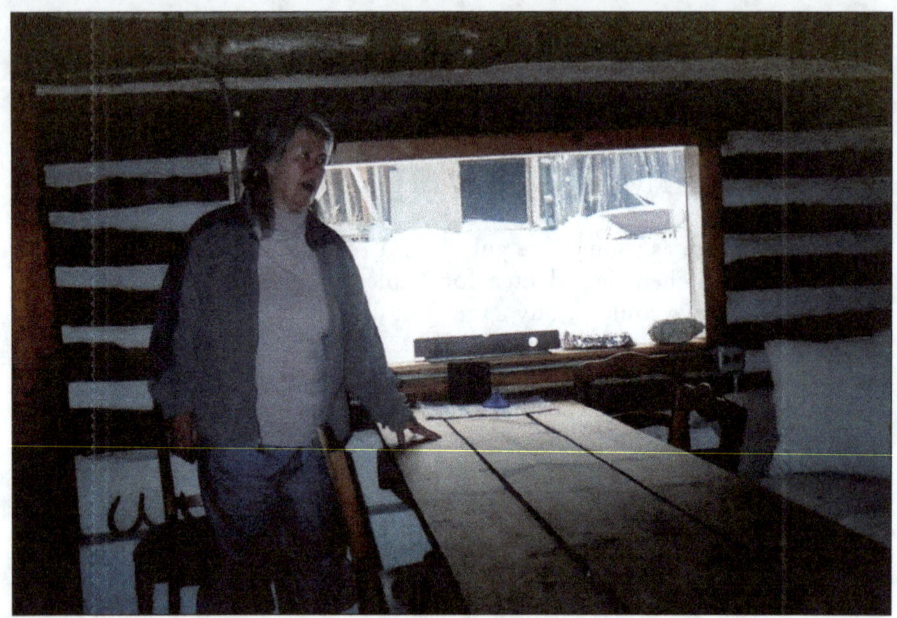

Jane with the Table She Made.

It was slow going. I would work on an open pair [of pages] and that might take the whole three or four days that Stan was gone and just get that done and then be able to close it to, because then the glue had to dry. I used, not Elmer's glue and not Scotch tape, but this tape called Mystik because it was cheaper and it worked kind of nicely. But I think all of that has, after fifty years, finally lost a lot of its virtue. That's one reason they made those copies of the scrapbooks at Yale. But that took many years to do those three scrapbooks. All three volumes are online; you can find them on my Wikipedia page, or on my website.

I'm skipping Rarc's birth, which was like six weeks after we arrived. We went to the hospital for that one too, because the doctor didn't want to come all the way up there, drive forty-five minutes to get to us. So we went down and it wasn't going to be our doctor, it was going to be his partner because our doctor was on vacation or something. We had to ask, "Could we bring a record player?" I guess, so that we could play the *Art of the Fugue* and "Could we take pictures? "And he said "Yes" to both, thank God. By this time though, Stan was not making another film like *Window Water Baby Moving*. He never did. Actually, Crystal's birth was in Part Four of *Dog Star Man*, Bearthm was in Part Two of *Dog Star Man* and in *Bloodstone* and *Blue White*. Neowyn had *Thigh Line Lyre Triangular*, which was covered with paint, expressing Stan's feelings and kind of hiding what he was having feelings about, but not entirely, that's for sure. But then Rarc, what was he in? He was in a *Song 5,* I think. After that we didn't have kids.

So we got used to the pattern of Stan going to Chicago and coming back; he'd be at home for two and a half weeks, and then he'd go for a few days and come back and so on. That was it for years. So then we had money; we were still frugal of course and didn't know how to spend money anymore. That was good because then we could add onto the house in '72. I don't know what to say now. I think we've done the poverty good enough.

Well, you've just swept all my notes into uselessness.

I'm sorry, I answered them all?

The final thing I wanted to talk about was the remarkable scrapbooks. I wondered if you would be interested in talking about the scrapbooks in relation to your previous history of crafts. Through these conversations you've talked about the different kinds of crafts you'd been doing, especially various things with fabrics. I don't recall fabrics in the scrapbooks, but they seem to be the kind of work that a woman would do in her home, like the crafts. Are you interested in talking about the scrapbooks as an instance of your own craft creativity?

Craft? Yes, well in our travels, I had seen a number of collages, including Jess Collins'* and some of the people in New York. There was this guy that sent things in the mail, little packets of collage items, I can't remember his name.† But anyway, I was interested in collage, and it was just a natural thing to take these things out of the box and collage them in, page after page. I'd take the two pages, and those two pages would be essentially usually one thing, although sometimes they'd just be two smaller ones. So that would be my canvas, what I put my collage on. It would have to be a thing in itself, a piece of work. All the stuff in the box was kind of mixed up together. It was not in chronological form, it was just in the box. I would just grab something because it matched, because it was talking about what was there on the page of what I'd put there. I put a letter, I don't know, from...

Robert Creeley?

Well, OK, yeah… Creeley was a close friend because we had gotten the families together several times and something that related to what he was saying, it could be a picture or I don't know. I keep saying a leprechaun. I don't know if I have a leprechaun in any of those pages, but that's what came to mind. Or various things that seemed to relate, or little comments that some other person had said. And I would cut them out of their context and put them in. There's a book that I was very excited about at that time, a 19th-century story called "Lucile" about a nurse, all in iambic pentameter.‡ I just loved putting it here and there in the scrapbook to keep the rhythm slow. If anybody wanted to read that, they'd have

---

* Often known simply as Jess, Jess Collins (1923–2004) is best known for his intricate collages. He was the partner of Brakhage's mentor, Robert Duncan.

† Probably Wallace Berman who sent select correspondents Semina mail packets. (PAS) Brakhage visited the Los Angeles artist, Berman (1926–1976) and admired his film *Aleph* (1976), restoring it after Berman's death.

‡ "Lucile" by Robert Bulwer-Lytton, published in 1860 under the pseudonym Owen Meredith.

to read it in iambic pentameter, which keeps you going pretty slow—because I do everything slowly, and it seems to be a great service to me. So yeah, as I say, the Mystik Tape and the Elmer's Glue were my constant companions, they were there always. And their kids had their own Mystik Tape and Elmer's Glue, and we would look back and forth at each other's work. They were wonderful at working together; it was a beautiful thing, seeing them working together. Sometimes one would take the page and do it, and there's me busy doing something else. Nobody helped me, I wouldn't let them help me, but I wouldn't let Stan either. Although they say it's Stan's scrapbook, it's *my* scrapbook, but I put him in there quite a bit, so that helps them make their case. But yeah, collage was really interesting, and I realized that I carried that on into my quilting years and years later when I was doing appliqué, which is the same thing as collage. So collage was it, and that was my craft of the day. When Jess Collins did it, I guess it was an art. But it was a craft, I guess, because it was on a scrapbook. So!

You just flummoxed me again. The next question I was going to ask you was, "What was the relationship to the scrapbook and quilting?" You've got me there.

[*laughs*] Well, I started quilting much later. That was way after Stan left. It would be 1998 or '9 when Carlos and I went up to visit his mother in Utah.* She was a great quilter, she was like a traditional prairie-schooner quilter, and she won prizes all the time. She said, "It's easy to win prizes in my county because nobody else makes quilts, at least not like I do." So she always got the prize, she went

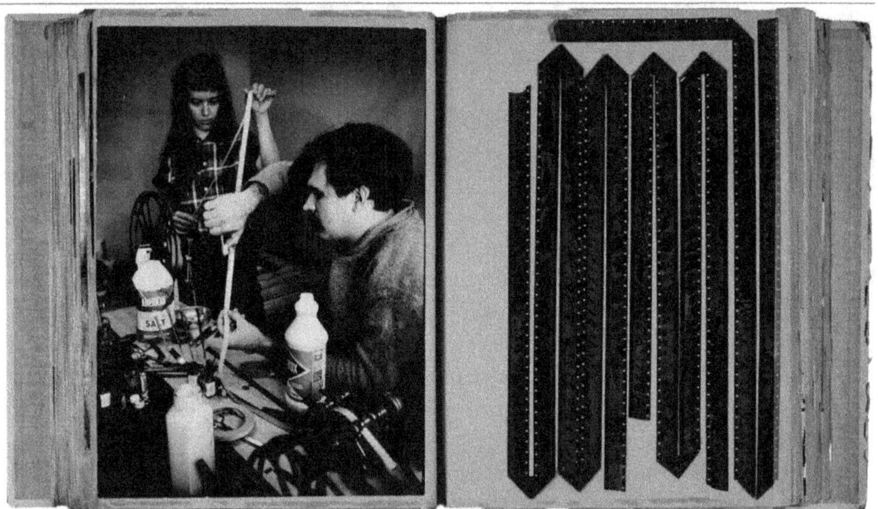

Pages from Jane Wodening's Scrapbooks: Jane and Stan Editing; Film Strip from *Mothlight*.

---

* Towards the end of her stay in the cabin in the Rockies, Jane met another ham radio afficionado, Carlos Seegmiller. When she came down, they lived together in Denver until his death in 2008.

and got one every year. She told me to go and get the prize one year when she was too old. I just was afraid that I wouldn't get it, or I didn't want to go to her county fair and try to get a prize from people that I *know* were excited, not about some collage quilt, but they were interested in the traditional patterns that were so ancient and well-loved. I did try some of the patterns early on, and I achieved them more or less. I gave all of those away and just went to making… I fell in love with dragons and whatnot. But we're talking now about the late '70s and the early 21st century. I was still doing collage, I was finding dragons and putting them onto quilts or making dragons. I had a dragon that I made that was quite nice. And another, actually, I made a whole quilt out of one serpent that just filled the whole quilt and then you had to sleep under it. So I don't know, have I gone on too much?

No, just the opposite. You've raised so many interesting points. Let me go back to one line where you really put me in my place when you said that I was implying that your collages were craft but not art, and I have to say a couple of things about it. You've described yourself and your quilting and your scrapbooks in terms very similar to the ways in which people have described women's craft in the pioneer days on the frontier. And one of the great things about feminist art history, I think, was that it has said, "Well, these things are not simply craft, they're art, and we should not denigrate them as simply women's craft." So I'd like to propose that in making the scrapbooks and the quilts you were really being an artist.

Stan got from somebody—I can't remember who, but I think it's very right— that one shouldn't step out the door saying, "I'm an artist." It's not for me to say that I'm an artist. That is for somebody who looks at my work to say, "Well, that is a quilt, so it must be a craft," or "But it's in a scrapbook, so it's a craft." I stayed always in forms that would not be called an art, just so that Stan would feel better about everything because he had a tremendous ego of course and wanted me to have a very small one. And I did, and I still do, and I think it's mainly a detriment, but it's of some use anyway. It makes other people feel better, I guess that's of some use. But yes, I don't think one should claim to be an artist. So I don't, but you called me "craft," you said, "Well, it's women's craft." And that was suitable. It's OK, you can do that. Or you can call me an artist if you want. That's fine too. You can call me whatever you *feel* is accurate. I don't know if you could even find that now after we've talked about all this stuff. Somebody else could maybe call me whatever they think I am, but not me.

Well, I'm going to take this opportunity of calling you an artist and of calling your scrapbooks and many other things that you've done art. So there you are. I've stepped out and I have a Ph.D… [both laugh] But this is important because the distinction between art and craft was so important for Stan, though not necessarily in gendered terms. Stan doesn't worry about craft being female and art being male, but he does worry very, very much about whether an artist has to be good at his or her craft and/or whether being very, very good at her or his craft makes him or her an artist. For Stan, there's a categorical distinction between those things that are art and those that are not art. I'm not going to go into my opinions, but I've always found that very problematic.

I would like your opinion, sir.

Well, I've already said you're an artist and your scrapbooks are art and all your other writings, of course. But I've never really understood what Stan meant by "an art" and the categorical distinction he made between a work of art and things which aren't works of art. I have often thought about asking P. Adams if he would hazard an extended comment about what constitutes a work of art for Stan.

Maybe you could put that into this transcription.

[laughs] *I'm sure he would do, but I was always afraid to ask him.*

I'm not scared of *him* at all.

Then you ask him what made something an art for Stan.

    P. Adams Sitney replies:
        Although I shrink from having the last word on what Stan Brakhage called "an art," or even from making a definitive statement, I shall nevertheless attempt a tentative explication of the idea as I came to understand it.
        It takes the form of a "negative theology" of art. Above all, Brakhage would assert that an art is neither personal nor commercial; that is, it cannot be made with any consideration of expressing a personal opinion, perspective or experience, nor can any aspect of it be adjusted to making money, or for career or personal advantage. Of course, we all know many works (and artists) that violate these principles, even works and artists that Brakhage adored.
        I now believe that he thought of works of art as medium specific: Poetry determined which poems were works of art, Painting which paintings, Music which compositions, Dance which choreographies. Therefore, there was, or might be, Film or a Muse of Film. The needs of Film had to be obeyed if a work of art were to emerge through the craftmanship of a filmmaker. Perhaps more important even than craftsmanship would be the ability (and the sacrificial cultivation) of detecting the dictation of the Art Form itself. Generally, it a kind of possession that humiliates, isolates, impoverishes, and makes a laughingstock of the very (few) human agents through whom it manifests. Any attempt to make the work comprehensible to an audience would be as destructive as crass commercialism to the potential to become art.

Thus, commercial cinema, most theatrical performances, the collaborative creations of Jazz, or making crafts would not constitute artistic work. Brakhage might have found a version of the distinction between Art and non-art latent in Gertrude Stein's theoretical writings, where she separated her writing for audiences and the "discovery" she made in the writing she created for herself. At the same time that she was writing her most successful "popular" book, *The Autobiography of Alice B. Toklas*, she was composing *Stanzas in Meditation*, her most obscure "epic poem" that fascinated Brakhage for more than half his life.

Probably following his mentor, Robert Duncan, he frequently cited versions of the Faust legend as if they were allegories of the dictates of Art, and its perils. He also frequently apologized for his own bad behavior as if he were obeying those dictates. More drolly, Jack Spicer made something of the same argument when he proposed that Martians need humans to speak for them, but in ways the humans could not possibly understand; so, they inspired the human poets to use odd expressions that encoded Martian messages. Genuine poets were not free to write whatever they thought they wanted; they had to obey the Martian instigations.

P. Adams Sitney, 2021 March 19-21

Let me go back a little. You raised so many issues, but there was just an amazing conjunction when you were describing the composition of your scrapbook: you said you had all this stuff in a box and you'd pick a piece out and put it next to another piece. That's exactly the way Stan described making the Prelude *to* Dog Star Man. *He had all this footage, he had no idea what to do with it, so he pulled out a piece and tried to find another piece that would relate to it in some sense. Right?*

I had forgotten that. It may even have been an influence on me.

Or vice-versa.

Well, he did *Dog Star Man* before I did the scrapbooks. [*laughs*]

OK. But I found that parallel very striking. Let's go back to some of the other things about that. Your exact phrase was, "I would clip them out and put them next to something else," which is exactly Stan's method of montage. What are some of the other things in the scrapbook that I noticed? Oh, the leprechauns! I noticed the recurrence of little colored pieces clipped out that looked like medieval romances of knights and ladies. I also noticed the extraordinary number of images of animals and birds; it seems that you kept every stamp that had a bird or an animal on it, and there are often pages where these are all put together. Another thing I noticed was that in almost all cases, when you have a photograph of a person, you cut it out. You don't put the entire rectangular photograph on the page. You do sometimes, but mostly you clip round the face or whatever, and then make compositions of these clipped-out things, which is again, exactly the way that Stan works. If he's making a portrait, he doesn't put the entire piece of film in. Instead, he clips bits out and puts them next to other things. Often those clipped-out photographs look like the flowers on a plant; there's a plant-like structure to the page as a whole that I thought gave a visual instantiation of your interest in animals and flowers and other organic processes. Another thing I noticed was how often you defeat the one-dimensionality of the scrapbook page by inserting something that has several layers. For example, there'll be a letter that has several pages and you'll put the entire letter in, which means that Yale had to take a separate shot of each page as the letter is opened; or you'll put a post-card in there, and Yale had to take a shot of one side of the postcard and then the other. So you made these pages not just two-dimensional but three-dimensional. You also made the experience of looking at the scrapbook an extended occasion in time, to some extent controlling the speed of apprehension. That reminded me of your saying that you wanted the experience of the scrapbook to be rhythmi-cally slow. You deliberately control the tempo of the spectators' apprehension of the scrapbook—as if it were a film. In all these ways—and I am sure in many others—the scrapbook itself is a very complex artistic creation.

Yes. It's also very interesting that all the time I was helping Stan [I was] learning how to be an artist or learning how to do something, learning how to make something. Then I'll have to say, "Well, it's OK to put Stan's name before mine in naming the scrapbooks" because I learned a lot. It's like you would say the teacher's name and the student's name. In science, you do that though you don't do that so much in art. Van Gogh spent his youth copying other people's paint-ings and really trying to become them and he always failed because he had such a brush stroke. But coming back to the scrapbooks, you said so many really interesting things there, and now I've forgotten them all.

I talked about animals and birds.

Oh, yes. And also I put in a whole lot of flowers, real flowers.

Yes, yes, yes!

There were a particular lot of magnolias because they would come in at an odd time of the year, and there'd be mountains of them. So I'd fill a sack with them and put them on a page and make a shape out of 'em that would be like a tree or something.

That's so interesting. First of all, Yale does not call them Stan Brakhage's Scrap-books, *Yale specifies as them as* Jane Brakhage's Scrapbooks.

No, it's Stan Brakhage and Jane Wodening.

OK, *but are you sure that Stan Brakhage comes before Jane Wodening in Yale's classification?*

I'm not sure. I just assume it because… [*laughs*]

Towards the end of the first scrapbook, which is the only one that I've been able to access, there are several pages in which you have a petal of various plants stuck on the page. These are very moving to me because as a child I collected wildflowers.

Oh, you did!

I pressed them and stuck them in a book with little pieces of Scotch tape. Then my mother would tell me their names and I'd write them out. So I made a big scrapbook of pressed wildflowers. And you have these pages of petals from various flowers, faded of course, but there are overlays of clear plastic or something, which is exactly the same as Mothlight. *And then two pages later, there are all these strips from* Mothlight! *It's uncanny!*

OK, OK. Well, that's very interesting. I am not surprised because when I went to New York City, I was nineteen I guess and saw art for the first time. I had thought that art was whether you could draw: if you could draw a chair that looked [like] it was in the proper dimensions of a chair, then you were artistic, you had talent. Then I saw Rembrandt, and maybe that was the only person I really recognized as art. It was just amazing. I mean, he *was* the prince of his craft. He was very, very, very good at painting. He knew how to do it, he knew how to make a pair of eyes with expression… talking eyes, in a way. He was very good at his craft, but at the same time—but totally elsewhere—he was doing this amazing spiritual thing that I call "Art." It's beyond craft, you can be just as good as possible in your craft and still not make Art because you're not feeling Art. I don't know; you're not crazy like artists are. [*laughs*]

That's such an amazing sentence; that sentence recurs in Brakhage's texts over and over again. "You can be as good as whatever in your craft, but are you making Art?" Brakhage never fills in the line that says what Art is; but you just did: "Because you're crazy."

Oh, crazy. Well, crazy, of course. I mean crazy like an artist is special.

But you've internalized the Brakhage unknowable concept of art. So Rembrandt was great at painting and drawing, but someplace else, he was off making Art.

It was all in the same place. It was all right there on the canvas. You could see how well he handled the lace work and all that stuff, even under all the dirt. But then he brought it alive. There's life in all of his works, even his drawings. It's just a different attitude. It's a different kind of person… I don't know. I think you're born an artist, maybe not. I've seen talent that was not an artist. It was extreme, wonderful talent and amazing, and not an artist. I'm bubbling right here… but I am trying to think what I was trying to say before. In spite of that quote he gave to me that nobody should say, "I am an artist"—and Rembrandt never did, he was a painter—Stan wanted to bring film into the realm of Art. That's what he was doing with his work. He was trying to say, "This is what Art is made of, and here I'm doing it." So he's saying, "I'm an artist," without saying it. He's saying, "This is Art." And so yeah, that was really an important thing that he wanted to say so that he could back up the fact [if] somebody would say he was an artist.

Well, as I said, you've totally…

I've wiped out your next batch of questions, I know. [*laughs*]

…demolished the structure of the interview. Let's just pick up on one or two things that you've said. You mentioned that you had a job earning a dollar an hour doing piece work or something. What job was that?

That was before I was married. I think it might've been a summer job or just after high school, or maybe it was after my, no, I don't know. Anyway, I had two jobs really. One was a soda jerk and the other one was making jewelry for Sue [Hoover?]'s mother.

We haven't talked about that.

No, we haven't. So I would take a ring base and glue a flat-bottomed piece of semi-precious stone onto it and then put it in a box of rice to dry. I'd do that fast enough to make at least a dollar an hour. Each one of those stones was something special. It might be a little busted piece of lapis lazuli or it might be agate of some sort or jasper or rose quartz or whatever kind of stone there might be around, so you could have a ring or a bracelet or a necklace or whatnot. I just put them together. I took out a piece and looked at it and saw it was OK and put it on the base and put it to dry. I don't know what I was paid per piece, but it wasn't much. So that was my job. And the great thing about it was I was to drive my boss down to New Mexico. I had just turned sixteen so I got my first long drive lesson driving her down to New Mexico to buy some more stones.

When you mentioned the visit by a nurse, the tone of your voice changed, as if that was a very special heartwarming occasion for you. You really liked the fact that she was visiting, and that made me think that you were probably very lonely in Lump Gulch, and this was very reassuring.

Yeah, I suppose the new neighbor was supposed to go around and visit the old neighbors, and I didn't. I was too shy. They didn't come to visit me, and so I didn't know them until the kids got to know their kids, or the dog came over, or my dog went there, or my goats went there and ate the tulips or whatever. And so it would be some occasion, like my dog got their dog pregnant. That was a big serious problem. That was terrible. [*laughs*] I had to say that I would give away all the pups after six weeks.

You talked about the lack of food. Did you have a vegetable garden?

I did, finally. I built a vegetable garden, and when I got a fence and could actually keep the goats and the wild animals — or some of them — out of the garden, I had vegetables, various things, potatoes. I'd stack up rubber tires and put them inside partway. I had a little patch of corn one time, and then a storm was coming. It took forever to grow corn up there. It was too cold, it was too short of a summer to grow corn, but I had gotten the corn to the point to where it had small ears. It looked scrumptious, but it wasn't going to grow any bigger, and I said to the kids, "Come on, let's harvest the corn." So we went out there and we ate those little babies, cob and all, we just chomped them down. Bear was so excited, he tore apart the stem and was getting the same stuff inside the stem; we all started doing that, but it was too hard. So we cleaned out the corn patch one late afternoon before the snow came. I was raising things, potatoes and corn and what else? Salads, I would try and keep fresh salad coming, but that's a hard thing to do. I don't know what else I grew, I didn't get into squash until much later. So yes, I had a garden. And then of course later we built the greenhouse. You didn't know I had a greenhouse on the roof.

Correct.

Oh my God! I was so frustrated, although that corn project turned out very well; in its way, it was a fine meal that we had. But still, I wanted to be able to grow things well beyond the two or three months that we were generally allowed at 9,000 feet. But that wasn't why I built it. The reason was that we had a ravine. The original house was a square, two-story cabin and then, when it was actually turned into a whorehouse, I guess, the long kitchen was added. Then shortly before we bought it, the back end, which had been a garage, was closed in and made into a kids' bedroom and playroom and the bathroom. But that made this roof that was a water trap, and all the water would go down from both sides and seep under the roofing and creep up capillary action and drip down through whatever holes it could find. At one point there were twenty-two little bowls or pans or pots catching drips from the roof.

So I went down to Don McCollum and he said, "Well, what you want to do is build a room up there and that would catch all of those drips and seal it." I thought that was a brilliant idea, and I tried to think what room I wanted to have and I decided a greenhouse was what I wanted. And so I got Charlie DeJulio and his buddies to make a greenhouse up there. They had to climb up and of course they needed beer, so I would hurl a can of beer up to the top of the pole where they were, and they would catch it. I realized that one beer was enough for anybody that was on a pole and I shouldn't give them two, no matter how thirsty they might be. They made a very nice greenhouse up there. It went from peak to peak of the roofs and then peaked itself so that it just went on down and out. I didn't have any of those leaks anymore unless I watered the plants too much, but I had plastic underneath the dirt and stuff. So the greenhouse was definitely a story in itself and [there are] several stories I could tell you out of that greenhouse. But I did grow lettuce and other tomatoes and other salad things in the greenhouse. It went very slowly in the winter, though; it was not totally satisfactory because it was so slow.

Perhaps now we can go back to the questions I thought to ask you at the beginning. You've talked about how your marriage changed after Stan took the job at Chicago. I wonder if we could talk a little bit more about the period before he took the job at Chicago, which is the first years of your time in Lump Gulch. There were things you raised last time that looking back on, I wish I'd asked more about. Would that be OK?

Well, would you ask more specific questions? I think I told you about poverty. We did have a car. Did we have two cars? Stan wanted to have a car so that he would be free to go to town, but I was interested in having Land Cruisers, the Toyota copies of the Land Rover, so that I could carry goats and straw and five children and things like that. I could go into the history of goats, that started before the Art Institute.

We rushed over your relationship with fauna and flora too quickly, so I'd love to hear about the goats.

Goats is a huge, huge topic. [*laughs*] I counted one time: I had twenty-three different animals and different types on the property. And they varied from time to time. I think we started fairly soon. We had a guinea pig that lived under the refrigerator, and that turned out to be kind of a bad idea because you move the refrigerator and the floor's all covered with guinea pig shit. You put that into the compost, but the story of compost comes later. I didn't know what to do with it at the time, but he was wonderful. His name was Luther and whenever anybody would come through the kitchen, he would holler at them, "Wait! Wait! Wait!" [*laughs*] Somehow that stuck in my head, that cry, shrill and demanding and yet friendly too. Generally people would come through the kitchen and give him something, just because it was obvious that's what he was saying, "Give me food." Another early animal, we had a dog when we arrived: Durin the Deathless, first King of the Dwarves, which we got from Tolkien. [*laughs*] I see you think that name is funny?

I was laughing because when I was a child, we had a black dog that I called Olaf the Lofty after some imagined medieval Norwegian tribe. I'm sorry, you were talking about your dog.

Durin the Deathless was from the Tolkien series. He would go crazy when there was a bitch in heat, and particularly crazy if it was a coyote: it was just impossible, we couldn't think. He was constantly whining and howling and yammering at the door saying he had to go out, wanted to go out. I knew that if he went out, he would be killed, because what the coyotes do: there's a bitch in heat, well, then there's food coming. And of course they'd kill him. It was not only a nice ambush, but it was also that a dog is not going to father their pups. They'd kill any dog that came. After three days of him screaming and hollering and we had important company coming, I'm very sorry to say that I said, "OK, do it. Bye." And I let him out. I mean, I had been going out with him on a leash and he'd been like, "OK, you want me to pee? Alright, I've done it, so now let me loose." Then he tore off into the mountains and was never seen again.

That was Durin, and before that was Brown Dog, which I got after Sirius was hit by a car. We got the Brown Dog in Princeton. I don't know why I settled on him. He looked right, he had a nice coloring, I liked his looks, he was handsome, but he was not the right guy because he didn't like kids. I noticed finally as we were driving around all those years that he would growl at the children. It was in Lafayette in summer, he took to growling at the children because they were a little older. I realized that I had to get rid of him. We had a pair of visitors that were film fans I think, and I said, "Do you want my dog? I have to get rid of him because he doesn't like children. And you don't have children. Do you plan to have children?" "No, we do not plan to have children, and we'd love to have your dog, and we will give him steak every day and bathe him in soap and water." So they took Brown Dog and they loved him for years. They took very good care of him, way beyond what I would've done. Then we got Durin. I can't remember where we got Durin, but we had obviously read some of the Tolkien. So that takes care of the dogs up to that point. We did have one cat that we had gotten, and then Stan confessed that he was allergic to cats. It was Pasht, named after the cat goddess of Egypt. She had kittens and we kept one of those, Emily. So that was the dog and cat situation. They didn't last long, the cats, and Stan was healthier when they left, when they died, and we didn't have any more cats in the house.

But then somebody was selling a goat for two dollars, so I bought him/her. It was a really weird hermaphrodite. We had him/her for a while, and him/her smelled strongly. And finally somebody said, "I really like your goat because he stinks, and that really is a good thing for a horse. I have a very nervous horse that would love to have your stinky goat." I wanted to have dairy goats really, so I got Tree who was not really a dairy. She was a good milker, she didn't give me a lot, but she stuck with it. She'd give me milk for over a year, so I would only breed her every other year. Tree was an incredible friend. She was, I have said many times that Tree was the best friend I've ever had.

Spelled T r e e?

Yeah, because she had a white blaze and then the branches or horns going back, so she was a tree. Stan named her that. She was otherwise mostly black with some white here and there. She was kind of a nasty goat, she was very, very sensitive. There were certain people that she didn't like and she knew what to do with her head and stab them with her horn. She would make a black and blue spot sometimes, but still, she was my best friend in all my life and that was because she was always on my side. Even if I was doing something wrong, she would tell me, she would turn against me. We had this great way of butting heads, and that would be a love statement. We'd butt heads and push a little bit, and that was like saying, you and me, we're together we are. She started my goat herd. I got her when she was like four weeks old and was feeding her with a bottle so I got formula—goat formula, not human formula—and fed her with a bottle, and that might be partly why we were so close. Then she wanted another goat really bad, and she told me very clearly, and I went and got Fawn, who was a beautiful goat, just gorgeous, but kind of dumb. The comparison between her and Tree was amazing, but they were very happy to have each other and be together in spite of being very different personalities. Still, they were both goats.

You want to take a break and do something besides goats. I mean, I could talk for days about goats.

Well give us another ten minutes of goats

And then stop? Well, let's see, ten minutes and some goats. Well, they grew up and I found a guy outside of Boulder who had a fine billy goat. He was a nice fellow who was a professor at the university and so I went to him from then on, first with Tree and… Boy, I don't remember Fawn having babies, and she was so pretty. I don't know what happened with Fawn. But they would climb up onto cars, you know, and sit on top of the car or on the hood, just curl up and look very comfortable. It did leave little marks in the paint, the hoof was kind of sharp like fingernails. I would take her down and get her bred, and she'd have the babies after five months. I would try and figure out when it was time and there were signs that she was going to have babies today or tomorrow. I'd be keeping an eye on her, and finally I would go and sit with her, and she appreciated that a lot and she never had any trouble with having kids.

Then I had cars. I had first one car, the one that we'd been driving back and forth, and it was going bad, huge clouds behind it. So we had either to sell it for $25 or—what I thought was better—was drive it into the goat yard and have it be a goat house so that they could settle in. There would be straw and nice and comfortable, and they could eat the upholstery, which they did slowly and thoroughly. And eventually I would take out some springs and put 'em in the trash. There were some coins. I wondered if there were any bills, but they would've swallowed the bills. The coins had been deposited on the ground so that they ate them, and then they went on through and came out polished. But you tell me when 10 minutes is up.

Just as long as you feel like. It's fascinating, but I don't want to make it difficult for you.

Well, I would keep the babies. Let's see, how did I do that? I'd separate her from her babies for half the day, and so I would get half the milk, and the babies would get the rest. That worked out very well, and that was fine for her. She was not a great milker that had to be milked thoroughly out twice a day. I don't know what she was mixed with, but she was a very strong and well-shaped dairy animal but no show-goat. I got involved with show-goats later when Cliff, the billy goat guy, gave me a show animal, and then she had a kid that was very pretty, and we tried to show her. But she was too hyper, too hyper to do anything. She was a very jumpy kind of girl, and so people voted against her.

Was Stan interested in these animals?

Well, he had them in some films, but he wasn't interested in any of the animals. I mean, he would include them, he would photograph them, but he didn't pet them or get to know them or feed them or babysit them or anything.

It reminds me of a later film called The Loom *that I've only seen once and I don't remember in detail except that it is about the animals in the pens around your house. Do you remember it?*

I remember the name, and I remember a picture of the loom that I had for a brief period. It took up so much room that we got rid of it but it was a lovely dream to be able to make something with a loom. But yes, he was very happy to photograph the animals. They were something to photograph for sure, worthy to look at.

We have a lot of other stuff, but I think it would best if we end here, it's nearly twelve. Is that OK?

OK, excellent. Yeah, well, it's been fun talking with you, and I kind of missed it last week, but I was all swept up with other things.

Did you have your shot?

It was a week ago Saturday. I think P. Adams is getting his second shot or just got it or something.

I think he told me that. You mentioned three feet of snow in the mountains. What was it like in Denver?

In Denver I called it seventeen inches. I couldn't shovel, it was so wet and heavy, and so I shoveled it partway, and then it took me three days to get my back back, and then I just broke trail for the postman out down to the road. Saturday was crazy because the snow was blowing in and I looked out the north window and the windows were covered with snow. The snow had glued itself to the glass, and so I went and looked out the east and it had glued to the glass on the east. And then I went and looked out on the south side, and it was glued to the glass on the south side and on the west side. I had the front door, and I went to the front door and lifted up the mail slot and looked out, and it came blasting right into my eyes. [*laughs*]

Well, this has been wonderful. I especially enjoyed talking about the scrapbooks, maybe we could look at some specific pages.

You look at some special pages, because it's huge to me, massive stuff that happened in the '60s. Thank you.

Bye.

Bye.

Nine

2021 March 24. The children; Jonas Mekas visits; Roscoe; Hollis Melton; Michael Snow; Jane begins writing; Barbara's death; Cheep Donkey; buying a car; P. Adams Sitney; *23rd Psalm Branch*; Stan's rages; Peter Kubelka; *Pasht*.

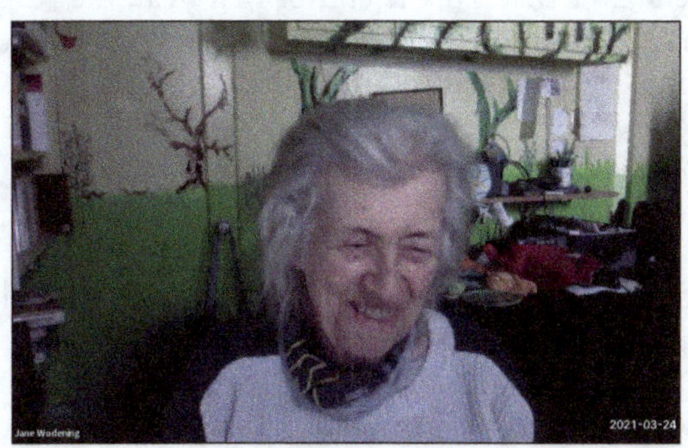

Hi, David,

Hi, Jane. Can you hear me OK?

Yeah, I hear you fine. Did you plug in, did you flick the switch or whatever?

Yep, it says we're recording. How are you?

I'm OK. I don't know. I seem to be kind of stupid this morning, so I can't remember things and it's rough, so I hope I do well.

We'll do what we can. Do you want to start out, or as usual I have a whole array of questions.

I can't think of a thing to say. So a whole array of questions or ask one of them.

OK. I'm trying to think about the time between 1964 and 1967. In 1957 you were without direction, possibly on the edge of suicide, and now you're getting towards a decade of being married and you have five children. I wonder if you can recall your sense of how your life was developing around this time.

Well, '64 to '67, that was the time where we were real hard-up. In that period Stan would go three or four times or maybe more on a lecture tour somewhere on the east coast or west coast. Another thing he did was get grants, they helped a lot. The kids were all little and Myrrena was going to school in Rollinsville. It was the last year that Rollinsville had its grade-school working so she went to first grade. She missed kindergarten, but she went to first grade, and I remember telling her, "You've got to do this, it's the law. [*laughs*] Kids have to go to school, so just enjoy it and have fun and learn as much as you can, and it'll do you good." That was my send-off for her. It wasn't far to Rollinsville, three miles or something, and the bus came and got her anyway. So that was one in school and the other four to mind, and that didn't make much difference. Except for her, she was alone in the world part of the time. I think it separated her; she always felt older than the others after that. At the end of that year, the Rollinsville school closed so they all had to go to Nederland. And the next year, Neowyn got to go to kindergarten while Crystal went to First Grade.

How did motherhood and having five children affect your sense of your own life? Did it give you a new stability, a new sense of accomplishment?

I remember thinking it was wearing me out. My hair was getting shorter by itself, and my skin was a little bit greenish—that was after Rarc was born—so I was feeling wrung-out. But I did think, "Well, we got to quit this somehow." It's just terrible not to be doing something wonderful. Being pregnant and having babies is wonderful, so I felt like it's going to be a great loss to give it up. But then, I have produced now or been party to producing a couple of dozen people— additional overpopulation on the earth—but I'm really fond of them: all the kids, the grandkids, and the great grandkids. Raising kids was no problem, I had so many so close to the same age that they really were happy to play together and hang out together. That took a load off of me. I think people who have one or two children get put upon more than I was because they were happy with each other quite a bit at the time.

The raising of the kids in Lump Gulch, it was so great. The kids could go out and just find their way around, and of course, they would stay close at first, and then they would find there was something a little farther, and then they never seemed to get lost because they didn't go far enough at one time to not know what to do next. They learned to find their way around, I think, well, one or two of them say they have a hard time telling which way is north. I don't know how that's achieved. I think I know which way is north because of the shadows pretty much. So I lose it at night, I get lost at night,

But the kids enjoyed playing outside, I would help them sometimes, play with them, or give them a useful project that was really fun. Like at a certain point in the spring, there would be puddles all over the aspen grove, each one breeding mosquitoes like mad. I'd give them each a container of Clorox to sprinkle into each of those puddles, and it really did cut down on the mosquito population for quite a while. Sometimes we would get equipment like sleds. We had a steep hill going down just from the house down—not all the way to the road, it stopped before the road—so that if there was any snow on the road, they could have a great time with the sled. There were a lot of enjoyments. We didn't have television, we never had television.* We just found other things to do.

I remember those scenes of the kids playing in the snow from Jonas Mekas' film Walden, *when he comes to visit you and you're playing in the snow and there's kids sledding down the hill. Do you remember Jonas' visit?*

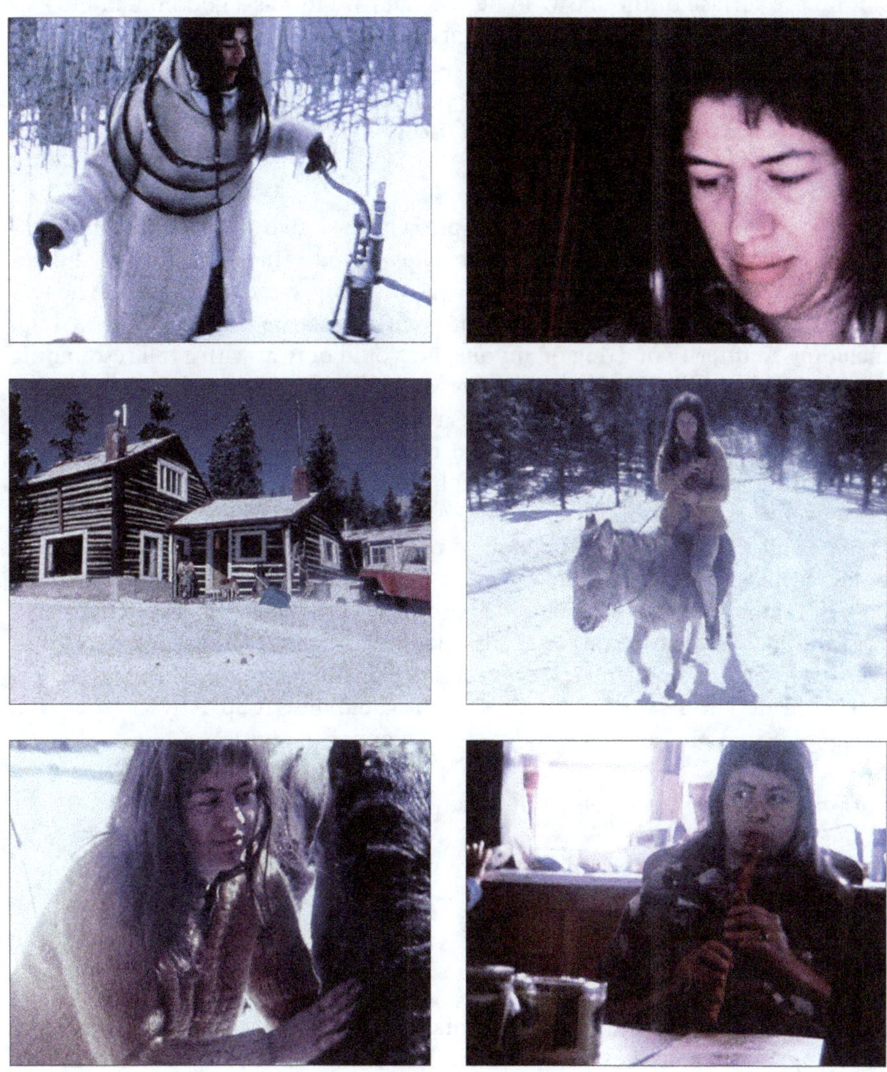

Jane in *Walden.*

* Actually the Brakhages very briefly owned a television when Stan was making *23rd Psalm Branch.* They got rid of it when Jane inadvertently or subconsciously left the electric plug in her waffle iron. (PAS)

A little bit. I liked Jonas. I think he was a little leery of Stan, quite a bit actually. He had to recognize that Stan was good at what he was doing and valuable to the avant-garde. But yeah, we went out, we went postholing out. The way you posthole is you have to step into deep snow and you make a posthole. We went out, I think, to the beaver pond, and that was quite a walk, postholing. That's what he wanted to see, I don't think he put any of the beaver pond into the film. It gave us a long walk and he found what he wanted to find, which was rabbit shit on the surface of the snow, so he was happy. He was a good hiker. He was strong and capable, and so he and I went out and I guess a dog or two.

You had Roscoe at that time. In Walden, *Jonas' film about the visit, he shouts, "Roscoe! Roscoe!" When did you get Roscoe? This was in the '70s, I'm getting ahead of myself.*

Roscoe had belonged to a happy couple who had two horses and a donkey, Roscoe being the donkey. The people broke up, and I think she took the horses and he got the donkey and the cabin. I was very impressed with Roscoe, he was quite a philosopher. Any creature that went across the road in front of him, including a butterfly or a dog or anyone, he would bray at with a full resounding roar, he could really sing in the donkey way. I was just crazy about him, I just couldn't stop looking at him. Donkeys aren't really pretty, but you can see their brains working as they stand there and nod. They seem to be very thoughtful or philosophical, and he was very thoughtful. I could ride on him, I had to have a stump to get up on him because there was no saddle. We'd go out together, Roscoe and I, and we would go along a road and he would be leading in a way, unless I pulled the reins in one direction or another. He would stop at where I couldn't quite see into the meadow ahead of us, the aspen grove or whatever it was. But he would stop and move his ears. He had very talking ears so I would respect that and figure that he was observing something that I wished I could see. But if I made a noise and tried to go see it, I would mess it up. Anyway, he was a great companion for a few years. He was a wonderful guy.

Do you remember when you got Roscoe?

No, no, I don't remember the date. He was a luxury, so it would have to have been after '67.

Did he live a long time?

Donkeys live thirty to fifty years, I think. He left me. I made a terrible mistake of taking him to a donkey race down in Rollinsville. I knew he could run very fast, but I didn't feel like I was horseman enough to ride him so I let somebody else ride him, and they were kind of mean. That didn't bother him so much but he fell in love with Buttercup, another one of the donkeys. And Buttercup, of course, won the race because he wouldn't pass her. [*laughs*] After that, he didn't want to do anything except break away from home and go to Buttercup's house. Finally I went to Buttercup's owners and said, "Would you like another donkey? Because he's in love with Buttercup and I can't handle him very well." And they said, "Sure." I wrote a story about him saying that he died earlier; but that was Buttercup that died, she was actually shot [when mistaken] for an elk. Roscoe went off with the owner's son and was hanging out with horses and having a great time and then he escaped them. He was a lone wolf. He was his own man. He would work for someone he felt like working for. I was honored to be that person for a few years.

Since we started talking about Jonas Mekas, maybe we should have a digression at this point and go through the whole of your relationship, or knowledge of him. You started out by saying that he was leery of Stan.

Maybe he just wasn't the kind of talker that Stan liked. They were kind of shy with each other talking, and so he was kind of looking forward to getting outside and taking pictures and stuff. I thought he was quite fun, but he was serious, he wasn't all that playful. Although he did galumph through the snow very amusingly. I didn't hang out with him much because Stan didn't. I remember when he was married to Hollis Melton, and she got mad at Stan because he didn't like Michael Snow,* and he said so. It wasn't Snow himself that Stan disliked; he didn't know him, it was his films. She tried to get him out of Anthology Film Archives, I think it was, or the Filmmaker's Co-op? Anyway, they didn't handle his work for a while.† Stan had, I think he might've, set up a lecture tour in New York City and wanted me to come along and do some diplomacy with Hollis and Jonas because I think he felt that they would just yell at him, but they would treat me politely. And I did. I went and did this diplomacy, and I persuaded them that that was just not anything you can do. You can't do that. They said, "Yeah, I know," and put him back on the slate. Jonas wouldn't have done that, but still, I don't know. They kept apart pretty much, they just weren't each other's type. We didn't really have a great relationship with Jonas, but he ran the thing, he did well, he made it grow and so on. So we had certainly a good view of him of him as a good working person.

Do you remember any other occasions when you met either Jonas or Hollis?

I don't think Hollis at all. I did meet Jonas just a few years ago when my book about Stan's childhood came out.‡ He was passing through Anthology Film Archives, and he was ninety years old. I ran over, I had to chase him down the

---

* Michael Snow (1928–2023), Canadian filmmaker and sculptor and Joyce Weiland's husband, lived in New York for most the 1960s. A pioneer of what became known as "structural" film, his most celebrated work was *Wavelength* (1967).

† There is an error here, perhaps resulting from Brakhage's persecution fantasies. The conflict and argument over Michael Snow's films is probable, but it would not have had any effect on the policies of the cultural institutions that Jonas Mekas directed. At the time Anthology Film Archives was closed; it hadn't been able to acquire new films since 1972. The journal *Film Culture* continued to publish positive articles about Brakhage's work. (PAS)

‡ *Brakhage's Childhood* (New York: Granary Books, 2016).

street and finally I caught him and gave him a hug. He was very nice. I don't know if he knew who I was, because I don't know what people can do at ninety. He had a couple of friends that were pulling him along. I was really glad that I did that, I got at least to give him a hug, that was important, to me anyway. We weren't close at all with him, but we didn't avoid him, he didn't avoid us. When I came for a reading, I invited Jonas and he said he lived all the way out in Brooklyn and didn't want to go that far to see me read. But a number of other people came from the film world.

You didn't have any contact with Hollis Melton after she and Jonas separated?

Another time we met was I went over to their house for a meal when I went first to New York after the breakup and I started traveling. So yes, I stopped there on my driveabout. I remember that he loved onions. We managed to have dinner together, and it was fine. Hollis was still there and a bunch of film people, I can't remember who all they were. They asked me how much I'd gotten for that house. It was a bad year, I really got about a quarter of what I should have at that time, '87. "$72,000," I said. It was a big slump in real estate. If I had waited a year or so, I could have gotten at least twice that much, but nobody told me that, and I really wanted to leave, not sit there haunted.

When you say that Stan didn't like Michael Snow…

He didn't know Michael Snow personally, but he didn't like his films. Not the person, he didn't know him. He [Brakhage] said something against [them]. He was too square for him.

Any more about Jonas?

I can't think of *anything* else. The first time we met him and his brother was at that meeting, and in that strange room. People were there like Jack Smith.

I've always thought that the section of Walden, *where he visits you, is really the film's high point.*

Oh, thank you.

Absolutely pivotal to Jonas's own development and sense of self and of the development of American film. It really is a beautiful, beautiful section.

Well, that's great. I think he really wished he was more of a country boy, but he had decided that if he was going to get somewhere, he was going to have to be in the city. He couldn't just go to the country and sit there. That's what you do, either that or you go into agriculture, in which case you wouldn't be up in the mountains. I felt that he liked being out in the woods, it was just a great joy. He wouldn't have come if it was just to see Stan, but he wanted to come and be in the woods.

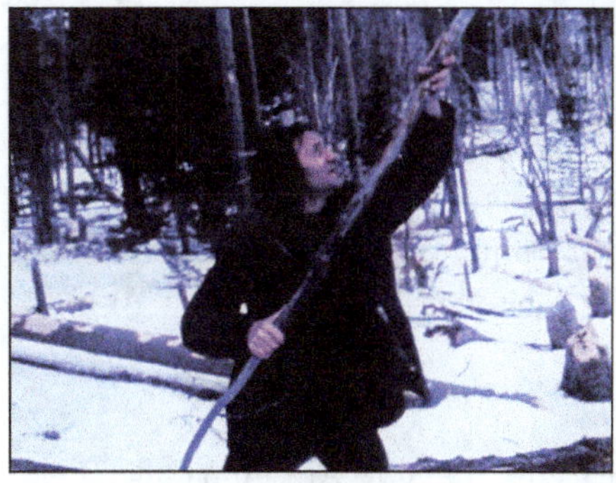 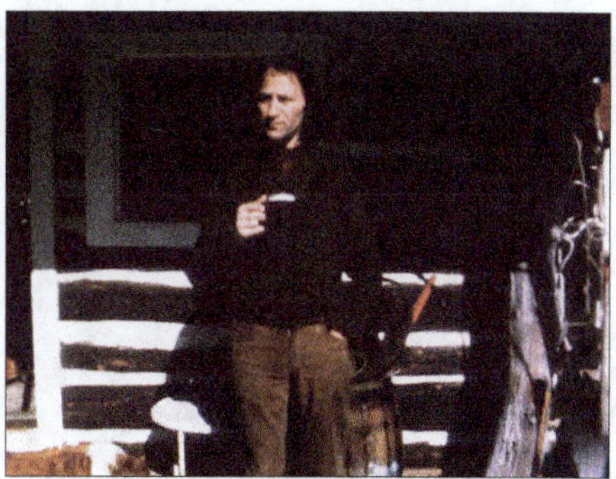

Jonas Mekas in *Walden*.

In the snow, in the woods, in the countryside, just like at home in Lithuania.

Yeah. I don't know what Lithuania is like, but I think it's certainly hilly, if not mountainous.

Still with some general things about your first decade of marriage: in my notes I have a quote from an interview [with Stan] that I can no longer find that reads, "I think Jane was very much more of a private person than she was permitted to be, not only within the family, but with respect to the world." Did you feel that Stan was forcing you not to be a private person?

Oh, no! No, he wanted me to be his private woman or one of his private women. He wanted me to be the private life, which was different from the public life.

But he was making you very much a public person by your role in the films.

Yes, yes. And he would mention me too. People say that he would mention that "Jane said this weird thing," and he was always quoting me. I'd like to have some of those quotes, nobody seems to remember exactly what they were.

We talked once about one of his applications for grants, where he reported that you could do closed-eye vision and open-eye vision simultaneously. That was a remarkable achievement that he tried to emulate. So he credited you with that!

He was trying to do that with *Thigh Line Lyre Triangular*. That's just something that I was able to do. I've never been able to look through the two sides of binoculars. I don't suppose that has anything to do with it, but I have to shut one eye to look through binoculars.

But you wanted to be more of a private person that Stan permitted you to be?

No, that isn't so. I would always look forward to company and to travel.

There's a lot about this in the interview with Hollis Frampton, and that's down the road a bit, so we'll maybe hold that over till then. Are you interested in or willing to talk about your consciousness of yourself as a writer, how that grew, how important it is to your sense of your own self?*

I am. I didn't start writing until I was thirty-nine. But I did write before that, I wrote that one story that Stan asked me to write about giving birth to Myrrena.

Which I said was a great piece of writing, the very first one that you did.

I'm really so pleased that you said that, that's great. [*laughs*] At Lump Gulch I was writing a bird journal, which just went on and on for maybe the first three years. But it was just a journal and I had the notion that all I could write was journal. It seemed impossible to do anything else until I had been talking with Barbara Gamow, George Gamow's wife. While the men were talking about who knows what, she and I were whispering together about how we both wanted to be writers, but neither one of us felt we could. She wanted to write poetry, but there was George all over the place constantly, and she couldn't concentrate. So there we were.

A few years later—fifteen, I believe—she died and I thought, "She never had a chance to write her poetry. She wanted to write, and she never did. And here I am, 39 years old, and I haven't either, but I guess I have some time." I got quite upset over her death. [Before she died] we visited her, and Stan was just so charming. God, he was charming and made her smile, and she wanted to see the kids. The kids had all grown up in those fifteen years, and so this great row of teenagers stood around her bed and smiled. They asked me, "What do we do?" and I said, "Just smile." So there were all these smiles, and then everybody left except me, and I couldn't speak. I wanted to say I was so sorry that she didn't write anything, but I thought that would be a rude thing to bring up. I just didn't have anything to say, and I finally stumbled out of the room. She was very understanding. She had these wonderful talking eyes, so she didn't speak but she was talking with her eyes. We had this intense conversation with our eyes. Then I went home and I couldn't sleep; I couldn't put my head back on the pillow because there was her head, her dying head and the pillow. So I got up and I wrote the story of Barbara. Now, how did I get into that long story? I just told you the whole story, which I should have made you go and look up. It's called "Goodbye to Barbara" and it's in *The Lady Orangutan and Other Stories.*

So at thirty-nine you wrote the story of Barbara?

I wrote it immediately, it took me a week to write. Then I called up Elfriede and I said, "I wrote this story, I'd like to read it to Barbara." And she said, "I'm sorry, she died last night." She probably died as I wrote my last words about her. It was a real story, not a journal.

---

* Hollis Frampton (1936–1984), filmmaker, photographer, film theoretician. Also a "structural" filmmaker, his best known work was *Zorn's Lemma* (1970).

So after the birth film story, the story about Barbara was the first story you wrote that's distinct from journal.

It was the first story I wrote, yeah, a real story with references and flashbacks and weird interruptions and so on.

If you were born in '36 and the story was written when you were 39, that would mean that the story was not written until 1975?

It was '76, actually. Eighteen years later.

So your career as a writer, as a self-conscious maker of art language began in 1976?

As soon as I realized that I had actually written an actual story, I thought, "Damn, I want to do that again, right now!" So I started writing every story I could think of. Actually "The Lady Orangutan" is one of the very earlier ones. I don't know quite chronologically where it fit in, but it was quite close, and a lot of the ones that are in *Mountain Woman Tales*. But yeah, then I realized I could write, I knew how to write, suddenly. I got it all from Barbara dying. While we were looking at each other there at her deathbed, she passed me the torch. That's how I became sophisticated [*laughs*], if you want to call it that.

OK. One last thing about birds. We did talk a lot about birds a couple of weeks ago, but you didn't mention your canary.

Oh, oh, Cheep Donkey! Yes. Cheep Donkey! We got him when Bear was very little and trying to learn to speak. I asked him to name the bird, and he said, "Cheep Donkey." I knew what he meant because he had just seen ducks. It starts with a D like donkey, so he was trying to say "ducks." And cheep means singing, of course, that's what a bird does, it says "cheep" except he didn't realize that canaries do better than that. So it was a singing bird is what he was trying to say: "Cheep Donkey" means "singing bird," even though ducks don't sing like that either. But yeah, that was a real good name. Cheep Donkey heard a lot of Baroque music from the time he came to us, mainly Bach and Vivaldi. He sang in the Baroque manner. I wish we had recorded it. It was just amazing. He was a great singer, the greatest bird singer I can imagine. It was an honor to have him in the house.

What happened to Cheep Donkey?

Oh God, it was so sad. Bobbie Creeley was visiting at the time, and I don't know, there was a breeze, and it might've been the breeze killed him, or I don't know what. He was singing in the morning, and then in the afternoon he fell over dead. It just broke me up, although I tried not to show it with Bobbie there. She came to visit by herself, I think she just wanted to get away, [she and Robert] fought a lot too, I guess. So maybe she got in the car, left, and came to visit us.

By the way, the scrapbook is in your name first. If you go to Yale, it's Jane and Stan Brakhage Scrapbook, not Stan, as you thought.

Oh, thank you. There you go! So I'm not so bad off.

Last week we talked about the letters that you preserved in the scrapbook. I wonder if you recall when you began systematically to save the letters that Stan received and especially the letters that he wrote.

I made him use carbon paper. He was supportive of my project. I think that was in Lump Gulch, so it started pretty late. But the ones we received… you know I had that box in the car as we traveled place to place. It was like a box that a sweater comes in, long and just a very few inches high, so it didn't take up much room. So that was accumulated across the years of driving from Princeton to this place and that place and the other place, and finally to Lump Gulch. So yeah, you seem to be a little upset about my putting a ten-page letter into that scrapbook, and then the poor Yale has to photograph it ten times.

No, just the opposite. I said, what a great intervention it was. [both laugh] Well, that gets to the end of the things that I had left over from last week. Just a little bit more chronology: Stan started teaching in Chicago in 1970?

'67 is way I remember it,

Teaching in Chicago in '67?

That's the way I remember. But you better ask P. Adams, he will be able to find out. He's just going to be late this week. I think he's going to skip this week, and then he'll have to catch up.

Maybe we'll skip next week. We'll see how he gets on. Let's just hope he comes out of hospital safely.

I haven't heard, have you? I think he was supposed to stay in the hospital and be watched for today. Wasn't it done yesterday?

I don't know. [pause] The add-on to the house was in '72?

That's probable, yeah, that would work. Or maybe two or three years later, certainly not before.

Was the greenhouse added the same time that you did the add-on?

No, the add-on was a little later, I believe. We were getting money. Well, God, you're right, like '70, we started feeling rich. I mean, we could actually buy a car, used of course, but we could buy one, and that was relevant to what we were doing. I bought a Toyota Land Cruiser that I could carry goats in and five children growing up. Also it could carry a year's worth of alfalfa hay for my goats. I had gotten goats so I needed a bigger vehicle. I got one goat during the poverty years, for sure. And that was Tinker Billy. He was a true hermaphrodite. If I may be so crass, he peed out of his vagina and it ran down his balls. It was just really amazing to see. Then he finally found a good home with horses, and I think I told you about this too.

Yes, he was the one who stank really bad.

Yeah, he smelled bad. I liked the smell of goats if it's moderate. He wasn't that moderate but he was a sweet guy.

So back now to our chronology: we've got to 1964 and P. Adams comes to visit that Christmas. Do you have any recollections of that?

Yes, I do. I told you the story about the dog and the horses. Also, we had just a mountain of presents that people from all over the country sent to our children. It took all day for the kids to unwrap each one and give it full honor. And only one present could be opened at one time, it was an exhausting ritual. P. Adams was very patient with the kids and nice. He seemed to like kids. He likes animals too, but I didn't have goats yet at that time, didn't even have Tinker Billy.

But yeah, we had a nice time except someone that P. Adams was very fond of died and there was no consoling him. That was really too bad. I don't remember who it was.* It was a nice visit. P. Adams was such a kid, very bubbly. He was very unsure of himself, and yet he was very knowledgeable too and very determined to be knowledgeable in the film field as well as the classics, of course, and the history of people thinking. He learned ancient Greek so he could read Plato, but that was later. I've always noticed that the very smart people are always kind of slow in plain ordinary stuff. He was a perfect example of that, at the time. He's kind gotten over that, I suppose it was hard to get over it.

And the next year, '65, you went to his wedding?

I did not. I don't remember going to his wedding. Stan might have.† I don't remember ever going to a wedding with P. Adams as the groom.

And, almost finally, how many times did John Cage come?

He came a few times, just for an afternoon, just to take a walk and have a nice talk with Stan. He really wanted to take a walk and see if he could find any mushrooms, because he was a mushroom fiend. He was very high on the echelon of mushroom people, an expert. I was sorry, it's a dry state. I mean, we don't

---

* Ron Rice. (PAS)
† Brakhage was Best Man at that wedding in Piermont, NY. Jane did not attend. (PAS)

have much rain, so no rain, no mushrooms. I should have thought about wet spots and stuff, but we found some mushrooms, and that was fun.

And the talk with Stan was cordial.

Yeah. He was able to talk like Stan liked, and so they had a good talk. John was not afraid of Stan. He would bring one or two people along with him. I remember meeting him in Boulder too. We would go to his concert. Who was that guy that played the piano on…

David Tudor.

Yes, David Tudor. David Tudor, also like Robert Kelly, liked his hamburgers just plain, but he only took one. That's what he really liked, and it would be hard for anybody to please him with home cooking. He didn't tend to come to the house and he didn't like walking through the woods either much. So he kept kind of distant, David Tudor did. But John was actually very warm and a pleasant person to be with.

Did Stan ever say anything about him when he left?

Not that I can think of.

Did Stan show him films?

I don't know if he stayed into the night.

Which would've been necessary to screen films?

Yeah. I don't know if we showed him films or not. I think it would've been attempted, for sure. I think John would've wanted to see a film. Just because artists are supposed to like each other… except for Korczac Ziolkowski in Custer, the guy that was carving the Crazy Horse sculpture. [*laughs*] I guess we talked about him already.

Finally here, I understand that at some point you thought about distributing Stan's films from home. Do you have any recollection of that?

Do you mean to rent? Oh, no, I don't remember that. We sold them from home. We did a lot of that, so I did a lot of packaging and wrapping and whatnot.

So an order would come in and Stan would have a print made at Western Cine. You'd pick it up, bring it home, pack it up, and mail it out.

Yeah.

Do you remember people you sent films to?

It would be mostly universities and whatnot. I don't remember so much in the way of human beings. I did all that, you know, the wrapping and some of the tele-phoning. He did some of the telephoning, he'd telephone with the boss person, and I would telephone with the secretary person. And I remember getting a great recipe for borscht from one of them. There was this very nice lady named Emma and I wrote a story about her, all about shyness. That would have been somebody at MoMA, I think or one of the New York museums.

Maybe we could talk about some films. We haven't talked about Two: Creeley/ McClure, *but that was shot before you moved to Lump Gulch. After you settled in Lump Gulch, Stan is mostly working at first on the* Songs. *He turned to 8-milli-meter and started making the* Songs. *It's many years since I've seen these, and I can't say anything intelligent about them, except I read that* Song 1 *was a portrait of you, a color film that Stan designated as "a portrait of a beautiful woman." Do you have any recollection of that film or of the making of the songs in general?*

I don't remember them either much, but except of course, the *23rd Psalm Branch*. [Among] the earlier ones, there was *Song 5*, which was Rarc's birth, and there was a song that was of Kirsten Creeley teaching me how to do the Twist.*

Wonderful. [both laugh]

We were going down to New Mexico, and so we could visit the Creeleys and I really wanted to learn the Twist. I didn't know anybody else that could teach me except Kirsten, and Stan filmed that.

So you'd not been doing much dancing since the days of the western square dancing.

For a while I would go to the folk-dance group and try to dance, and it didn't work out well. I really wouldn't say I ever gave up dancing. But interestingly, Crystal has taken it up, folk dancing particularly, and is extraordinarily good at it. I think it is extremely good for keeping strong and able. She said there are two ladies in their nineties in that group, well, one of them died while she was dancing. I guess I didn't do much dancing, I think it was pregnancies and so on that cut me down for that six years of not being fit to dance. I forget what the question was about dancing or what was it?

We were talking about The Songs. *Do you remember anything of* Song 1, *the "portrait of a beautiful woman?"*

---

* *Song 19.*

No, somehow that has not been shown much. As I say, I went to a lot of trouble to forget as much as I could [about Brakhage's films], and you can see that I really succeeded rather well. I had spent thirty years memorizing Stan's films frame by frame, but also where they were chronologically and how they fit in, and how much they cost, and on and on, all the details of the business of them. Also, what films they were related to and what came before and after, on and on and on. I just really didn't have much room in my head unless I got rid of that and just filled my head with absolutely anything but film. So I haven't gone to any movies either. I've gone to movies and I've seen some on the computer now that I've got a computer. Also, Stan at our divorce made me sign that I would not make any films. So I told everybody, "I am out of the film world." I still love my friends though. Let's see if we can talk about something else.

I don't want to push you to talk about anything you don't want to…

Oh, sure, but I think of them. *23rd Psalm Branch*, I really should talk about, because Stan was so warlike the whole time, and it took about a year for him to do it, even though he didn't photograph. I don't think any of it is photographed. He was mean to other people besides me, but he was mean to me pretty constantly. From then on, he was getting rid of people a lot more than before.

No, there's a lot of you and the kids in it. Stan said that you bought a TV but a few minutes ago you said that you'd never had a TV.

Somehow the wire got into the waffle iron, it was very soon. That destroyed that television set, and we didn't buy another.

But you did have a television for a period?

Well, yes. Maybe a week or a month or something, yes.

Stan said that one of the motives of 23rd Psalm Branch *was that he was so upset by images of the invasion of Vietnam on the television specifically. Do you remember that?*

No, I don't. I don't. Maybe I didn't see it, it's possible. Or he might've seen it also at a hotel.

So what are your recollections of the period of making 23rd Psalm Branch?

Well, the *23rd Psalm Branch* was a time when Stan was war-like. He was fighting, he was yelling. He was just constantly at war with visitors and certainly with myself and the kids. He was just angry. It could be that he was expressing anger about something else, and so chose to make that film to blow off some steam, which people very often do with artwork.

What do you think he was mostly angry about?

Everything. He was angry about me. Anything I did was wrong.

Would you rather not talk about it?

I can't remember what he accused me of. I can't remember what he yelled about. I do remember finally realizing that essentially when he'd go on a rage… I mean, he said he was having holy rages, and it was not very holy from any viewpoint I could see at all. But he felt it was holy, and I think that was because he felt rage in his heart, and so it needed to be blown off. It would be unholy not to, I guess, I don't know. But I noticed that he would just simply rage at me without meaning. He would be saying things that had nothing to do with anything or even wouldn't be full sentences. I tried to record one, and he of course turned it into an aesthetic argument, which really was of no value to anybody. But it was meaningless harangues. He would just yell. So I don't know, it was not fun at all, it was very rough. And why he thought the *23rd Psalm* would have anything to do with war, I can't think.* It may have had to do something with religion, I don't know. I don't know what he was mad about, but I was very good to yell at, I think. It wasn't any specific things; he would just yell. And he yelled always, always. The only time he stopped was the one month that Peter Kubelka† came and stayed with us. He wouldn't yell when people were visiting, but usually people visited for a day or two. Peter stayed for a month, and that was a great relief to me.

Could we talk about Kubelka's visit?

Well, we could, yeah. He showed his new films, of course, and Stan showed his films. And so we were happy filmmakers together, and that was nice. Peter did some work at Western Cine. And Peter gave me a strip of the lion attacking him; if you remember in his film *Unsere Africareise*, there was a lion that was running to attack him. The people that he was with let him run for a while so that Peter could get the footage. But he got rather more than he needed, and then they shot and killed the lion, which was too bad. But it had to be done, I guess, considering. Anyway, I got one strip of it. What did I do with it? I put it in one of the scrapbooks, I believe. He loved to cook, so we were eating a lot of meat when he was there. He liked to cook, and he liked the meat to get old. I didn't want it to get as old as he wanted, so we cooked it earlier in my honor. [*laughs*] Whenever he cooked a supper, he would hand me two or three strips of bacon that I was to fry very lightly, just a little bit, and give it back to him to eat while he was cooking.

He'd eat rare bacon while he was cooking? [both laugh]

---

* The "23rd Psalm" was recited at the burial of soldiers during WWII. (PAS)
† Peter Kubelka (b.1934), Austrian filmmaker, very much involved with Mekas, Brakhage and the U.S. avant-garde.

He had crazy taste in food, but he was also an exceptional cook. He would start cooking dinner by… have I got it right?… butter and onions, and I think carrots. I'm not sure about the carrots. It made an exquisite smell. There was something else.

Celery?

No, that's not fattening enough. [*laughs*] He's lost weight now, he sent me a picture not too long ago.

So you're still in touch with him?

Not very much. I wrote this one little short story about him in my last book, *Animals I've Neglected To Mention*. I wanted to send him a copy. It cost me like $25 to mail it to him. It was really outrageous, and I never heard whether he got it. So then I bothered Don Yannacito* and asked him, "How do you get ahold of Peter?" So I wrote to him, and I don't think he answered me. That might've been because he didn't like the book, perhaps, but he didn't dislike it enough to not send me a picture of himself. "Here's looking at you," he said.

I had some other things to say about Peter's visit. He played the recorder and he was really, really good at it. He would go up on this rock pile that was sitting ways away from the house, and he'd play the recorder there early in the morning while Stan and I were still asleep. And he gathered the animals around him, the animals, the birds and the squirrels, everybody was getting to him. It was quite wonderful. [*laughs*] For a long time, he didn't mention it, but then when he was about to go, he mentioned it.

I liked his recorder playing so much that I started playing the recorder. Also, I was quitting smoking at that time; I needed some oral entanglement, so I learned to play the recorder too. He sent me a recorder of German silver that I have still, and it plays very purely. He called me up shortly after he mailed it to me from Austria and asked me how it plays and could you play it on the telephone? I played a few notes and the telephone broke off. He said, "Go up the scale," so I went up the scale, and at D, the telephone broke off. He called back and said that if you really hit a pure D, it turns off the telephone. [*laughs*] I haven't heard anybody else say that, so I don't know if it is true or not, but it worked on that occasion. One other thing that I noticed: he and I were out in the front of the house, I can't remember what we were doing, looking at the sky, and a hummingbird came down. I was wearing a red bandana, and it just hovered for a second and then flew straight up. And Peter said, "What! Was! That? I said, "It's a hummingbird, I think it's a male, Broad-tailed." And he was just thrilled because they don't have hummingbirds in Europe, and it's a great loss. I think it's a wonderful thing to have. I guess you don't really have them much in the west coast.

---

* Don Yannacito taught filmmaking at U.C. Boulder as well as being a film programmer and curator of the First-Person Cinema Program.

Hummingbirds are outside my window here all the time.

That's great. Yeah. Strange and wonderful creatures. Yeah, he was good about talking about animals, about his trip in Africa and how he didn't like those people but he did enjoy the animals. Particularly this one giraffe that he talked about, and that's the one I got the story about. So it was a very pleasant visit. He was a good guest, and as I say, he cooked for a price: three strips of slightly cooked bacon. [*laughs*] He was very pleasant and nice.*

To have people like Kubelka and Stan in the same tiny house for a month, that must have been a little bit pressured.

I think finally he felt from Stan that he had to go. Also he just wanted to get out, it was kind of a trap for him. There were no women available there, and there was nothing much to do except be a guest of Brakhage. He didn't like to take walks, I don't know why, he should have, but he didn't. I don't remember taking him on a walk, but it was very nice. Then he left and Stan started yelling again. It was kind of a daily problem. He just was, he had a lot of rage. He had a lot of rage, and he wanted to keep shouting. My children have all suffered from it a lot. Every one of them, except for Crystal, who never married, has divorced and remarried.

Did he rage at the kids?

Not so much as me. I would just tell 'em to go to their room, and they had each other to play with.

[long pause] *The other things on my list for today were* Pasht, *1965, which you mentioned because the cat gave Stan the asthma that disappeared after Pasht died. Do you remember the film?*

About Pasht? I do a little bit. She was a beautiful cat, a tortoise shell and just a very lovely person. She once caught a bird and I caught her and pressed her jaw to open her mouth and let the bird out. She realized that I didn't like for her to catch birds, and so she never did, at least not in my sight again. But she went to war with a ground squirrel and lost. She got really kind of sick from that, I think that was what killed her. She got some kind of infection. But first she had a batch of kittens, that was in California. She had those kittens in California. How did we take the train back with two cats? We kept one of the kittens, Emily. None of her kittens were pretty like she was, there were no tortoise shells. That was too bad. Emily was a black and white cat, but she ran off at some point, and then Pasht died. So then we didn't have cats, but we would have other animals. I had all those animals in the backyard. First years we had a couple of goats, and they stayed pretty close to home. But one spring, the two goats went out and ate my

---

* Jane seems to have forgotten that Kubelka spent the month in Lump Gulch using Brakhage's equipment to prepare the A and B rolls of *Unsere Afrikreise* for printing. (PAS)

neighbor's tulips. So we had to build a fence, and that was too bad, but we had Charlie build it. It was a palisade, and it was quite wonderful. It had room for a vegetable garden in one part of it, and it had a hay shed, and it had the goats and it had chickens and geese and ducks.

After I lost Roscoe somebody was trying to get rid of a donkey and gave me the other donkey whose name was Jack. And he was pretty useless. I couldn't ride him, he was not rideable. I mean, you'd have to be a bronc rider to get on his back. One time we were all in the second meadow except for Bear. I guess the animals were loose, or Bear had taken Jack out of the fence. Anyway, he tried to get on his back and Jack bucked him off, but he held onto the rope, and the rope was wrapped around his body, so he couldn't unwrap himself from the rope with any speed at all. Jack was dragging him at a gallop right towards me. I had bought a big strong knife and I had just reached in—it was not a switchblade, but the kind that you open—and I just cut that rope off where it was taut between the donkey and the boy. So Bear fell and the donkey ran into the woods and came back eventually. Everybody was OK, but Bear would've been whacked against a tree or rock or something if I hadn't done that. Bear was a little mad at me because he was having the time of his life. Many years later, Bear asked me to give him the knife I saved his life with. I knew just what he was talking about, but I couldn't find that knife. I've been trying to find it so that I could give it to Bear as the knife that I saved his life with. But I haven't found it. I don't know what happens to things. They get lost.

I don't know where that came from. We were trying to talk about something else.

Pasht.

Pasht was lovely. Pasht was a very sweet creature. And I don't know, I should have given her away, I suppose. But it was really early on that she had that fight with that ground squirrel and it was a nice place to have a cat, I thought. But why she got into a fight with a ground squirrel, I don't know. Maybe she thought it wasn't much of a deal, but it was. It was big as her and much tougher and wilder.

When you talk about your animals, you also talk about your relationships with other animal owners. You gave this donkey to this guy who got that goat from that guy. Before you said you didn't have much social relationship with other people. It seems animals were a means of communication amongst the other people in the area.

Well, let's see: Roscoe. Stan had a local girlfriend that liked animals, so that's where I got Roscoe. The other donkey was from people that I didn't know. They'd heard about me and how I liked animals and had a donkey. So it might've been that the guy I gave him to had said something. Chickens, I would some-times go to the auction; during the summer anyway, you could go to the auction in Longmont, I guess, a town not too far from Boulder. I could buy chickens or geese or ducks there for not much money at all. I don't know how I heard about Cliff, my goat friend. I can't imagine how I found him. He was a professor of

German at the university. Oh, I know it was Ester who, you remember, used to visit us on her horse in Chrisman. And she knew people that had goats, and I think she introduced me to Cliff. Sometimes I'd sell baby goats to strangers. I didn't want to have more than a few goats. So yeah, there were people involved, but a lot of 'em were strangers.

Well, it's 12. I was going to talk about Scenes from Under Childhood *today, but maybe we could postpone that till next time?*

Yeah, that sounds good. Alright, so we'll do that next time, pleasure, as always.

So great to see you. Goodbye.

Ten

2021 April 7. Long sentences; more goats; *Scenes from Under Childhood*; the children at school; Bob Branaman; shooting pool; Bruce Baillie; Donald Sutherland; painters; *The Act of Seeing With One's Own Eyes.*

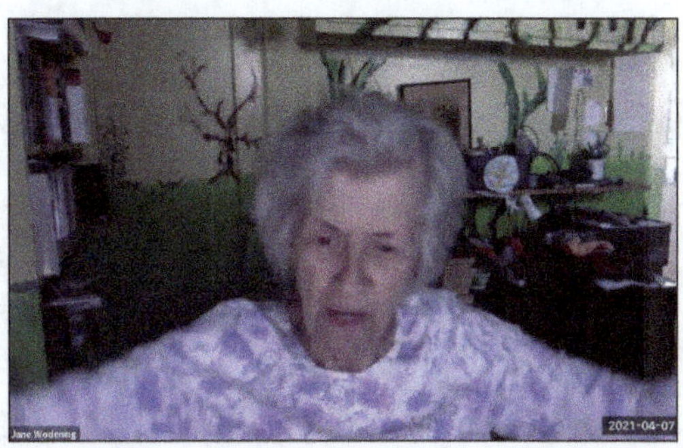

Just a minute. Let me get your sound up. How have you been?

I've been various. I've been very energetic and very weak in the past week. And now today I'm feeling pretty good. How about you?

I've been fine, thank you. Thank you so much for those books. I read all about Sunshine, *and this afternoon I read "Goodbye to Barbara." You spoke so movingly about that last week. That was the one that got you started writing. And that was the first story in a way.*

Oh, yes, yes.

But also the amazing What the Ambulance Driver Said. *It's extraordinary. I remembered your saying you liked long sentences and this proves it beautifully. Can you recall how it came about?*

Well, George told me. He was an old guy from the 1930s. He told me some of the stories, he was good at telling stories. He also had a fine tenor voice, and he and I used to sing "Tumbling Tumbleweeds" and other songs like that.

Cowboy songs?

Cowboy songs, yeah. He knew them, every word of every verse, and as I say, he had this nice tenor voice. Are you getting a clear picture of me?

Yes, very clear.

OK. Well, I'm not getting a clear picture, but that may be my… I've been told that I need cataract surgery, so everything's fuzzy. But yeah, George was quite wonderful. He was the best old guy for telling stories and stuff, and that was a story that he told about driving the ambulance. He was crippled so he couldn't do all the vigorous things that he would've liked to have done. He would've liked to have been a volunteer fireman, but all he could do was drive the ambulance and that that was a help.

How did the one sentence story crystallize?

I've done a few, actually. There's another one about an iceberg, "What the Iceberg Said at Dawn." But I just like them because they take a lot of stuff and show it to be one thing. I mean, it clearly is one thing because a sentence does begin and stop so that you get a feeling of separation between each sentence. If you don't separate, then you have everything together kind of in a bag. But I did prove with that diagram that it was not just in a bag, it was organized.

I don't fully understand the diagram of the sentence, but it's a beautiful object in itself with the blue lines and the words in space. It looks very much like those field poems that Olson and Dorn talked about.

I think they stopped teaching diagramming of sentences, which I think is a great loss. It's just like they're stopping teaching cursive writing, which I think is just horrifying because I spent years off and on dabbling at trying to learn handwriting analysis. I can see things about people in their handwriting, and that isn't so in their typing. It doesn't show so well on the computer, so people are hiding behind the computer there.

Absolutely. How did it come to be published in this form? Granary Books, 1998. Was there a specific person behind this?

You don't know Granary books?

No.

Granary Books is a wonderful publishing house. The guy is Steve Clay, he lives in New York and he makes books. He makes things out of pieces of writing. He just came out with a collection of Wally Berman's stuff, and I'm sure it's very much the way Wally Berman made it, which was all in scraps in a litter across the table. I knew you'd know him because he's from the West Coast. You met him? Yeah, he died young. But, yeah, Steve made a big book of Carolee Schneemann. Mostly he makes maybe twenty-five copies or something, and he has maybe fifteen places where he can sell it. Then there'd be other people that would be special to that one piece. He's just making a facsimile of just a few pages from my scrapbook.

Wow.

About twenty-five pages picked out of the big collection. For pretty, I think partly, but they are a spectacular collection of pages. So that's coming out, but if you want one, why, that'll be three-and-a-half or four thousand dollars. I'll tell him you want one, because then he'll make one more. [*laughs*]

Who chose the pages?

Well, I chose way too many pages, and then he chose amongst the ones that I picked.

I see. And that's coming out soon.

Yeah, whatever that means. He's working on it now.

You mentioned Wallace Berman. Did you meet him?

No, I never met him, but he did send us some things, and I scattered them throughout the scrapbooks. They're in there, but I don't think I even initialed them or anything. They're just there mysteriously so that made them anony-mous. I didn't mean to, it was just how they came in. They were themselves.

Stan knew him.

He didn't go to LA very much, but he did once in a while, I guess, and got to know him.

He made a wonderful film. But he never visited?

No, he never came to the house, I don't think. Or if he did, I don't remember.*

Last time you were talking about the Longmont auction, where you went to buy chickens, geese, or ducks; and you mentioned your friend Cliff, the German professor who was a goat man.

He had the billy-goat that all my goats went to when they needed a billy-goat. Cliff knew his business, and he was also really sensitive about goats and very knowledgeable. I liked him. I liked his wife too, but especially I liked his goats. All the goats were like pedigreed, and even though the buck was pedigreed and

---

* Berman rarely left California. Even when the Jewish Museum brought him to New York on the occasion of his exhibition there, Berman never left his hotel room. (PAS)

mine were not, that was OK by him, it didn't mess up anything of his. He gave me a goat once that was very pregnant. "Frühling" was her name, springtime in German. I can't pronounce anything properly. Frühling was a very good milker and good goat, but there was Tree, always the great goat. Tree is very special. But certainly Cliff was a very useful friend. I had to give him the stanchion I won at a raffle. I won a portable stanchion that you could carry in your truck and take it to goat shows. I had to give it to Cliff, I don't know if he ever found a use for it. That was the one raffle of my life, winning that stanchion.

You must have enjoyed going to those auctions and finding a lot of other people who were animal friendly.

I found the goats. Different people who have goats have them differently. Different people have different senses of what a goat is, and of course, they have a long history of, I mean, what is it, 10,000 years or more? 15,000? 20,000? I think I've seen a new drawing that they found that was 20,000 years old. Some think of them as exquisite pedigree creatures, and I've never figured out the value of that. Frühling had one very beautiful daughter who lost at the pedigree show because she was a wild and gloriously beautiful creature, but she didn't have the broadness of hip and the mass of a space to build milk in. She was too dainty a creature, I think, to pass their rules, and I can understand that they have a set of rules. [*telephone rings*] Oh, yeah, the water. People always call when we're talking. I buy water in bottles because they're from a glacier, and I just love glacier water. Sorry about that.

The dainty goat whose hips were not sufficiently wide?

No, she didn't have the right kind of hips, but she was a very beautiful creature. [*laughs*] I looked at the goats mainly and met people. I don't think I got to know anybody there really. It was just like going to, well, going to an animal show that I was involved with that had creatures. I didn't bring any of mine except that one, Tilly. I was interested to see what kind of creatures won and what it took to win. One of the things, of course, would be discipline, they had to be well-behaved. Tilly wasn't that either.

Were your children involved with the animals to the same degree that you were?

Not to the same degree, no, but they were involved, and they all knew how to milk a goat, and they were doing it sometimes. We all developed this little bump of a muscle on the arm, which shows that you know how to squeeze the teat of a goat. It's not the same as milking a cow where you pull and pinch, because a cow's teat is not very big. The goat has this big old handlebar and you've got to squeeze all the milk out, which is a different technique. [*Jane demonstrate the gesture on Zoom.*] Am I showing the technique on the picture?

Yes. You're showing it now. This last two or three weeks, we've talked a lot about animals and birds Any other things that you'd like to add about your relationship with wildlife and domestic animals?

We had a lot of different animals out in the yard. Charlie DeJulio, who made the greenhouse, also made the fence. The fence was a palisade, and he picked up the poles as he'd be driving around the county. He lived in the county and he was a fine painter, well known from the Drop City group.[*] If you've ever heard of the Drop City group, they formed Criss-Cross and things like that. Charlie was an artistic guy, and he was very happily collecting poles to make my palisade around my animals, and that was a lot of poles. He would stop and pick up another load and then put them into the fence and then go on about his merry way. It took a while to build the fence, but it was a beautiful one, and I really appreciated it a lot. The animals had crannies and places, and there was a fenced-in garden at the back end and also a fenced-in hay shed. So there were a lot of places where you could hide from each other and keep separate and not fight over space.

I'd have several goats, and that one year I had half a dozen rabbits and never again, but that was that year. I had chickens, ducks, geese. The geese were wonderful. I liked them a lot. I could pick them up and carry them around and put them on my shoulder, for instance, and they'd stay there, and that was good. The ducks were more demure. There was a guinea fowl that was quite wonderful. We called him "Bird." Bird was a watchdog, he was a watchbird. He had lost his whole family to hawks, so he was always looking up in the sky for hawks and he was always yelling loudly. He sounded like a peacock. If you've ever heard a peacock, that's what he sounded like, just very loud. I'll try not to quote him, but he made me realize his skull was particularly formed around a tiny little pea-sized brain, and he had a pointed crown, a crest that reached up. I kept looking at him and thinking, "He's thinking all the time. He's looking around, reaching out with his thoughts beyond his body up into the sky and everywhere around him in the yard. And that's just a whole lot of thinking to put into a pea-sized brain." My feeling is that he was doing it, that the brain reaches beyond the skull and it reaches actually beyond the feathers of whatever crea-ture it's in. I found him very inspiring because he was so smart and reasonable and sensible and conscientious and paranoid about hawks, not about people. We could pick him up, but he was paranoid about hawks. As you probably have figured out, I could spend a long time talking about animals.

Well then, let's talk about films a bit.

Oh, films! OK.

The next one up is Scenes from Under Childhood, *of which I've only been able to see again Part One recently. It occurred to me that for one part of your and Stan's*

---

[*] A counterculture artists' community, Drop City was formed in southern Colorado in 1960. Some of its members later moved to Boulder to start Criss-Cross, a similar artists' cooperative.

career, you were photographing the births of your children, and now there's a period when you're photographing your children's childhood. As I understand it, at least part of this project was Stan's attempt to recreate childhood vision, maybe his own childhood vision, even though he realized that that was impossible. Did you talk about the Scenes from Under Childhood *project? Did you talk about childhood vision? How did the project come about?*

Well, he really felt strongly about being a kid and what is it like to be a kid, and the child's view, the child's-eye view. So he'd say, "Let's do some shooting in the front room." I think he preferred the front room because the light was interesting there. I would gather all the kids and say, "Come on, get your diapers on whatever, and let's go in the front room and do some shooting." I think *Scenes from Under Childhood* was a strain on all of them. They all have kind of complained about it in a way.

What did they complain about?

We were all devoted to the films, and I don't know if the kids had a recognition or an acceptance of that. I did, but they didn't seem to, they don't seem to have had that recognition and acceptance of being part of the film work.

You'd just take the children into the front room and Stan would say, "Play" or something.

[*laughs*] They had a sense of what was expected of them. But then they also were kind of rebellious, and one would just sit and suck his thumb or something that would seem rebellious and he would photograph it. That would be good, because being rebellious was his memory of his childhood. He was rebellious quite a bit as a child, and so it worked out for the film just fine.

But he was also a lonely child. And in the film the children seem such a happy family together that it's almost an autonomous world. There's that wonderful scene where one of them—sorry, I don't recognize them by name—is feeding the other with a spoon from a jar of jam or baby food. They seem to be delightfully involved with each other and getting sustenance from each other.

That was the truth. They were very much their own world. They were together and that took a load off me because if they wanted to be entertained, they would go to each other instead of come to me. They didn't do that particularly for food. For food, we'd come together and have a meal usually, and I'd be feeding the youngest one out of a jar or maybe out of a bowl of whatever I made, as soon as they could take their own spoon in their own mouth, they were pretty independent. [*laughs*] But yeah, they were together. They had a world and it was amazing to me that they broke it up when they grew up. They just broke it up, it went blowing.

They went their separate ways?

Yeah.

The photographs you've sent me of Thanksgivings and things like that, they come together again sometimes?

The photograph I sent you of the table, that was Neowyn and some of her family. She's the grandmother now, and I'm the great grandmother. I don't go, it's too far to drive.

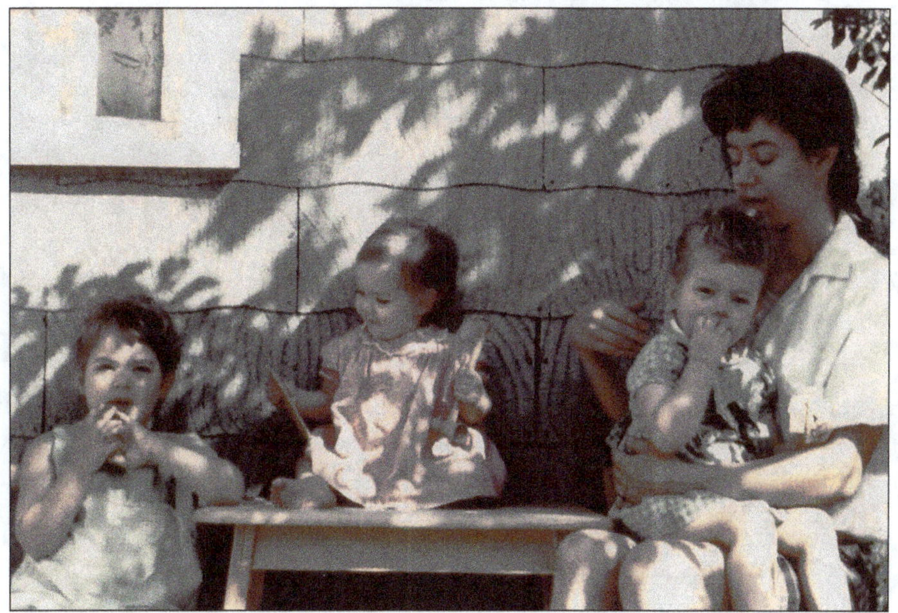

Myrrena, Neowyn, Crystal and Jane.

Since childhood, your five children now largely keep themselves separate from each other?

Yeah. I have tried really hard since the divorce particularly to make particular friends with each one and gotten to know each one and how differently they have turned out. That surprises me too, that. But they did learn something, I'm sure, from being together. They didn't have a lot of other friends commonly. Some friends would come, like the Barteks would come for two weeks, a little later than *Scenes from Under Childhood*. They came annually and camped in the second meadow. That was really fun to have them next door for a couple of weeks. And they all got to know the Bartek kids very well.[*] But as to me carrying

---

[*] Neowyn was married to Ethan Bartek; their children are Iona Bartek and Quay Bartek. (PAS)

them back to Nederland after school, I didn't do that hardly at all. That was a strain on them. They did make friends in school, but then they didn't have a way to go to after-school events because I'd be busy at home with Stan.

When we were talking about your social life in Lump Gulch, you said that the people thought of you as weird and that the children were weird and they had a hard time in school.

Yeah, they did, especially early on. Then they did get to know some of the kids and became friends, but yeah, they were weird. They didn't dress quite right. They didn't think right, I don't know what.

In the Brakhage Scrapbook,* *there's a really angry letter written by Stan to Dolores Daniels, who I assume was a teacher at the school. She complained that the kids were not bathed sufficiently often.† Do you remember that?*

Yeah, vaguely, that was very early on, I think. And yeah, I don't know. I don't know.

It was published in Film Culture *in 1966. I don't know why Stan would want that to be published, but I guess he felt that the principles of self-sufficiency and self-regulation were important too.*

Yeah, something like that, I don't know. I look sadly at some of the things that transpired during their childhood. I could have done something. I could have gone to bed early and got up early and given them all five baths and made a proper breakfast myself. They were all saying, "Don't wake up for God's sake. We know how to fix breakfast. We can eat breakfast our own selves and pack a lunch." They were taking care of themselves, and perhaps I depended on that too much.

When we first began, you talked about periods of unhappiness in your childhood. And Stan, as you document, had a very difficult childhood. Did you have clear ideas about how you wanted to bring your children up differently from the ways in which you were brought up?

The main thought that I had about that was that I wanted to hug my children, I wanted them to know that they were loved. I wanted to hug them because I suffered, I was crazy to be hugged. So I went to the dogs and they would lick my face, and that was good. They would wag their tails, they would follow me. They were really friendly, but my parents were not friendly; they were cool and not affectionate. So, it was affection that I was most aware of, the lack of affection.

---

* *Brakhage Scrapbook: Collected Writings, 1964-1980* (New Paltz, New York: Documentext, 1982).

† Daniels wrote about the bathing, and the subsequent ostracism only of Myrrena, the eldest Brakhage child. (PAS)

Did Stan have clear ideas about what children needed?

Oh, security of course. Security, for God's sake. Also, he really would've liked to have found some people he could talk with, that would understand how smart he was. That was really hard to find. He finally found Jon, if you remember Jon in the book. And Jon was a joy for him for a while. He was the one with a deformed hand. Stan was asked—or all of them were asked—to draw a picture of somebody in the classroom and have it be recognized as to who it was.* He knew that he could draw a picture of Jon with that hand showing, and everybody would know who it was. That was really cheating and a very harsh thing for Jon to take. Jon couldn't take it and got rid of Stan, although he came back once to visit. I don't know what they talked about. Jon kicked me out, I couldn't stand and listen.

Did you like Scenes from Under Childhood *when you first saw it?*

I thought it was very good, very good. There was a sense that I didn't relate to— that he was myopic so everything was fuzzy and out of focus. I didn't have that memory of childhood, in my childhood things were sharp and I was farsighted, so that separated me from it. I didn't relate as a child to it. Aesthetically, it was a good film.

Did your parents ever visit you in Lump Gulch?

They would stop by, not usually. We went down there, actually. They would babysit for us, we'd drop the kids off there to go to a movie or shopping in Boulder. That was very nice to have them there as babysitters.

Did your children like your parents, their grandparents?

Yes, they did, they liked them. They were both teachers, so they were both respectful to them as smart little kids. As they grew, each one of them picked something that they could help with as they were growing up, they were both happy to help teach. But mainly they just went in there and got plugged into the television set, that's where they saw television, at my parents'.

Did Stan ever film your parents?

No.

He never expressed any interest in it.

No, far more to the contrary: "Try not to bother us with your film work."

---

* See *Brakhage's Childhood*, pp.129-31.

Tell me if any of these questions are improper. So your parents never realized how important your and Stan's work was?

Right. They noticed that we were getting money out of it, and that was nice. But that was eventually, and that was really out of the teaching. They probably did notice that it was out of the teaching, not out of the films themselves.

With Scenes from Under Childhood, *we're well into the second decade of your marriage and, if you're willing, I'd like to talk more about that. But as I read through the* Brakhage Scrapbook, *I noticed a couple of things. There's a letter to James Broughton in mid-December 1964 in which Stan says, "Our contract to marriage, probably finally legal, this coming anniversary," which implies there was perhaps something incomplete in the first marriage statement.**

No, we did go to the county clerk in Central City and got legally married. And although he'd asked me to marry him, he wanted to be free and have a little unsureness about that, maybe just to make himself feel free. I don't know. I think he's saying that if we were only a common law marriage or something like that, I don't know… If we were common law married, then we were married, I mean…

So the 1957 December 28th marriage was somehow incomplete as far as the legal position was concerned?

As far as *he* was concerned. That's what he says. I think that he refused to go down and sign something two weeks later or something. I'm not sure.

So it didn't become completely legalized until ten years later, until mid '64?

I think it's all OK. I think that legally we did get married in 1957. In the county court by the, what was it, the judge or something, the county judge.

A bit later on, there's a letter to Andrew Myers about Bob Branaman's films. Do you recall anything about Bob Branaman?† Who he was? [Jane fetches painting by Bob Branaman]

It's Bob Branaman. Well, you'll see a lot of him in the scrapbooks, and there's some original paintings glued in there into the scrapbooks. He was someone we met in California while we were in San Francisco, he and his wife would come and visit. They lived in Big Sur. I should hold this up while I'm talking about him. They lived in Big Sur. It's kind of distracting to hold it up because I have to keep it in this little tiny square rectangle above you.

I've taken a screenshot and I can send it to you.

____

* *Brakhage's Childhood,* p.20.
† Bob Branaman (1933–2024), Beat Generation poet and filmmaker.

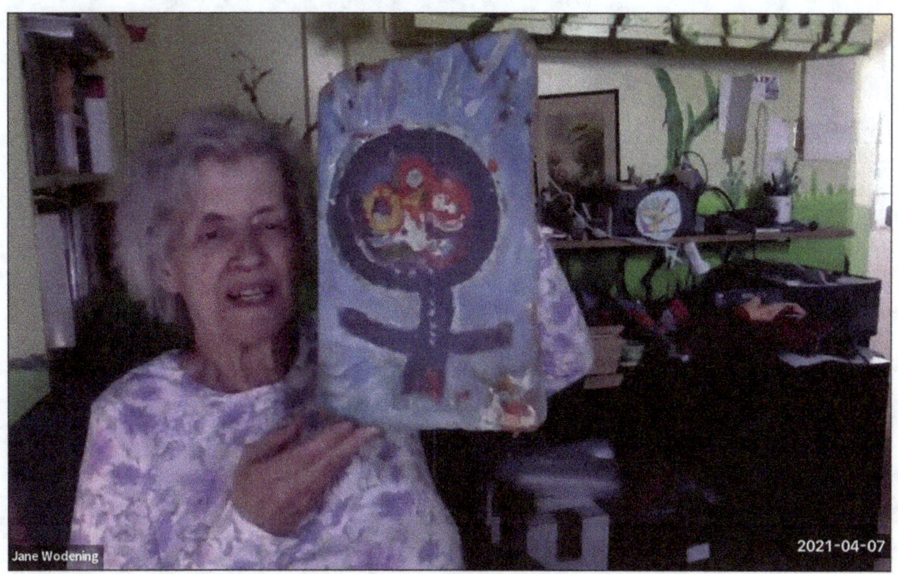

Jane Holds the Painting by Bob Branaman.

Oh, OK. [*laughs*]

He was associated with the Beats, is that the connection?

Yeah. He was there in California and he took a lot of drugs and both he and his wife were very beautiful, and his children were stunning. He had two or three children, little girls, I think. They'd come in a group and play with my kids. He was a lovely man and they had this beautiful life in Big Sur. It was just that they took a lot of drugs and they were real happy about that, so I couldn't argue. But I liked them. He was not a talker like Stan liked, but they would come to visit anyway, and on occasion we'd talk about nature and the ocean and the mountains and all kinds of things.

Did they visit you in Lump Gulch?

No, we only saw them a few times in San Francisco, but he wrote to us quite a bit after that. He liked us.

And he made films and sent Stan films?

I think so. I think he worked in maybe Super-8, I'm not sure about the Super part. He was always down home, everything was very much like kids' toys. He was fine with that. He made an art out of… I don't know what kind of crayons or something. He had this wild sense of image and of love of life. I think he lived quite long, and I don't know if he's dead yet. Even now, I think he might still be alive.

Is that painting you showed me a self-portrait?

It doesn't look like anybody particular, I think it looks like it could be like every man or something like that. It's a face, it could be every woman too, it looks very sensitive. But he was very sensitive. He was tall and thin, and his wife was tall and thin too, and everybody was delicately made.

In the same book, there's a letter to Ed Dorn in 1967, in which Stan complains that every time he goes to a bar, somebody tries to talk to him, insists on interrupting him and explain things to him. Then he talks about how he eventually joined in a pool game and they were amazed that he could play pool. He remarks that we've got a date set up when Jane's going to come back and go to the bar and play pool. He writes as if he expects you to be a very good pool player. Do you remember anything about this incident?*

I don't know anything about it. This must have been after we broke up or something.

No, 1967.

1967? No, I didn't hear anything about this. And Ed Dorn, I'm sorry, I just don't know about dates, but Ed must've been in Pocatello at that time, and so he was with Helene and their kids?

This is a letter that Stan wrote to Dorn about the problems he'd been having in Lump Gulch.

Yeah. In 1967 the kids were going to Nederland schools, and so Nederland became noticeable in Stan's eyes. I cannot imagine him shooting good pool because his eyes were really different, they were really different. They were not straight and true, he wasn't a straight-line kind of guy. And I have played some pool and I was able to do some shockingly good things on rare occasions, but that's as far as I got. That was fun and I got excited about pool; it's such an intellectual game because it's so geometrical. You have angles going against angles, and you have to really see a straight line. I just can't imagine him being good at pool at all. This is a dream that he's telling him, surely.

No. He says that he confesses to not being good at pool but says how amazed they were that he was able to hit the ball or something like that.

Well, yeah, definitely hit the ball. He could hit the ball, I'm sure. I never learned pool until after Stan left me. That was something I did to hang out with the kids for a while.

---

* *Brakhage Scrapbook*, p.139.

There's a letter to Bruce Baillie in which he writes "Jane said: 'Oh!... I like him.'" We talked about Bruce Baillie.*

Oh, Bruce Baillie† was very nice. We didn't see much of him when we were in San Francisco, although he was there. But he was very busy with a nine-to-five job carrying bananas from one boat to another, or from the boat onto the docks or whatever. He worked with his muscles all his life, that's what he did for a living. Other people taught, but he would do physical things like carry things around. And the bananas were somehow the topic of the day always, at least when we were there. I don't remember meeting him then, but I met him at Lump Gulch, and he stayed with us for a few days, a week or two maybe. During that time, he got acquainted with a stray dog, a very beautiful silver German shepherd type and smart too, except not smart enough to keep away from a porcupine. So one adventure that he and I had was that we had to pull the quills out of the dog's nose. It was quite a few, but that dog put up with it and was a hero and took it. When he left, he left the dog behind, thinking that Lump Gulch was such a free and wonderful place that the dog would love to be there instead of being tied up in his backyard. So he left the dog and the dog was shot within a week, and I sent him this curt message about it: "I'm sorry, he died of what they call lead poisoning." That was the major meeting, I don't remember other meetings except maybe at a party or something.

We didn't go to California much, we'd go to New York and Bruce would come at another time, but he did give me... I'll give you another show and tell. I don't know if you can see this. [*holds up a gift from Bruce Baillie*]

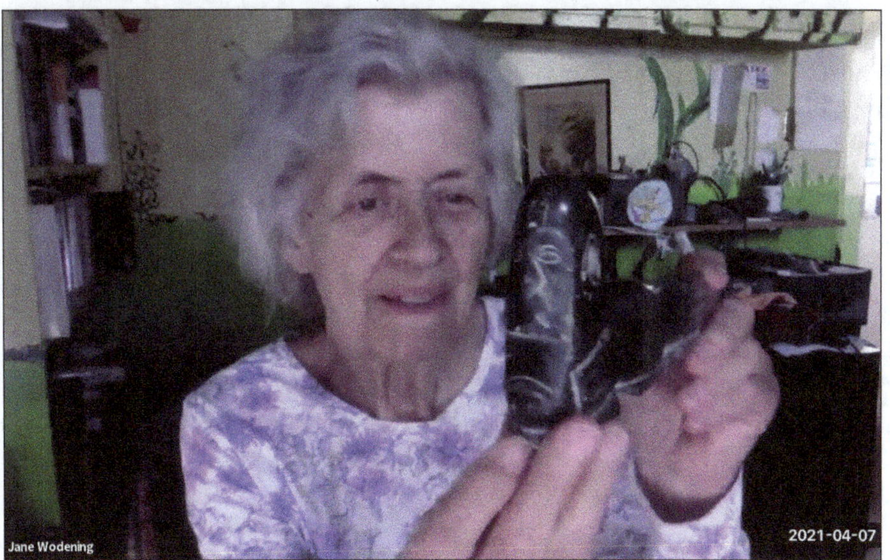

Jane Holds a Gift from Bruce Baillie.

---

* *Brakhage Scrapbook*, p.150.
† Bruce Baillie (1931–2020), filmmaker, highly-regarded by Brakhage. He co-founded Canyon Cinema in 1967.

OK. He is a God, if you can see... I think it's a fish, he's some kind of a fish God. He's not altogether friendly. He's got this grim look on his face, but he wishes well to everybody who does well, and that's what I think Bruce was giving me. If you do well, you'll do well. I found it a very interesting gift. It was like, I think maybe he was afraid that he wasn't doing well, and he wanted to get rid of it. The complexity of the psychology, I never figured out, but I treasure it tremendously: a good creature, and it lives on my mantelpiece.

It's beautiful. It looks like it's made by indigenous people in the Northwest.

Yeah, definitely, it's an Eskimo work. Could be Tlingit around Juneau. I'm not sure where Bruce went, but Juneau would be easy to get to from San Francisco.

So Bruce visited at least once in Lump Gulch, maybe more?

Very possibly more. I just don't remember anything except that very special time with the dog. He cared a lot about animals and felt very strongly that they were people too and worthy of as much respect as anybody got, so we had that bond. It's a rare thing for people to think that.

Do you recall Stan saying anything about him or his films?

I think he liked his films, he admired his films, but Bruce was not a talker. He would go walking in the woods. Maybe I took him. I took people for walks a lot, just to exercise and get some fresh air and get a break from trying to keep up with Stan's talk. Stan liked to have a break too, I think he did anyway. I don't remember walking with Bruce any particular place, but I'm sure we walked together since he was there for several days and the dog was there. I would usually take the animals, take the goats and the dogs, and go for a walk. And the donkey when we had Jack Orozco.

There's several letters to Donald Sutherland, and you talked about him in the interview that we lost. Would you like to talk about your recollections of Donald Sutherland?

OK. Donald was not the Donald Sutherland the actor, but the scholar.[*] He also wrote plays, and his wife was a lovely person, but she stayed in the background quite a bit. Donald liked my story about giving birth to Myrrena so much, and he said that "If Ernest Hemingway had had a baby, he couldn't have done better."

I wanted to go on record as having said it was a terrific piece of writing before anybody else did, but apparently Sutherland got there first.

---

[*] Donald Sutherland (1915–78), classical scholar and translator, Professor of Classics at University of Colorado at Boulder. He wrote "A Note on Stan Brakhage" in *Film Culture* 24 (1962), pp.84-85. Brakhage designated his film, *Burial Path* (1978), as an elegy for Sutherland.

I am afraid [*laughs*] I really put you out of shape. Oh, wow. He said that and I was embarrassed, and then he said to Stan, "Did I say something wrong?" I was just so shy at that time. I was unable to speak hardly at all. I liked him and he didn't know it because I was too shy to join the conversation. But he was grand, he was quite a delight. Then he was dying, he was on his deathbed and he was taking oxygen and smoking. He wasn't going to stop smoking just because he was dying for God's sake. What's the use of that? He wasn't going to save his life, and if he went up in flames, why, that would be quicker than sitting around waiting for death. I just really liked him. He was humorous; he was objective; he gave me a clarity of how to look at one's own death and face it. I cheered him on for smoking, even though I was smoking too at that time, but I wasn't cheering him on as though it was like a good group to be a part of. I just worried about the house or his wife. He fought valiantly, for his last weeks he was fighting valiantly to maintain his habit of smoking. I think he drank too, but the smoking was the more hair-raising one with the oxygen there.

At one period in my life, I was trying to be a poet, and I wrote a poem about Marlboros. It was one of the first poems I ever wrote, and Ed Dorn published it. So I have some sympathy for people who have commitments to smoking cigarettes. I eventually quit, but I was involved with Marlboros for many years.

Of course, you would smoke Marlboros. [*laughs*] But I would like to say that if Ed thought your poetry was good, then it was.

Thank you. Reading all these letters, I'm struck by how thoroughly immersed Stan was in contemporary poetry, but he almost never talks about painting.

That's right. That's right. Painters were a different breed. Painters were more ballsy, more physical. He just wasn't that type. As a child, he was like the fat boy in the gym class that couldn't do anything. He couldn't climb a rope. He couldn't jump because if he started jumping, he'd have an asthma attack, and he just couldn't keep up with the kind of people that are painters. And I'm really sorry about that because I would've really liked to have known some of those people, but he just avoided them.

He avoided them?

I think he avoided them or they avoided him, I'm not sure, I think that he avoided them. I don't think any of them were allowed to come over and visit. He'd be rude to them. I don't know.[*]

Did any of them indicate a desire to visit?

---

[*] Later in his life, Brakhage wrote about Canadian painters, extolled Joan Mitchell, and befriended sculptor David Rabinowitch. (PAS)

Some of them certainly indicated an interest in his films; they saw his films and they liked them very much and felt related to them. But he didn't want to because they would see that he was that little fat boy that couldn't climb a rope because he'd get an asthma attack. I think he would've gotten an asthma attack at the sight of one of them. He didn't like people who were athletic. There's Jackson Pollock hurling paint around and wearing his Levi's, even though he'd been in New York for how many decades. All those guys were hurling paint around, even there was one in Denver: Kirkland, was that his name?

That rings a bell. Maybe it was mentioned somewhere in those letters.

It's a museum, actually. It's an art museum in Denver, and I think that it is named after this artist, Kirkland. There was something in the museum where he had kind of a swing that he could pull himself around and dab paint. The painting was on the floor, and so he would go over around on this swing and pull the ropes, all very much like a sailor climbing the mast. Stan just didn't do that kind of thing.

The reason I was reading those letters, is that I have a recollection of letters that Stan wrote to you from Pittsburgh, while he was shooting The Act of Seeing With One's Own Eyes *(1971). I can't find those letters. Do you remember seeing them printed somewhere?*

I'm sure P. Adams will know.

He didn't, he couldn't find them either. Stan talks about how traumatized he was, especially when he was visiting the morgue. He went to the morgue for all of one day and then wrote to you at night that he had to go back to the morgue the next day. Do you remember receiving those letters or am I making it all up?

I don't remember receiving those letters. That particular corpse was surely photographed just at one gathering because they were cutting her open at the time. It was a very time-specialized thing. The thought of going back to the morgue would only be because he hadn't photographed a corpse being studied.

Do you have any recollections of the films about the police or the hospital? I did see the police film, Eyes *(1970); I didn't think it was up to Stan's standard.*

No, because they just wouldn't go anywhere. They turned off the radio and didn't want to be photographed doing their thing because they might cuss or who knows what. Then if they cussed or punched somebody in the nose, a legal suit could be made against them and they'd lose their whole career. I think that was a real limitation for this film. It was just a ride around Pittsburgh really, and it didn't come too much. Then when they dropped him off, they turned on the radio and Stan heard—or he says he heard—them being called, "Come quickly," and they put on their siren and off they went to something real.

The police film and perhaps the hospital film suffered from that limitation but in the morgue film, he became very involved.

He was thinking of the corpse: she was a pretty lady. That is the one that sticks in my mind too.

These films were arranged by Sally Dixon. Did you ever meet her?*

Oh yes, we got to know her very well. She was a very nice person. She ran the film part of the Carnegie Museum and really made a place for it. Then she moved to St. Paul and married Ricardo [Bloch]. He was a bright and charming Mexican guy who needed a green card. She rented Molly Ball's house in Lump Gulch for the winter, and there she met Ricardo and fell in love with him there in Boulder so they got married. She became an aunt to both Myrrena and Crystal. Each of them, separately, went to the Twin Cities. She was just a really good help to each one. I went there after the divorce and visited with her too. She was highly honored by a lot of people, and rightly so. She died a couple years ago. Crystal was in touch with her still, they would talk on the telephone as she was fading away. She had a fading away kind of death. Finally, it still seemed as though Sally could understand what she heard, but she couldn't respond to it. Sally was a very bright and useful member of the film people. It's a funny thing— not surprising—but the West Coast film people are one world, and the eastern half of the United States is connected with New York. So there's not much of a connection really between the two, although Bruce Baillie is seen in New York and James Broughton, sometimes... Wally Berman and a few others from the West Coast. Anyway, Sally was certainly one of the important members helping the experimental film people. She was very useful, very bright and imaginative. She could also draw, she had a good hand at drawing.

I'm not sure what's the best way for us to proceed. I've been asking questions, because I had the chronology. Shall we just go ahead and you reminiscing about what happened in the '70s.

We could start with that, if we have some time.

Shall we start with that next time?

In the '70s I have a number of items. There were two trips to Alaska. There were two trips to Europe. We bought my car one year, his car the next year, both of them used. We didn't buy any new cars. We added on to the house. There are all these things happening in our life that ought to have connections to the films in some way. *Creation* was filmed in the earlier trip to Alaska
     Another thing that happened in the '70s: I started writing.

---

* Sally Dixon (1932–2019), museum curator and supporter of avant-garde film. As Film Curator at Carnegie Museum of Art in Pittsburgh, 1970–75, she facilitated Brakhage's *Pittsburgh Trilogy.*

Eleven

2021 April 14. Alaska; flying; England; *Unconscious London Strata*; Amsterdam; Van Gogh; palm trees; *Weir Falcon Saga*; *Sincerity*; Paul and Gregory Sharits; Hollis Frampton; feminism; Annette Michelson; more feminism.

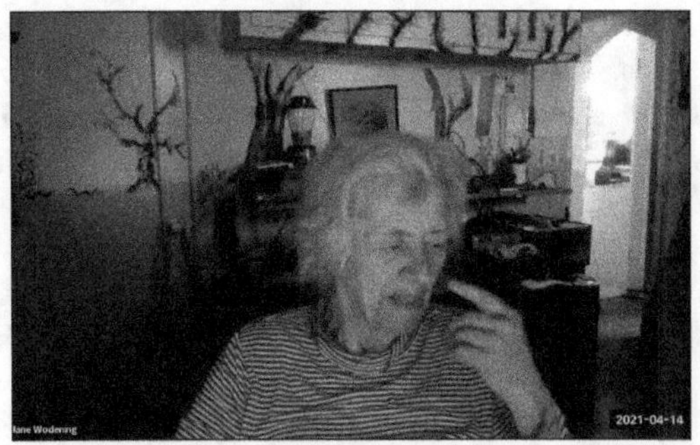

Hi, Jane. Can you see me? Can you hear me?

Yep, I can hear you. Did you turn it on?

Yes, it says it's recording. How are you?

I'm very good, thank you. What are we doing?

Last week we said that we'd go on to the '70s and you had a list of things you wanted to talk about. But I have one question, if I may.

What is your question?

I wondered about your role in Stan's photography. In the early years of your marriage, you played a prominent role in the filming and we talked about your photography in Wedlock House *and* Dog Star Man. *Indeed, Stan spoke of his films as coming not through him alone, but through you and the children Brakhage, as if the whole family were generating them.* Did your role in the photography decline somewhat in the late '60s?*

---

* The complete quotation reads: "'By Brakhage'" should be understood to mean 'by way of Stan and Jane Brakhage,' as it does in all my films since marriage. It is coming to mean: 'by way of Stan and Jane and the children Brakhage' because all the discoveries which used to pass only thru the instrument of myself are coming to pass thru the sensibilities of those I love. Some day these passages will extend thru the sensibilities of those I now can only imagine loving. Ulti-

I wouldn't necessarily say that. Things changed. I didn't shoot the 8-millimeter camera, but there were things, I can't remember the film in which I took care of all the sound. I didn't, of course, edit it because I didn't know how. There were other things, but I don't think I did so much with that.

So now we move on into the '70s. I remember you saying that when Stan got the job in Chicago in 1969, it brought difficult times for you. You mentioned that he got a mistress and you were miserable all the time. Would you like to talk about that or shall we put that aside?

I think I did talk about it, and that's all that needs to be said.

Of course. So, let's go on to the end of last week's session where you said you wanted to talk about the trips to Alaska and Europe, buying the cars and adding onto the house. Then: "Another thing that happened in the '70s: I started writing." I think it'd be good if you would take the lead in the discussion.

Well, I don't remember the chronology, which came first, but yeah, so my car came first: we could actually buy a car and that was nice. There's not much you can say about buying a car, but I could buy a car. Going to Alaska, we went to Juneau the first time, that was when Stan photographed *Creation*, the film you saw when I went to L.A.

That was photographed almost entirely in Glacier Bay, which we had to fly to. The only way to go anywhere in Alaska is by putt-putt airplane. A lot of people had an airplane, and so we got a ride with somebody who would take anybody where he wanted to go. He must have waited for us while we took a ride on some kind of boat for tourists to get close to the glaciers and to see the icebergs floating and hopefully to see a calving.

Mainly I was interested to see the seals lounging on the icebergs, looking very comfortable, and I wanted to join them. It was quite lovely, and there were some interesting birds. I didn't see any other mammals—yes, yes, I did. There was a particularly charming humpback whale; that was kind of a shock, then he was gone for twenty minutes and back up for air. They go down for up to twenty minutes, I guess, and then they have to breathe. I don't think we hung around for that, the boat didn't know where to wait and so on. That was a great occasion, that trip to Glacier Bay, and it was fun to fly. Did I mention flying with my Uncle Marsh when I was a kid?

No.

I didn't! Oh my God. I left out a lot of things in my childhood.

Let's hear about Uncle Marsh.

---

mately 'by Brakhage' will come to be superfluous and understood as what it now ultimately is: 'by way of everything.'" *Metaphors on Vision*, p.96.

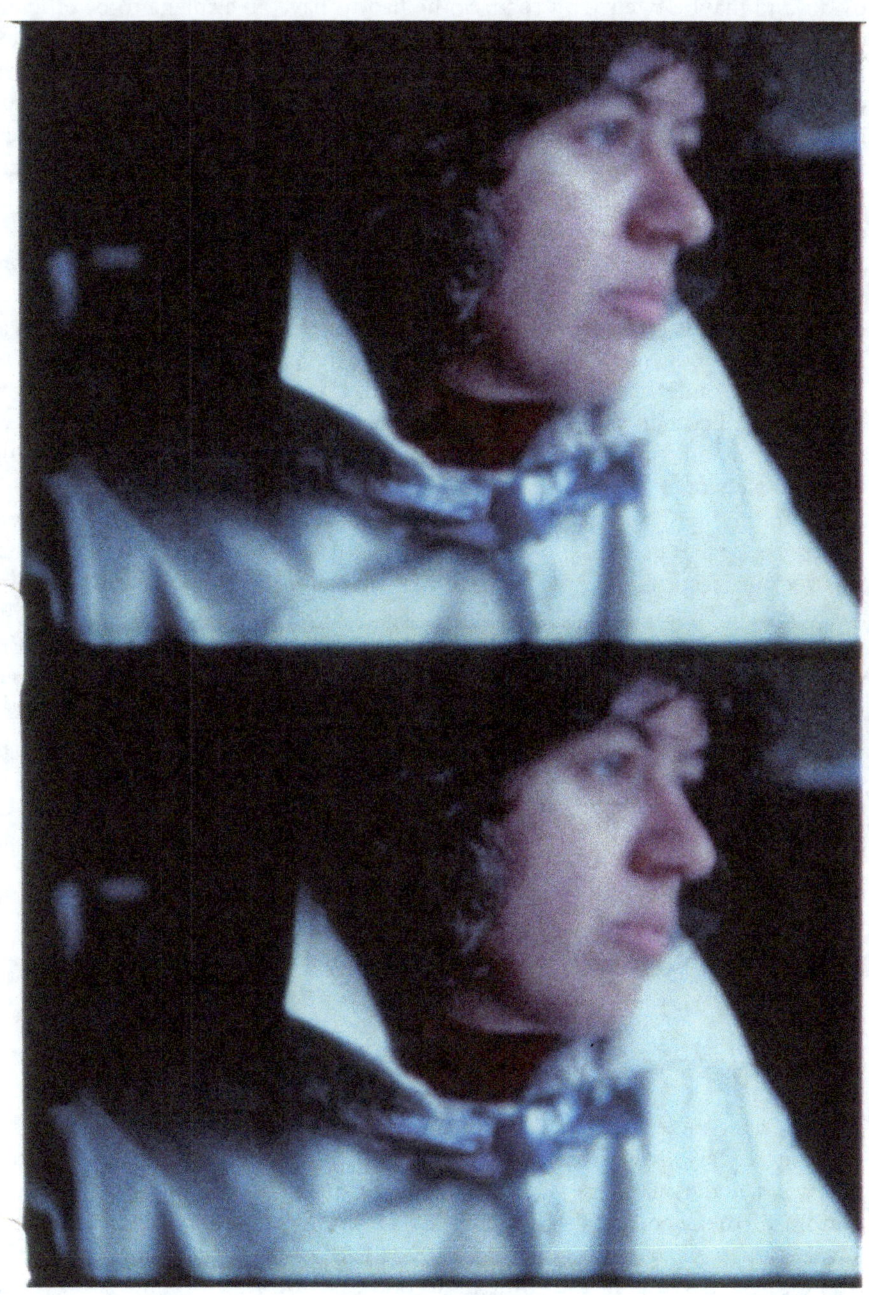

Jane in *Creation*.

[*laughs*] OK. Uncle Marsh had to have an airplane because he made grain elevators. He'd go from one grain elevator to another, which might be two miles away by air and maybe twenty by road. So he had to have an airplane to be efficient in his work. Before we left Illinois—I think it was still during the war—he flew to Western Springs, Illinois where we were to visit his sister, my mother, and he offered me a ride in his airplane, a two-seater. It had two little cockpits, each had room for one person. He was in the front piloting, and I was in the back and he told me, "If you're scared, if you want to go down, just tap me on the shoulder" because it was so loud. You can't speak to each other, especially with your head sticking out of the airplane. We went up and I was just thrilled. I loved it. I loved flying and looking down on the streets of Western Springs, Illinois. But he was very unsure or Mom had expressed her worry, and so he came back down *way* quicker than I wanted him to. But I had a chance. While I was up there, I was wearing a leather helmet, just like Amelia Earhart. And goggles too, of course, so I really felt wonderfully dressed up. I told him I wanted to go up for longer next time, please. I couldn't speak to him when we were up there except to tell him to come down, and I didn't ever want to come down. Across the years, he would visit and we would go up in the air.

One time he took me on a trip to Lima, Ohio, which is a sad little town. I guess they were having a conference of people who made grain elevators, that was very interesting. But he had shaved his hair all off, and I complained to him about that. He said, he heard that if you accentuate your flaw, then women like you, and my flaw is that I'm bald on top. I said, "No, your flaw is that you're short, and the baldness on top accentuates that, but you've got to grow your hair to make it work." I got his hair back for next time. [*laughs*] He was a very charming and extraordinarily lovable uncle, he was just great. This one trip in Alaska was another moment of joy in the air. I'm not at all interested in flying in big airplanes because you're really blocked from the world, you're just enclosed in something that has pictures on the wall that move. But it was fun riding in an airplane there.

Do you remember the year you went to Alaska?

I thought it was '72, but maybe not.

You went there specifically to go to Glacier Bay?

No, we went there specifically for Stan to show his films and speak in Juneau. Also, there were crowds of eagles along the shore, especially at one section, and that was wonderful. There was another boat ride that I took in a kayak. At the bottom of the Mendenhall Glacier near Juneau, there was a lake, so we went kayaking. I went with some strangers that had a kayak. She was in the back running it and I was in the front in a good seat for viewing things. We were going towards an island that belonged to the Arctic Terns. It was full of nesting Arctic Terns, and they started coming towards us to chase us away, and they were dropping their bombs closer and closer. They would shit closer and closer to the kayak, warning us. I did have a nice sailor hat on. Somehow we never got bombed, or at least not badly. But that's what they were doing, they were chasing us away and that was wonderful. We had to be careful not to run into an iceberg.

Do you remember anything about the screening in Juneau?

The screening? No, I don't remember much about the people. I'm sorry, I have a flaw in my character there. I remember Juneau somewhat. It was a funny little town with a lot of boardwalks because it was steeply going up the hill. It was really no place for a town, but it was the state capitol, so it had to have some way of getting around.

You said that you went to Alaska twice?

Yes. Another time was a few years later, not many. We went to Anchorage and again, Stan was at the college showing films and speaking. I don't remember going out into the town or anything. I remember that we had a balcony in our hotel room and that it was springtime. In Juneau, it was the height of summer, so there was very, very little darkness, really just a kind of a heavy twilight. In the spring in Anchorage, there were five different mountain ranges going around, so that the views, if you were up always which we were, were fantastic: views of different mountain ranges, doing geometric things with each other and the light seemed like it was never quite daytime. It never was bright and sunny. It was just not quite day yet. The whole time, it would be slowly coming towards daytime, and then it would be slowly going away from daytime. That was just fascinating. I just loved sitting out there in that porch, watching those mountains, watching the light. The light was just stunning. Also, I heard there was a moose loose on the college campus, and everybody was warned because moose are a little tricky sometimes, you don't go up to them and pet them. So, I was kind of left out. I was brought and left in my room, and there was a beautiful view, and I didn't mind.

Did Stan photograph anything there?

Well, I think that somebody gave him a ride through some of the mountains; he took some pictures of mountains, and I think some of those got into *Creation*. I'm not sure. I just remember the glaciers and the places where they were melting. Anchorage was a city. I do remember a street in Anchorage, but it was just like Colorado Boulevard [in Denver] used to be but isn't anymore.

You mentioned trips to Europe that you wanted to talk about?

Yes. Let's see. We went once to Amsterdam for a few days. We went to England first and we were there for a week or two maybe. I had Windy [Newcomb] taking care of the house, the kids, milking the goats and everything. I had to train him to milk the goats. Of course, he had our library to enjoy so we were OK. In

England, I remember going to the Tate and there was a room with only Rothkos on every wall. I remember Big Ben and I remember we went to Kew Gardens. We were trying to get out of London, it's big. We couldn't get out of London. We'd go and go and go and go, and then we'd find ourselves at Kew Gardens. And so we'd get out and look at Kew Gardens, and there was just down the street, Keats' house.* They had a Rembrandt in Kew gardens. I didn't think it was a real Rembrandt, but maybe it was because I was so used to the portraits and not so much use to his landscapes or seascapes. This was a seascape. There were some people there who didn't know how to get out of Kew Gardens, it was so big. So I said, "Well, we're just going, I'll just lead you." I didn't know how to get out either, but I know how to get out of places, so I just led everybody out of Kew Gardens, including a couple of strangers.

Did Stan shoot any film in Kew Gardens?

I don't believe he did. I don't remember him doing so. Maybe he didn't bring his camera.

Well, when you were in London in 1979, he shot the footage that was later edited into the film about London called Unconscious London Strata.

Oh, well, maybe then he did. He made a film there, and I've forgotten it. I remember I was looking for old coins. There was a bridge named after a family in my huge genealogy, Hungerford Bridge, and there was a coin shop right under it. Maybe there was some photographing of London Bridge. The film, you don't remember it?

No. But Stan also talked about the influence of Dickens on his life. He was excited to go to London because of Dickens.

Yeah, Dickens. As a kid when he read Dickens, he felt that that was his kind of life, that's how he lived.

Were there screenings in London?

Yes. Yes. There were screenings in both London and Amsterdam, more than one in each place.

Do you remember any of the people you met in London? Do you remember Simon Field?

Yes, I remember that name, but I don't know as I remember a face that goes with it. But Field, definitely. I don't remember the shows. I don't remember what else we went to see.

---

* In fact, Keats' House is in Hampstead, the other side of London from Kew Gardens.

Your visit to England was very important for English filmmakers, so I just assumed that you would be surrounded by people who wanted to meet you.

It's very possible. At a show the people would gather around, especially afterwards and ask questions. The show would close and a lot of people would leave, and then there'd be the people that would gather around and ask questions. I may have been standing by Stan at that time, probably was. I would've been with him, so if there were questions of me… doubtful, but it's possible.

Sometimes people did ask you questions?

Sometimes, yeah, they would ask questions of me, but not usually, because there'd be Stan right there, and so they'd ask him.

So this first trip to England was specifically to show films and talk?

Yes, that was why we went anywhere actually, I mean on an airplane. We did it two or three times there or more.

Was Amsterdam a separate trip?

Yes, it was a separate trip, and it was at a different time, later. We went to Amsterdam first and met these nice people. So many people in Amsterdam can speak English very well. They don't have much of an accent, they don't have a German accent, it's quite interesting. But as we would walk around the streets—and it was a very nice weather, so we were doing that—I would have my handkerchief hanging on my back pocket, and evidently that was totally out of style in Amsterdam. Total strangers would tell me to tuck in my handkerchief. Then there were the cigarettes. In England there were the matches, these wonderful Swan Vestas. I wanted to buy a whole box of them, I mean a big box of them, but I didn't. Then I was sorry because then I ran out of 'em real quick. In Amsterdam, everybody wanted to bum a cigarette, and so I was giving away cigarettes one by one to strangers on the street and lighting it for them. It was a strange thing, but it was kind of nice because there was a chance to speak to somebody. They must have had some reason why they were bumming a cigarette from an American. It was so interesting in Amsterdam, the canals. You didn't walk across the street, you went over the bridge. And it was not perfectly clean as I was expecting the Netherlands to be; the canals had junk in them so it was kind of disappointing.

But there was a fantastic Van Gogh Museum there, and that was a great joy. I really am fond of Van Gogh. And there was Rembrandt's House that you could go to. There was not a single Rembrandt in that house because they didn't have a lot of money, not even a drawing, but they had other things that they were showing. It was kind of a big house, except that it was all heavily varnished, just really shellacked all over. It looked like it was trying to be behind wax or behind a glass box. But I was really glad to see his house, although it was amazingly hard to relate to him in there because I'm sure he didn't like it.

We also went to Utrecht and did a show there, and that was interesting. We drove in and there was this little parking lot of yachts, boats, various sizes and so on, just a whole lot of boats. And evidently it's right up against the ocean, I'm not sure what the deal is. Utrecht was a very different city. It was not a tourist trap so much, it was a bit more Dutch, and we did pass a lot of windmills. Some of them were modern and others were old fashioned. I thought the people were a lot of fun, and they knew English so well. Everybody—people on the train, on the bus, people everywhere—knew English and to joke around with us, and I enjoyed that a lot.

You didn't mention seeing Rembrandts in Amsterdam.

There was another museum that we went into that had a few Rembrandts, I guess that was the big one.* The main one that excited me was the not-so-little one of Van Gogh but the big one was great. It had some Rembrandts, some that were unusual, and a couple of Van Goghs and [Frans] Hals and all those people and other people from around the world. The museums in Amsterdam were very good. We went to the Red Light District and looked them over. It was shocking, the Red Light District. There were women in shop windows and making lascivious gestures at us as we walked by. I remember looking down an alley and one was hanging out of the upper window and making lascivious gestures. [*laughs*] It's all perfectly legal and approved of somehow and, of course, also a tourist trap.

So we took in the sights and met, as I say, just a lot of nice people there, especially in Holland. The British are more shy and polite and stuff, but the Dutch were gathered around us, even if we didn't know them, even on the streets. I think they wanted to practice their English, but they were so good at it, all of them.

Do you remember any other trips in the '70s? We've got two to Alaska, one to England, one to Amsterdam.

Those are the four [when] I was taking the trips. After that, Stan would take one of the children on a trip. The next trip was Pocatello, to stay with Dorn and Helene, his first wife, and their kids, and do a show and speak. That was a wonderful occasion for everyone. It started Helene sending us beautiful things in the mail, some of which I put in the Scrapbook. She was such a delicate artist, working with collage and paint and so on. I didn't see them until much later. I saw Ed with Jenny later when he changed to his second wife. And then I saw Helene in Gloucester much later when I was doing my driveabout. She and I became friends there, I'd see her practically every day. I was there just two weeks.

Do you remember your trip to Riverside?

---

* The Rijksmuseum, the national museum of the Netherlands dedicated to Dutch art, holds the largest collection of Rembrandt's work. The Van Gogh Museum is close by.

Riverside, California?

Yes.

That's where I got my palm tree.

Exactly. We talked about that before.

I don't remember what happened. There were several shows in Riverside.

He was teaching there for several weeks, but he'd go home at the weekend usually, except one weekend, he didn't go home. You came to Riverside instead.

Is that how it went? OK. I remember walking around town alone, he was busy doing something. He'd usually want me at his shows but not always. I was walking around town and coming across a vacant lot that was full of palm trees of various sorts. They would all be like three or four inches tall, since the last time it was mowed, which might've been months before. The backhoe was there just waiting for the guy to come and start mowing down all these beautiful baby trees. I found a nearby hardware store and bought a trowel and some plastic bags and started digging up palm trees and putting them in plastic bags so that I could take them home and maybe share them around with people. I brought back some other plants too that were so fascinating. You have amazing plants down there in that hot and dry area. San Bernardino was great, inland quite aways, but a big city. I just was interested in the palm trees, and so I packed my bag full of all this greenery and gave away eleven of the twelve trees that I dug up and planted the twelfth one in my greenhouse on the roof. I've written a story about that palm tree—it's in *The Lady Orangutan*—because it was a very impressive tree, it was just a wonderful tree. That's about all I can say about that trip to San Bernardino.

Those were the things that you wanted to talk about. I have a couple more questions about the '70s, especially the film, The Weir Falcon Saga *(1970). Stan said it was about the illness, convalescence, and recovery of Rarc.*

[He had] the flu, I think. I remember him taking him to the doctor and he was sitting in the back with the other kids and he was drooping and the other kids were sitting bright and interested in things. We went to our pediatrician who we had for the whole time of their childhood, and he was a very charming and pleasant man for them to go to. That was a good thing. I think Rarc had the flu and the pediatrician recommended various things, maybe some pills. Beyond that, I don't remember the film, except that Rarc did recover after a few days and was playing with the kids. That was the image of the recovery unless he was hobbling around. He was kind of young; he might have been four or something.

The illness wasn't life-threatening?

No. It was Rarc playing Stan. Stan had been sick a lot when he was a child, and so he was hard-pressed to find sick kids in our family. Rarc was pretty good for that, sometimes.

After that, the main body of films were the autobiographical series Sincerity *and* Duplicity. *I've not seen those for many years. Do you have any recollections about that series of films?*

I just didn't see a meaning in the name *Sincerity* or *Duplicity*. People teased him so much about the name *Sincerity* because he was never really doing that. He wasn't being sincere, he was always being complicated and duplicitous. It was, I think, Paul Sharits* that shouted out from the audience at one point, "Why don't you call it *Duplicity*?" Of course, Stan made it with different things, having influence on other things, and so that it was all tangled up... It was not straight-arrow like you would think of sincerity; like one asks a question, and the other answers "Yes" or "No," or tells the answer.

Did you meet Paul Sharits?

Yes, we knew Paul and his brother Gregory. Gregory was also a filmmaker but he only worked in 8-millimeter, and he was younger. They grew up in Denver. Gregory went to New York and became a helper in the Film-Makers' Co-op. He was very useful there, I'm sure. I think they really wanted him to get into 16-millimeter but he was always poor and didn't have a 16-millimeter camera. He wanted to stay small. He was beautiful; I wouldn't say he was handsome, he was beautiful like some kind of an elf, but he was a beautiful creature, gentle and shy and all the women fell for him, to the right and the left and I don't know as he noticed that. Paul, on the other hand, was interesting-looking and brash.

When Gregory came home from New York, he was a big dope taker. He was taking LSD in Indianapolis at the bus station. It was six flights up and then he could jump off of the balcony and fall six flights and he did. But he didn't die. He almost did, the whole world was trying to save him, you know just sending good prayers. Anyway, he woke up and survived for a while; he was crippled then, and had trouble having really hit his head so he couldn't make films, and he had trouble talking, too. He was still beautiful, so he got along. People would help him, they would go way out of their way to help him. He was gentle in every way, so that helped. He then moved to California and he was in an apartment and he somehow got a hold of a gun that had six bullets in it. He shot them through the ceiling of his apartment or through the walls to the outside and they were gone, you know, the six bullets, and that was that. Then a policeman came and he was sitting in the doorway looking down the hall, as though he was waiting for that policeman to come, and he raised his empty gun and pointed at the policeman, and the policeman killed him. So that was

---

* Paul Sharits (1943-1993) Filmmaker, initially a student and protégé of Brakhage's, he developed a highly personal style of filmmaking based on the rapid alternation of single frames.

suicide by a policeman, I think, because it was his own doing by raising the gun. Their mother had committed suicide by cutting herself in the bathtub, and other relatives had committed suicide, so it was a kind of a family problem. That was Gregory. I know you'd asked about Paul, but I just wanted to give Gregory his space. I think his films were lost.

Paul was much more responsible, he was the older brother, he wasn't near as handsome but he looked fine. I mean he was a good-looking guy, but not like Gregory. He came and visited once or twice. I think I tested the palm tree on him and it worked. He had schizophrenic tendencies, I guess. But he made really fine films and he was sharp, an interesting talker, although he wasn't a talker like Stan; he was more like he would come out with some perfect statement or something you know. I don't know what you call it, but he was good with words in a way, but he wasn't fast with them like Stan was. He once came to Colorado, and he got to know some people on the other side of Nederland who were hospitable to him. Almost all the people live out in the country, you know, at least in the mountains they do. He wanted to visit them, but they weren't at home and so he thought he would try and climb in through a hole in the roof, a chimney. Anyway, he fell down and broke his leg badly. I guess then a friend, not the homeowner, came and found him there with a broken leg, called 911, and he was carried off to the hospital and he had his leg in a cast hanging from a rope for quite some time.

He had a friend who came to help him out and take care of things, and Paul told that friend, "Well you go to Stan and Jane's house and they'll give you a place to sleep, and something to eat and you'll be fine." He arrived after dark, and we had already had supper—I don't remember what his name was I'm sorry —but I didn't have anything really that would be nourishing to give to him to eat except I had some eggs. So I gave him a fabulous omelet with lots of vegetables and some meat in it, and he was shocked, he said, "You don't have omelet in the evening, you have to have it in the morning." He was quite startled, even horrified but he felt obliged to put up with it, because it was after dark and he didn't know any place to stay. But he said that, before the ambulance came, he and his friend had taken off Paul's Levis to look at his leg and then put them back on again. Then when the people in the ambulance came, they cut his Levi's off of him—those same Levi's that they had pulled off, they cut off carefully and he realized that he maybe had done a wrong thing there. Paul came out of it with two working legs, so that was OK in the end. But yeah, he broke his leg in the mountains of Colorado trying to break into his friend's house.

Did Stan show him films or did he show films to Stan?

Oh yeah, they showed each other films, when he visited our house, two or three times.

I think Stan once filmed him making love with his wife. Do you remember that?

No, I don't remember that.

It might have been in the Sexual Meditations.

I'm not sure. Probably, that's what jumps to mind.

When did you first meet Hollis Frampton?

It would be in the '70s, he came and visited once or twice. It was spectacular when he would come, he was so lively and funny and he had me in stitches the whole time. Crystal even now says he was the funniest and the funnest guest we ever had. He was terrific but he smoked four packs of cigarettes a day and died young.

I think he finally died from cancer.

I guess.

Did Stan feel in competition with Frampton?

I don't think so, I think that he felt that Frampton admired him so much, I think that was so. In sections of the interview with Stan and Hollis, I had the sense that Stan was really being polite and respectful. Well, I don't know! Certainly, he admired Frampton's mind, and he was somebody who could talk, Frampton was, and so that was a very valuable thing to Stan. I don't know what he thought of his films.

Did you ever meet Frampton's wife?

I don't believe I did, no. He didn't bring her and I didn't go to wherever they lived.

Did you go to New York at all in the '70s?

I just don't think I went to New York in the '70s. I did in the '60s, and in the '50s and in the '80s, but not in the '70s. We would go through it on the way to Europe, of course, but generally that's just a stop at an airport and then go away in an hour or so or maybe make a phone call.

By the mid '70s, Stan was being criticized by feminist filmmakers. Do you recall this?

Yeah. The feminists were trying to get me to say things that they liked to say and I didn't like to do that. I don't see that much difference between a man and a woman as far as brains and ability and so on, so it seems silly to say, "My gender is better than your gender!" [*laughs*] I don't know. I also did notice that they had said that men get paid higher than women for the same jobs. I thought that was unfair, but it wasn't a big enough deal for me to make a scene about, so

I didn't play their game. They just thought I was happy to be a housewife, and maybe that was so, but they were political. And yes, they gave him trouble for what he was doing to me. I guess he did like to praise me sometimes or quote me on stage, that I was interested in helping him out. And he suffered, I guess, and I don't think he knew what to do about it because he had very few women that he could talk with. Bobbie Creeley and Gloria Bartek, both of those were smart in a verbal way like he was. So he knew that women could talk, because of them. But I don't know about feminism. I've kept out of it because I keep out of politics. I just don't do politics and that's what it is.

In the early '80s, I became somehow the head of the county library board. The county library was actually housed in a little log cabin by the side of the road. It had a few books that people would like to read and it had some of the local history books and whatnot and mostly used things. We'd have our annual book sale to get rid of things that weren't used much and so on. And Gloria Bartek was saying, "You can do things, you can start from grassroots, you can fight for the goodness of books through grassroots politics." Even though she talked to me for three hours straight one time about how to do that, it was not the kind of thing that I could do. It was something that she could do. Politics is just not something I can do. Although the feminists were shouting at Stan at about how badly he was treating me, I wasn't defending him or myself about that.

Was Stan distressed by the attacks on him by feminists?

I don't think so, not much. He liked to debate and he liked women and so it was fun.

Do you do you recall the period after that, when the "structural" filmmakers started to criticize Stan?

I'm trying to think what a structural filmmaker was.

One of P. Adams' many significant contributions to film history was to point out that there was a group of filmmakers beginning with Michael Snow around 1967 who were very different from the period of...

Give me more names and then I'll know.

P. Adams says that Warhol was the founding figure, but then it would be people like Hollis himself, Michael Snow, Ernie Gehr, Paul Sharits.

OK, that's good. Stan didn't have much use for that kind of thing because it was so clean, it didn't seem to be from the soul or the feelings or anything. It seemed to be geometrical or whatnot. And there were some others around Colorado too that were not even filmmakers such as, you know, the Drop City people. He didn't relate to their work much, he didn't feel that their work related to his.

There was Warhol making a four-hour film with no movement, and Stan working away to make a 15-minute film that had all kinds of movement. I don't know, it just seemed like a little depressing that Warhol would be admired for this.

Did Stan ever tell you the story when Jonas Mekas told him to watch a bunch of Warhol films and Stan watched them and said, "I still don't like them." Jonas said, "We'll go back and watch them at 16 frames per second instead of 24." And he did and came back to say they were really good. I think this story's apocryphal—what Jonas would have liked to see happen, but never actually did.

I can imagine Stan doing that or saying he had done it. It would be a lot easier to say that he had done it, and that's probably what happened. I wouldn't have seen a difference except that one was longer than the other. That doesn't mean I'm the final word!

I don't think Stan ever approved of Warhol in any way.

No, no. I don't think he felt that they would have much to say to each other, but I'm sure he admired his salesmanship.

*Do you know Annette Michelson?**

Yes, yes indeed, she even came to our house once.

Really?

Yes. She was very shy with me. [*laughs*] If you could imagine Annette Michelson being shy.

I can't, no.

[*laughs*] Oh she was very shy with me, and she would always ask me how the children were and I guess I was not one of the talking people, so what can she do. I liked her actually. Not many people do. I liked her because she was shy, and I saw that and I like shy people. She came to the house and I can't remember if it was just her and Stan talking, and I drove her up and then I drove her back. Homer was a noisy vehicle, so I didn't get much chance to talk with her and she couldn't raise her voice loud enough to compete with my car's engine. That was difficult to talk at all when we were driving. I did visit her one summer, about four or five years ago. Tony Pipolo brought me over. She was in this high-up apartment that was—I don't remember how many floors up—six or eight or ten or something; it had three views of the city and that was wonderful. She led me from room to room to show me them and I enjoyed that. She was so polite to me

---

* Annette Michelson (1922–2018), art and film critic and academic. An editor of *Artforum* and founder of the journal *October*, she was an important supporter of Brakhage.

that I didn't quite know what to think, but I guess it was because she didn't want me to be mad at her. [*laughs*] I couldn't be mad at her. She lived in her world of words.

When she visited you in Lump Gulch she didn't stay overnight?

She must have.

Did you take her out for walks into the forest?

No, I don't think so. I think I took her up in the afternoon, and she stayed for the evening, I think that was it. I can't imagine her walking through the forest. She stayed… Where would we put guests? I think we couldn't put them in the children's rooms, maybe in the living room. She was doing her thing with words and just dancing in a kind of an Alice in Wonderland game of dancing with cards, you know dancing with words. It was a chance to use her amazing vocabulary.

There was a screening in New York, where Stan attacked some of the "structural" filmmakers; I think he attacked Michael Snow for the camera work in a film called La Région Centrale, *when it was fixed to a machine and Stan said words to the effect that this film cannot mean anything, since it's not governed by the immediate needs of the filmmaker. Then Annette Michelson stood up to defend it—"dancing with words," as you say—and Stan said, "Well you know your problem, Annette, is that you can say things so beautifully and you've such a gift with words that you can make anything sound good." And she said, "Well! Wha! Wha!" in distress. Then Stan even attacked Peter Kubelka's* Arnulf Rainer *film, the very famous one. He said, "Well I've seen this 13 times now, and I still don't think it's any better than seeing the whole array of the frames on the wall… Frankly I don't think it's all that interesting."*

Stan liked to abuse his friends. He was not loyal to his friends, didn't know loyalty.

Do you remember a film he made called Him to Her *about you, filmed in the greenhouse?*

In the greenhouse, yeah, me in the greenhouse, three minutes. That was his supposed portrait of me, but it was really just the greenhouse and me reading a book. I had been saying, "Do something about the real me," quoting from the Michael McClure play, no, I don't think I can get it right, "If you if you want to know the real me…" I can't get it right. From *Billy the Kid*, it was something that Jean Harlow said. I suppose it could be looked up and put in here, I think that would be nice.

   P. Adams clarifies: "Before you can pry any secrets from me, you must first find the real me. Which one will you pursue?" (from *The Beard*)

This reminds me now of the interview that Hollis Frampton did with you and Stan that I sent you. There's a crucial exchange among you, Stan and Hollis over the representation of you. Perhaps I could read a bit to you?[*]

OK.

> Brakhage: It's my problem, at the moment, that I am once again, or let's say especially for the first time, trying to make a portrait of Jane. This is, after years and years of Jane's image being central to film after film after film. And this is weighted with the problem that every now and again Jane will say, "Well, you've never gotten an image of *me*." So here I go for the first time — again.
> Frampton: Why is it that he can't make a portrait of you, Jane?
> Jane: He just uses me.
> Brakhage: Oh boy, now I'm in trouble! The whole women's lib movement at this instance descends on me like a puddle of Harpies!
> Jane: He just photographs a woman having a baby, sweeping the floor, or making a bed. It's the making of the bed, not how *Jane* makes the bed or what *Jane* does with it.

A bit further on, Frampton is talking to you.

> Frampton: You felt, then, that you had no life outside of your cinematic myth, that you were becoming a movie star, in fact, that kind of object.
> Jane: Yes, an appendage.
> [*then a bit about Rembrandt and his wife Saskia*]
> Jane: I didn't resent it. I just feel that that's the case, that's how it is.
> Brakhage: I'll be the first to say "bullshit."
> Jane: That was years ago that I did care, and now I don't, and now you can make the goddamn film because I don't give a shit.

You remember this?

I started cussing, didn't I. He had me doing things that, of course, that women are supposed to do, like have babies and make the bed. I was driving the car sometimes and minding the kids. Anything else that I might be interested in, except for animals. He did photograph the animals, the animals were there mysteriously. So I don't know, I just had this feeling that he was using me as "the woman of the piece." That was always the case, that it wasn't *me* that was doing that — that was what needed to be done by the woman, and so I did it for him. I don't know why I joined in that conversation, maybe just because I felt that I could, and that that would be all right.

---

[*] Frampton, "Stan and Jane Brakhage, Talking." *Artforum*, XI, 5 (January 1973), pp.72-79.

It seems that you are expressing that anger that you've been feeling for many, many years. It reminds me of when we were talking about Wedlock House *and Stan said, "OK, take your clothes off." You said he figured that every artist had to make a portrait of a nude woman at some point and this was his. Your resentment at being used as a figure for the female, rather than as a representation of you, yourself… that that distress was long standing and it erupts in that interview so powerfully.*

I was thinking also at that time about all the nudes in all the paintings and whatnot and films that were just like, "That was a nude." It didn't matter what her name was or what she cared about, who she was or anything like that. And I was talking to the artist, not to him, himself; it was the nude talking to the artist. [*laughs*] I think that nobody caught on to that. It was me saying, "You know, you're not doing me, you're doing *the woman*, or you're just doing Womankind, or the female of the species or whatever it is."

That feeling certainly comes through in your exclamations in the interview.

OK. Did I sound angry?

You sure did, it was great. [laughs] *My sense is that every woman who reads it says, "Right on Jane, that's right!" You really assume the feminist critique of Brakhage, even though you ally with him.*

I was really saying that Gauguin didn't do any better, and all those other people who did so many nudes. "Nude Descending a Staircase," who made that?

Duchamp

Oh yeah.

Where do we go from here?

Well, you are the interviewer.

I remember the film Stan made for Donald Sutherland. It was called Burial Path. *It begins with an image that is mostly birds flying and then an image of a dead bird—it looks as if it's being buried. Do you remember that?*

No, I don't. It was *Burial Path*?

Yes, Burial Path *in 1978.*

That might have been a film expressing his sorrow over a friend dying? Donald Sutherland flew away like a bird and they buried him. Symbolism was really good with Stan, even though he was not a Jungian, he was a Freudian.

We've gotten to the end of the '70s and you were separated from Stan in 1986. I would imagine that the next few years were very unhappy. Shall we leave till next time whether you want to talk about them?

Is it time to shut down?

In five minutes, yes. Do you want to think about it for another week?

OK, yes. We didn't mention me starting to write, which we had mentioned before, so I don't know if talking about it again would help. I was doing that in the '70s. Sutherland was actually very helpful to me, and so was Guy Davenport.* Stan was jealous of Guy Davenport so he got rid of him. That Davenport liked my writing was just horrifying to him. But Stan really had to say that my writing was pretty good too anyway.

A couple of weeks ago we did talk quite a lot about your writing the story "Goodbye to Barbara" in 1976, and how that really kicked off your career as a writer. So, if it's OK with you, perhaps in the next week you'll think if there's any more to say about your career as a writer taking off in the '80s. I don't want to inquire into areas that are unpleasant and painful.

Well, mostly during that time I was writing, not fighting any more than usual, I think. There was less fighting than usual, since he was not there. Because I was busy writing, I had something I could do, as I'd had the Scrapbooks earlier.

Let's pick it up there again next week.

OK we'll start in 1976 or so. I don't want to endlessly talk about other women, that just seems more irritating and not creative. When I went to L.A. I was very thoughtful, I wanted to write about being creative. I didn't want to write about being kicked around, and I want to stay that way as much as I can.

One last question. You said you tested Paul Sharits with the palm tree. What did you mean?

Well you'll have to read the palm tree story.† The palm tree was responding to gentle attention. He was one of the people that tested it and, of course, being a sensitive man he succeeded fabulously. Just get the book and read that one.

I will do. Right now.

Thank you, thank you, bye.

---

* Guy Davenport (1927–2005), writer and painter who was a close friend of Brakhage's and a commentator on his work.
† "The Palm Tree" in *The Lady Orangutan and Other Stories*.

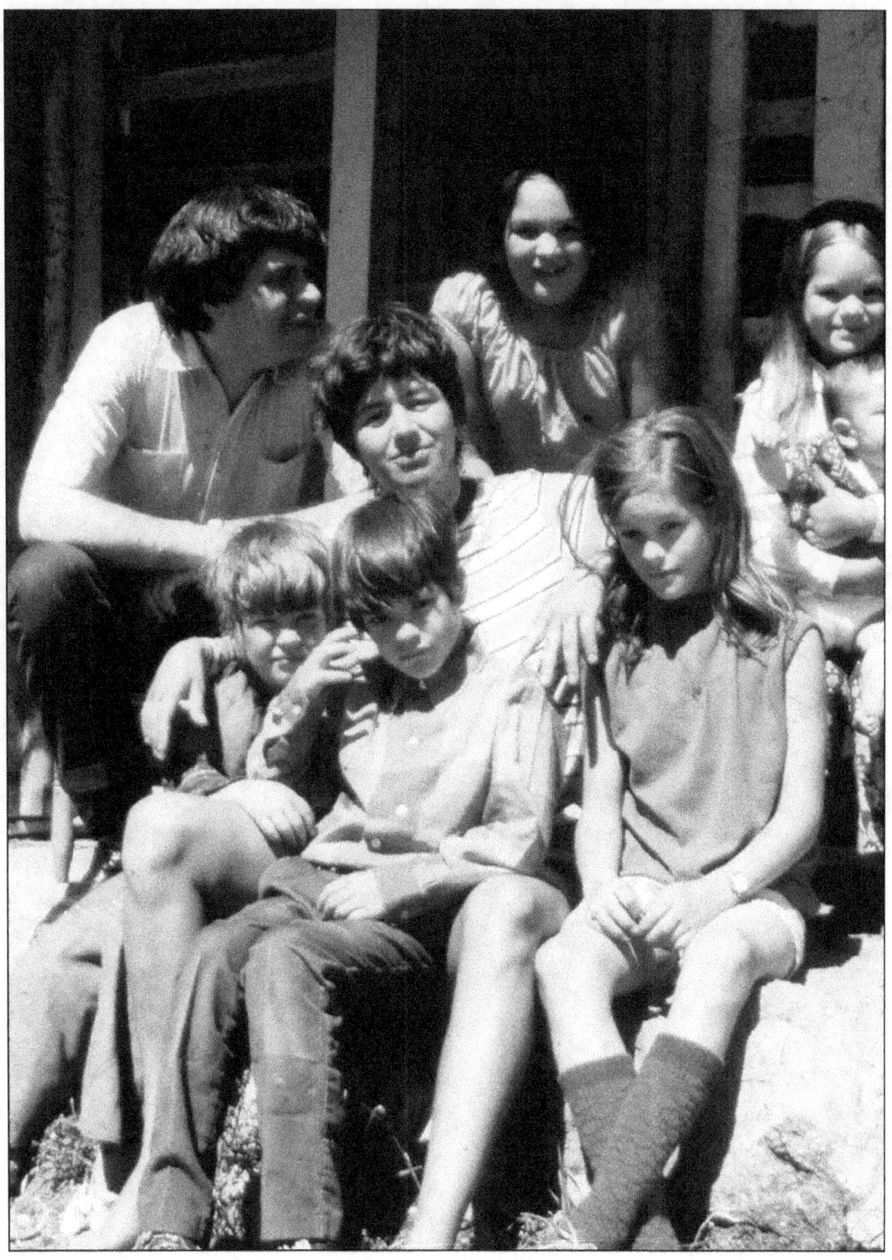

Jane, Stan and Children.

Twelve

2021 April 21. Monster movies; *Lump Gulch Tales*; Jane's next stories; the driveabout; Ed Dorn; Lucia Berlin; becoming Jane Wodening.

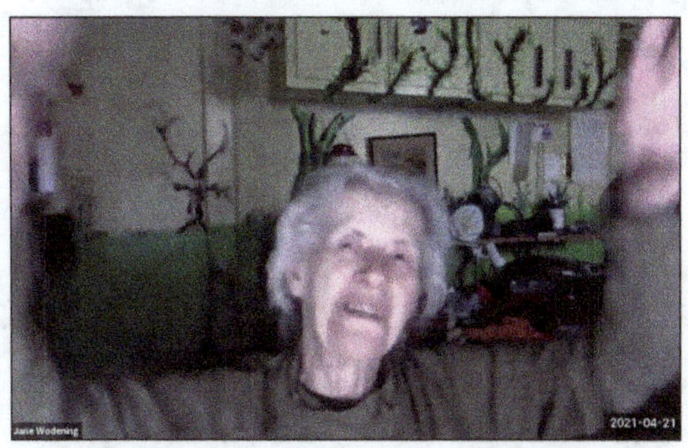

Hi Jane! Can you hear me?

Hi, David. Hi. Yeah, how are you? [*laughs*]

Fine. How are you?

I'm struggling. [*laughs*]

Oh dear. It's hard times we live in.

Hard times!

You look well and you look happy.

You look happy too. I'm happy to see you. [*laughs*]

Me too. Well, I sent the files to your friend Jeanette, and I also received your email.

Yeah, OK. She's gone to the eye doctor and she's in Boulder, and so she'll be back late this afternoon. What are we doing today?

Do you want to take the lead? Or I can, I've got a framework.

Please. I have no framework. I can't remember what we talked about last time.

OK. I'll get to that. But if it's OK with you, I'd like to talk about the letter you sent me saying, "Is this about Stan or me?" My thoughts were that it started out being about you and Stan because the purpose was to accumulate all the information we could in case in the future somebody would write a biography of Stan. You are obviously the most important person for such a biography. I wanted to get your side of the story on record so that any future biographer would do you full justice. That's what it started out as, but it looks as if it's turned into a biography of Jane Brakhage. One idea I had was, I could see it ending when you became Jane Wodening. So this would be The Autobiography of Jane Brakhage *by Jane Wodening.*

I hadn't thought of that one. That's a third choice.

Do you want to put your two main choices on record then?

Well, no. Just as I presented: is this about Stan or about me? So when would we end in that respect?

I thought when you said third, I thought you meant on the third level of preference. Then another thing in your letter, you said, "I don't want to go into Stan's womanizing fighting. I'd like to relate some of his fighting to some of his favorite movies as a child, but then I'd like to drop it. He just got more and more into the Sunday Associates and less and less into his home and then just went away. I don't want to name any of his girlfriends or overwhelm the interview with misery— just to admit it was there and go on." My preference is irrelevant, but I'd like to follow that as long as you feel it's appropriate.

One thing I wanted to put in here is that there was another terrible problem he had on top of his endless womanizing; he went into rages, mostly at me, although other people suffered badly from it and he'd get rid of people by telling them they were not artists—as Duncan had told him he was only a mediocre poet. But with me, I think it was something different.

As a kid he had always loved monster movies and he was in his mind always the monster. His favorite monster was *The Mummy*, who was weak and sickly and who staggered around strangling women. And I was The Woman in his films and his fantasies, so he would yell at me and then start to strangle me. I wasn't afraid that he would kill me, ever. That was not done in the movie, I guess, but he did this often, keeping me down. Perhaps worst of all, the children were his audience. Sorry. I just felt that a biography of Stan must at least mention that. Charlie DeJulio said, "He's just mean." Although at times he could be quite gracious, he loved to rage, to act out the monsters, to make people cry, especially me. But I gained so much from being married to him and had five children to raise, so life just went on.

It was interesting because at the end he was distant. He wasn't there much, and when he came, he would have planned an entertainment like, OK, he was going to read from Tolkien to us. As I said before, he read the whole Tolkien series, which was quite a lot, during that period. He saw that we were having quite a few happy times that had been thought out, and he wanted to make himself accepted, as though we were people he didn't know very well.

That seems to bespeak a degree of consideration or affection?

I know what it bespeaks. I think it certainly is theatrically correct, and we all appreciated it greatly, me and the kids. We loved him, anyway. He loved to read aloud and he was very good at it indeed. This must have been earlier, because the boys were quite young and the girls were still at home.

Shall we end there or do you want to add anything more?

No, we're on record, so we're being recorded and presumably typed up. Do you want to start here?

OK. Well, let's go back to where we ended last time, with your saying that Stan was jealous because Guy Davenport admired your writing. Then the fighting lessened because your career as a writer was taking off. You wanted to talk about being creative, not about being kicked around. And several times you've said how the story "Goodbye to Barbara" started your writing career in 1976. Is that correct?

I was 39. Well, that was in '76, my first real story. But I don't connect to the word "career"! I did send my stories to many small press magazines and they all published them, no money exchanged. I just feel that in a career, one starts bringing in the money and, although later people bought my books, I always paid more for them than I got back, except for the one time Marilyn Mason did a review of *Lump Gulch Tales* in the *Christian Science Monitor*. It bought my groceries for that whole summer, and the buyers were rural people all over the country.

So could you talk about your writing taking off and being creative and not kicked around?

Well, I will talk about it anyway, a little. I got to writing every story I could think of, and I made a collection of those and then I was out of stories. I thought, "Well, I really think that Lump Gulch is good for a collection of stories that I bet you the neighbors, the ones that have been here, forever, could give me stories." I went and knocked on their doors and interviewed them, and they were just as happy as clams to talk to me about the old times and these fond memories that they had and to think of having them written out. They were all coming at it from different angles. You remember we were talking about George Merchant, who was the ambulance driver; he was a crippled fellow and very charming and bright. As I said, we liked to sing old cowboy songs together. I knew a lot of the verses too. And there was a family that had been in the canyon really since the beginning of Lump Gulch being involved in the gold mining—actually, Lump Gulch had more silver than gold—but they had a long history. One of them told me about the founding mother of the family in Lump Gulch, and she had been obliged—she'd been courted by this Berger Nerheim. Anyway, I wasn't to put that story in the book because they felt that their children would not be pleased that she hadn't married for love, and she certainly stuck with the family and was a good mother and grandmother and so on. So anyway, there were tales… Have you read *Lump Gulch Tales*? You did? OK. So that was really fun and encouraging that people would be glad to give me stories. The word got around that I was collecting stories and so other people told me other stories and that enlarged my… It was not Lump Gulch tales, but it was other stories: "Why Gracie Turned Out the Way She Did," and the one about the porcupine and the wolves. The wolf story was given to me by three people separately so they each gave me a different angle on it. I turned it into a book,* actually, although there was a story which I got first, and it is not a bad story, so I put it in *Animals I've Neglected to Mention,* and I felt that it should be mentioned.† I was running out of things to talk about, and because I'd only been writing about things that came to me, not things that I'd make up.

I thought, "Well, I'll have to ask Stan for his childhood because his childhood was so interesting and he had such good stories about his childhood." I wanted to put it in chronological order because you'd just get it one story at a time and was confusing. He and I made that book, kind of like this interview, yeah, it was really like an interview. I would ask him, "Well, I want you to tell about McComb, Illinois now." And he'd say, "OK, give me a month." I'd have to do other things during that month, then he would come and one day he would just tell it to me. I'd take some quick notes, just oneword or two-word notes, and then I would go immediately and write down all the stories that he had told me that day. By just a few days later, I'd be ready for the next one, but he wouldn't. So that was quite fun, but then we came to a point where I was eager to get to the high school stories, and I don't know, it was very confusing. I think he didn't want to tell his high-school stories or I don't know what it was. He had told some, and I could have put a few sketchy ones in, which might've been a nice thing, especially the one when he gave up singing and threw away his glasses and decided to lose weight. I had one bad decision: that was a good story and I didn't put it in the book, maybe I should have. It would've been kind of a weird lump at the end. I could tell that now because it's about Stan and I don't know, has it been told before? Is it in the archives?

I don't know. I've not been to the archives.

The story I got was he was like maybe fifteen or maybe even sixteen years old, and he was still singing soprano and he had this clear soprano voice. He thought they were trying to teach him how to sing tenor and he was balking at that,

---

* *Wolf Dictionary.*
† "Elsie's Story of the Last Wolves," *Animals I've Neglected to Mention,* pp.143-54.

balking at the whole thing because a tenor has not got the chutzpah that a boy soprano does. [*laughs*] He realized he didn't want to become a tenor, and so he slammed the door on the singing teacher and went stomping out. I don't know if it was the exact same day, but it sounds like something he would do immediately—he took off his glasses and hurled them into the gutter and set out across the street and almost got run over by a truck. Then he realized that if he's going to throw away his glasses, he was going to have to be more careful about crossing the street. It was difficult for him for quite a while to adjust his eyes to where he was able to get around. He did not have good eyes. He was wearing thick glasses as a kid, but he got himself to where he could see well enough; he could see people in the audience and he could read. I never saw him put on glasses so he could read, but he was nearsighted, that was his thing. Then he was losing weight, then he was pulling together a group called the Gadflies, which I think a lot of people have heard of. They were doing plays and a lot of theatrical things because a lot of them were interested in theater. One was a poet and there were two who were real actors and got into theater in their adult life. Then came the little theater, the Yellow Door Theater in Black Hawk or Central City, Colorado. So that carries it on quite aways, but just to kind of bring a story to thundering something [*laughs*] and the beginning of something else. Yeah.

Exactly.

I don't know. It's a hard thing talking about Lump Gulch because it was twenty-three years, it was all kind of in a big wad. It seemed that way, but there were people that, I don't know, we didn't cover nearly enough people, but perhaps we couldn't. We've mentioned a few.

Could we go back to that story about Barbara?

OK.

First of all, the story is called "Transformations."

Oh, no, no, you didn't read the right story. The story of Barbara is called "Goodbye to Barbara." "Transformations" is about the second story in that book.

"Transformations" is the second story in the book.

And that's the one you read. And it wasn't "Goodbye…"

I also read "Goodbye to Barbara."

Oh, OK.

"Transformations" reads, "There was a woman I used to know. She and I used to say we'd send each other our writing when we wrote it." But that also was Barbara, right?

Yes, it's Barbara.

OK. I said the story is called "Transformations," and it's not the same as the story about Barbara specifically, but Barbara is present in it.

Yeah, she's present. Yes, she is.

Then you write that you failed to exchange your writings with each other and that you visited her when she was dying: "That night I woke in wild terror and my head on the pillow was her head on the pillow, and for the first time in my life, I knew I would die someday, and if I didn't do something, I would die without having done anything." Then in the next paragraph you write, "I thought this piece was finished. But two days later, my husband of thirty years left me. For several months, I worked with all my energies to get him back, but he couldn't bear the thought of it. Again, I had to transform." If you don't want to talk about this, just say "Shut up, David." But it seems like you've condensed the period between '76 and the mid-'80s into those two days.*

Yeah. [*laughs*] The story starts, actually, when I'm eleven, so there are some very big gaps between transformations! Those ten years just got squished away. And yes, those ten years I did a lot of writing—as I've described—these short stories that I found in my head. Everybody's got a lot of stories in their head, but they don't usually tell them. But I was eager to form them into stories and show them, so I did as many as I could think of. Recently, going through my stuff after my archive had been packed up and sent off to Yale, I found a book that I had been writing stories in 1997. Not stories really, it was a little half-page-size book, and that half-page was in handwriting. I would just fill that one page with something, with an image or a thought or something. So I started reading it. There were forty-three different images there or stories or whatever. They were little tiny things, and I don't know if any were a single sentence, but they were small. I like to grab some little image and make something out of it: show it, just frame it or I don't know. And then, during those ten years, I did essentially the wolf book from the stories… [*glitch on tape*]… the wolves. I was thinking, "Well, should I do it from Elsie's point of view?" That was the one that was the best, so I put that in the animal story. I think the other two I threw out at some point, or maybe I'll still find them, or maybe they're over in Yale somewhere. I just found a lot of things to write about, but it was hard slogging. I had to think of something to write about. I would find something or remember it, or…

So it was ten years of writing. Probably my most productive ten years of writing in my life was right then and before Stan left. When he left, I switched to

---

* "Transformations," *The Lady Orangutan and Other Stories*, p.7.

writing a journal, and that journal later became *Driveabout*. It took me decades to figure out what to do with that journal. I had the thought when I was driving around, it seemed to me that I'd be going alone, and I would say, "Well, the sun is going to be going down soon. I need a place to sleep there," and there on my right would be a little mysterious road into the woods. I would take that road and I'd get a smaller road from it and a smaller one and a smaller one, and I'd find myself in a beautiful place to sleep. It would be often the case that somehow, I'd be asking for something and it would be there. Or I would be asking, wondering about something and I'd stop for gas, and the gas-station man would say something inspired in relation to what I was thinking.

Or I remember one time I was thinking, "Gosh, I'm lonesome. I wish I had had somebody beside me." And then there was this hawk that came along and was flying beside me for a few miles. [*laughs*] It was a long ways, and I was extraordinarily satisfied. I was very proud and pleased that I felt like I was being given what I needed. That was an interesting thing. I wished... and I got the idea that everything was connected, there was a lot of connection, and we were all one. It wasn't that it was all for me, but it was that we were all one and we were as a world together. It wasn't like coming to somebody and they would be the enemy—even if they said something grumpy, that would be still something to learn from.

But I couldn't pull it together. I couldn't write enough. I would've had to spend all day writing and then maybe drive a little ways and write all day after a few hours of driving and it would mess up what I was trying to achieve in my psyche, that is to get over it, to get well. I was struck down and I needed to get well. What I wrote was more like a journal at the end of the day, telling whatever story I could think of. I had a collection of stories so I said, "Well, I'll have to be content with that because I can't do that other thing, which would be so grand." And P. Adams said, "Oh, well, that's what James Joyce did." It wasn't *Ulysses*, it was *Finnegans Wake*, I think. I don't think I could achieve that, but I had it flowing through me for a while there. Jane's *Finnegan's Wake* but it didn't work out. It's come to a nice little adventure story all around America.

That grand thing that you couldn't do, that might've been to write a novel?

It would've been to write exactly what happened and how I related what the gas-station man said to what I was thinking. I'd have to say what I was thinking and then say what the gas-station man's response to it was and what I was thinking and the eagle's response to it. I think it was a hawk actually, but anyway, it was somebody wonderful.

Your account of driving off the road and off the next road strikes me as incredibly courageous, brave. It reminds me of two things in the Orangutan *stories. First, it reminds me of the time when you left Princeton and you drove off road, and in the middle of the night, both of you had this horrible terror, and you drove out in the middle of the night to escape this horrible terror.*

You've been reading some of the other stories I gather.

I've read almost the whole book.

Oh, have you! Yeah, of the unknown. It was not in the night though, it was in the daytime, and we wanted to rest and have a lunch and so on, but we couldn't do it there. That was for sure.

The other thing it reminds me of is the story "Pilgrimage," where you write about this harrowing ascent up Long's Peak, and especially when you go up the wrong track and you have to crawl down again, and you put this line in, "I didn't want to allow my fears to govern my life." As I hear you talking, it seems that you so bravely and nobly confronted all those fears, it's just so remarkable.*

Shortly after I had started writing, I was writing quite a bit—after Barbara handed me the keys to the kingdom, then I could write. Stan thought that I should take a class with Ed Dorn, and I liked Ed Dorn, so I thought, well, that would be alright. I could take a class, but not poetry, please. I can't do poetry. He was doing a prose class for freshmen, so I went to that class and joined it. At one point in that class, he would tell us to write about this or that, like the teachers are always supposed to say, "Tell us about summer vacation." Then one day he came in—and he came in late, which was common for him, but he was worth waiting for—and he said, "Now I want you to write about fear." And my heart sank. What are all the symptoms of fear? I suppose I turned pale anyway, yeah, my mouth went dry, everything. I thought, "What'll I tell about fear?" So I told that story of the unknown, but then I couldn't stop. I got involved in writing about fear from one direction and another direction and another direction. You've been reading those stories, and some of them perhaps you haven't noticed. The one I ended on was "Dear Emma," which is a story about shyness.

Yes, I remember, "Dear Emma." It's not the final one, but I remember her.

There were several about fear, and of course, climbing Long's Peak was one of them. I waited seven years before I wrote that story because I was too scared to write it. Yet after I wrote it, people were saying, "God, what a fun trip that was. And let's go back. I'll go with you and let's go together." And, "No, I'm not going up again!" But yeah, that was another one. I blank them out because they're so scary. There were scary stories that I waited until I felt… actually that the pilgrimage story could be laughed at all the way through… that there were funny things about my fear, that it was so funny, the way I had to crawl backwards to get back to the path, the little shelf that we were walking on. Then, when Stan had left and I was trying to figure out what to do, I called Ed up and I told him, "OK, you gave me an assignment to write about fear, and I've been writing about fear and I'd like to stop. Could you give me another assignment?"

---

* "Pilgrimages (Long's Peak)," *The Lady Orangutan and Other Stories*, p.51.

[*laughs*] He said, give me a couple of days, so he thought about it for a couple of days, and he called me back and he said, "Aggressive self-assurance." I said, "I'm not aggressive, I can't do aggressive. How about assertive?" "Well, all right," he said, so I took off in my car with striving for assertive self-assurance.

So instead of writing about assertive self-assurance, you manifested assertive self-assurance. You performed assertive self-assurance.

Yes. The thing is that I'm still shy, only I've gotten over showing it in conversation. I've learned to converse so that I can converse because it's interesting. It's important to me to say things. Up until then, people would say things to me and I would want to correct them. I would want so much to correct them or say something back that was lucid and right and useful, but I couldn't. I remember when there were some English people that I was talking with. I was down from living on the mountain, and so I probably looked like some kind of wild creature or something. They were asking, "What do you find up there?" "Well, I find, of course, the beauty and this and that." Then I was talking about herbs [pronouncing *erbs*] and they said, "It's *herbs*." I was so shocked that I couldn't say anything. I couldn't even say "Oh, I can pronounce my h's. It's just that whoever came over to America with herbs were dropping their h's. It took on and it took off like wildfire across America, and that's how it was pronounced. And so that's how it's still pronounced." That's the story I made up to explain it, but I don't know if I told it, maybe I didn't tell it. But anyway, I heard them say, "H's are so difficult"; they were trying to be sympathetic. [*laughs*] That story about the herbalist that came over was one that I never got to tell, and we just didn't have much to say to each other after that because we were obviously from different levels of society.

The stories in Lady Orangutan *seem to be a mix of several different kinds: the ones we've been talking about, about personal transformation and fear, and then there are the others which are sketches of things in nature, like the story about the beetle and the story about the hen that are just so beautiful and precise. I love those stories.*

Thank you.

Did you ever show those to Ed Dorn?

To Ed Dorn? Yes. He had the idea that my story about the hen, "Biography of a Hen," and Lucia Berlin's story… You really should know Lucia Berlin, you've got to find her books, you should know her because she's a very well-known writer, but she got known after she died. Anyway, he wanted to put her story about the laundromat,[*] the two books, the two stories together, backwards to each other. I think I mentioned this.

---

[*] Lucia Berlin, "Angel's Laundromat," *A Manual For Cleaning Women* (New York: Farrar, Straus and Giroux, 2015), pp 3-8.

Yes, we talked about that.

So he knew some of my stories anyway, and I don't know what all he read before he died.

I haven't got to the end of the book, but I noticed that Lucia Berlin does appear in the penultimate story called "Visions of My Death." I haven't read that yet. Maybe we could talk about that at some point in the future.

She's in that story, "Visions of my Death?"

[reads] *"My dear friend Lucia Berlin came from California to teach a course in prose writing at the Buddhist-inspired school called Naropa in Boulder and she let me sit in on a class."**

Oh, yes. I don't know what that has to do with "Visions of My Death." But anyway, yeah, she was one of the funniest people I ever met, and she really knew how to laugh, She was a really fine writer in the way of writing about things that happened to herself. I was very sad when she said she was going to write a book about her mother. She wrote and wrote and wrote and wrote and wrote for months. Then, she said, she threw it away.

Threw it away?

She threw it away. I said, "What did you do?" And she said, "I hit delete." I think I know why. It was because her mother turned out so bad. There were so many things that she did that were… well, like killing herself was one. I don't know. Just, oh, drinking, being an alcoholic was another, and Lucia was an alcoholic, although I always called her Lucia [LOO-sha]. There were three ways of calling her. One would be her mother called her Lucia [Loo-CHEE-a]; the old group back in New Mexico, I guess, or maybe it was California, they called her Lucia [LOO-sha], so I called her that; but now everybody feels that the only proper way to call her is Lucia [Loo-SEE-ya]. And so there's three ways, maybe there's others I don't know. But there's only one way to pronounce Jane, I think.

Terrific phrase. I can imagine that being a title of a book, There's Only One Way to Pronounce Jane.

[laughs] *One Way to Pronounce Jane.* Well, there's David.

Dafydd in Welsh, I'm half Welsh.

David, your other name. I can't think of another.

____

* *The Lady Orangutan and Other Stories*, p.320.

Do you want to talk about when you became Jane Wodening?

Well, that's part of *Driveabout*.

That's another one I haven't read yet.

OK, so I'll tell you a bit about that. I really felt the burden of the name of Brakhage. I wanted to erase not only all the films—my brain had been arranged to keep an eye on the films, to know if I see one frame of a Brakhage film, I knew not only what film it was from, but where exactly it was and what other pictures were around it, and the name and date and everything of the film, and how much it cost and what we were selling it for, and whether I have a box to put it in, if I sold one and other films that related to it, and all the things that you would've enjoyed having me tell you if I had remembered them. But I needed to find a life of my mind. [*tape unclear*] I didn't want to carry around any Brakhage either. And Carolee said, "Well, you deserve it!" And I thought, "Oh, what a curse." Certainly, she was saying that I did fine as a wife, but I didn't want to be a Brakhage and everybody say, "Oh, are you related to Stan Brakhage?"

So I thought, I am going to go out and maybe I can find an Indian who would call me White Cloud or something. At first I thought, "Well, I can think of a name. My favorite color is brown: Jane Brown." It doesn't somehow sound very sparkling. It doesn't have a lot of life to it. My favorite thing in the sky is the moon. How about Jane Moon? Just then Reverend Moon killed a bunch of people. I don't know if you remember the story, it was one of those cult things. So I couldn't grab that name, that was denied to me. I also took my wonderful family tree, where I think I told you I'm descended from King Alfred the Great and all the people in between. I put it all on adding-machine tape in pencil, and I hung it on the wall. It was on the kitchen wall for many years. I took that down and put it in a box and put it in the car. I got a small car where the seats fold back so I could sleep in it. It was a Honda Civic of 1979 or '80, I think it was '79.

So I sat out and drove around and went places all over the West first. That was wonderful because I could just drive off into the desert and find a place to park and sleep, as I described, going down a little road and a little road and a little road. There were fewer of those in the East. East of the Mississippi, there's a lot more people, and they're just constant, you can't get away from 'em. They're farming, of course. In the desert, you can't really farm well, so that leaves it some places wild. It was a long time before I got to Boston where my friends—actually the suburbs of Boston—where my friend Carol Weston, the poet, lives and she's a fantastic person.* She's just a poet from one end to the other, and she has a big smile, and she's marvelous. So we ran around together and she told me, "Well, there are people reading their poetry at Charlie's Tap." I called up and I got a place to read. I got an evening to read in Charlie's Tap. So I went to Charlie's Tap and I read the story, "The Birth of Godot." I was determined to read that. I'm not sure why, but there was a young man who said, "Please don't tell me about birth

---

* Carol Weston (b.1956), writer and advice columnist.

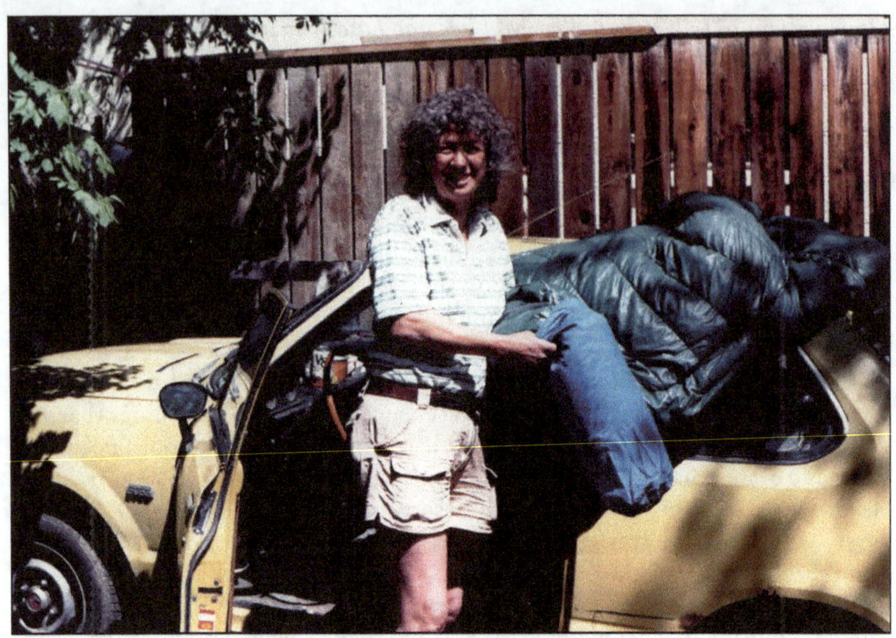

Jane with her *Driveabout* Car.

because I'll have to leave." But I said, "I have to read this story." I'm not sure why, what it was, so I did read it. There were, I don't know how many people there, thirty, maybe at the most, in a little room off to the side. After I finished reading, I guess I did some other stories and then he was gone, of course, I'm sorry, I chased him out of there.

This eccentric-looking man started talking with me, saying that he had ten languages and his favorite language was Old English and his favorite person in all the world was King Alfred the Great. I said, "Well, I'm descended from him." He fell at my feet. [*laughs*] He truly fell at my feet, I think he thought that's definitely the thing you're supposed to do. Then I don't know, did I help him up or something? I said to him, "Maybe you could give me a name. I need a name. I just got divorced and I need a name. I can't have my maiden name because my brother has it." He said, "Well," and I quote, "Give me a couple days," just like Ed had said. I gave him my phone number, and he called up and asked me to come over for a cup of tea and gave me the name of Wodening. I had to show him my adding machine tape full of ancestors. He kind of sprawled them out on the table, and it was too long, it was dripping over in all directions. I said, "It's only in my handwriting, so I could have made it all up." But he believed me and gave me the name of Wodening, the child of Woden. The reason he felt that that was relevant—I don't know if it's really relevant, but I mean, I would've preferred Jane Alfred or something just to remind me of Alfred. But he was being accurate, in that Alfred himself was concerned very much that you had to be a descendant of Woden. And Wodening means a descendant of Woden, so that's what he named me. At least if I ever meet King Alfred the Great, I can say, "My name is

Wodening," and he will say, "How do you do? You must be a relative." I took off my first name, "Mary," because I was not pleased with being called Mary Jane and I never used it, people were teasing me about being Mary Jane, which was just a variation of marijuana. Then I went to the county courthouse and got the county judge—I believe it's the judge that has to do it—and he had a little time, and so he signed the papers. So that's the story of my change of name.

That was my new name: Jane Wodening.

That strikes me as the perfect conclusion, so I suggest that we end here for the time being. I will assemble the whole thing and I will also minimize my questions so it's almost entirely you speaking.

I don't want that.

Excuse me?

I don't want that.

I'll just do a little bit if it strikes me as…

The way you talk… If you're embarrassed about the way you talk?

OK. If there are places you want to elaborate or develop more, we'll meet again and maybe talk about areas that you think you'd like to talk about more. Does that sound sensible?

Um, OK. That's what we'll do. So this could be the very last bit?

I hope it's not the last time that you and I meet and talk.

Me too.

It's been a great honor and a delight for me, and I'm very grateful to you. I want to say one last thing: I feel guilty that I couldn't find a woman to do these interviews with you. You might have been able to speak very differently with a woman than with me. But nobody else would do it, so I did it.

I'm really glad, I'm really glad, because I actually find it easier to talk to men than to women. I don't know why I've always liked men, you know, just as they are. I like the way men think. Maybe I relate to… my father, my father's way of thinking more than I do to the way my mother thought. So I am so glad, I'm glad you couldn't find a woman for me. I would have preferred you. You're the top.

I don't know about that. But I certainly hope it's not goodbye. I'm sure we'll be in touch with email. But I'm worried about P. Adams. I felt his absence in today's conversation. I always look forward to sending the interviews to him, but I'm not going to send this one, and I hope that you and he return to an ongoing cordiality.

Yeah, we did, I called him up again, so we can call each other up whenever we want. I don't know what he'd want to call me up about, but he will.

I'm very glad you said that he will. OK, Jane. We'll be in touch. Thank you for everything.

Thank you for saying, "It's been such a delight," and I'm very sad that it seems to be over.

I don't think it's over.

OK. I'll be less sad. Bye.

Bye. Do take care of yourself.

Thank you. You too.

Appendix One
Jane Wodening's Family

Parents
Harry Holder Collom: 1906 April 2–1983 December 26
Margaret Jack: 1905 June 26–1997 December 16
Married: 1930 January 31

Siblings
John (Jack) Aldridge Collom: 1931 November 8–2017 July 2
Mary Jane Collom: 1936 September 7–2023 November 17

Husband
Stanley Brakhage: 1933 January 14–2003 March 9
Married: 1957 December 28; divorced 1987, finalized 1988

Children
Myrrena: b. 1958 November in Princeton; appears in *Window Water Baby Moving*
Crystal: b. 1960 February in Boulder Hospital; appears in *Dog Star Man, Prelude* and *Part Four*
Neowyn: b. 1961 June in Crisman, Colorado; appears in *Thigh Line Lyre Triangular*
Bearthm: b. 1963 February in Boulder Hospital; appears in *Dog Star Man, Parts Two* and *Four*
Rarc: b. 1964 August in Boulder Hospital; appears in *Song 5* and *Three Films: Blue White/Blood's Tone/Vein*

Appendix Two
Books by Jane Wodening

From the Book of Legends
New York: Granary Books, 1989. Second Edition, London: Invisible Books, 1993

Lump Gulch Tales
Nederland, CO: Grackle Books, 1993. Second edition, Boulder, CO: Baksun Books and Rodent Press, 1996

Mountain Woman Tales
Nederland, CO: Grackle Books, 1994. Second edition, *Mountain Woman Tales and Bird Journal,* Boulder, CO: Baksun Books, 2000

The Inside Story
Boulder, CO: Baksun Books and Rodent Press, 1996

Moon Songs
New York: Situations Press, 1997

What the Ambulance Driver Said
New York: Granary Books, 1998

Book of Gargoyles
Boulder, CO: Baksun Books, 1999

First Presence
Boulder, CO: Baksun Books, 2000

Living Up There
Boulder, CO: Baksun Books, 2009

Egypt and Me
Boulder, CO: Baksun Books, 2012

The Lady Orangutan and Other Stories
Nederland, CO: Sockwood Press, 2014

Brakhage's Childhood
New York: Granary Books, 2016

Wolf Dictionary
Nederland, CO: Sockwood Press, 2016

Driveabout
Nederland, CO: Sockwood Press, 2016

Animals I've Neglected to Mention
Nederland, CO: Sockwood Press, 2019

Appendix Three
The Birth Film

Being an artist's wife is strange, and when the artist uses moving pictures to express himself, it is very strange indeed. Then, when the artist say he is going to make moving pictures of the birth of the first child, we are both very excited and talk about it long into the night many nights. For there were plans we had to make and things to arrange, and he had to be in the delivery room, and the doctor and nurse had to help in many ways, and I had to be fully awake all during the childbirth, because I didn't want to miss a minute of it.

So, first of all, the right doctor must be found, and we found him quite easily and went to see him together. He was much in favor of natural childbirth. The first step had been taken, and things were going well. When my husband, Stan, came into the office and was going to ask him about the film, before he even had time to say, "How do you do?" the doctor said, "How would you like to make a film on natural childbirth?" We were thunderstruck, and we all sat in the office and were very excited and talked and talked and the doctor said he'd try to get the hospital to agree to it and everyone was enthusiastic and happy. But then, it didn't continue as it had begun, and the doctor talked to the hospital, and the hospital had conference after conference about it and, finally, talked themselves out of it.

Thus, it was that we decided to have the baby at home, and we were very glad because I never liked to go to the hospital, and we were glad because Stan would have more freedom at home than in the hospital, and we were altogether glad in every way. There was much fuss about getting equipment for the doctor and hiring a nurse, and the doctor and the nurse were glowing with excitement because this was an adventure they'd never had before.

Stan and I went to classes and learned about childbirth, and I learned all the exercises to make my body strong and right for having a child.

Then we waited.

By the afternoon of November 12, we had taken some moving pictures of the baby moving and kicking before being born, and that night there were contractions, and we were very happy and took some more film of our happy faces and some of the cat and played games and watched the clock and then the doctor came with his nurse and all his paraphernalia and said, no, this wasn't labor and to call him when I stopped knitting.

The next night, I stopped knitting, and we called him, and he was at the hospital with two other women in labor, and he told Stan to give me a drink and put me to bed. And the next night, we went bowling, and still there were contractions and then several days running around and again bowling with a score of 130 and still contractions. Till we were going mad, and we didn't believe what all the people said, we believed in the stork, and the heck with it.

Then Friday and my appointment with the doctor, and I was very gay and didn't care what happened and he said, "You'll know when it's for real," and I said "How?" and he said "You'll suddenly say, 'Oop,' and then beat your fist on the chair arm, and then you'll get up and be fidgety and walk around."

And then that night, for the first time since all this began, Stan did some work on another moving picture he was working on, and I was sitting at the kitchen table getting up the energy to do something or other, I think, the dishes, and suddenly I said, "Oop," and beat my fist on the table and then I was very happy, but, by this time, I didn't believe in it, and I got up and did the dishes and "Oop" and "Oop" very regularly and told Stan, who didn't believe and went on working. And a bloody show and still he didn't believe and "Oop" and "Oop," and I believed and started trying to figure out how to be most comfortable during the contractions "Oop" and after a couple more hours I was very adept at relaxing completely when it came, and then it wasn't "Oop" anymore but a strange sinking into a beautiful and frightening world then rising again and a moment of bliss, then normalcy. If I didn't relax completely, then I wasn't shown the strange world or get the moment of bliss, but then it was pain.

Finally, when Stan was through working, he believed pretty much, and he read Proust to me, and, at 2:00 or 3:00 A.M., he called the doctor, who was sleepy and sent the nurse who arrived around 5, and it was dawn, and we had stayed up all night.

Again and again into the strange world for hours and hours. Stan filming and the nurse checking this and that, timing contractions, boiling water, shaving me (that was the worst, most uncomfortable part of the whole experience), telling us it will be a long while yet. Stan and I go to the mailbox to get the mail between contractions. The doctor arrives, Stan films and films, and I go again and again into the strange world and again and again have a moment of bliss. The doctor leaves, Stan and I sleep for an hour or so while the nurse reads in the kitchen. Then, the doctor arrives again and says it will be yet several hours. The nurse is tired. They both drive off. Stan and I are alone for a moment. I relax while Stan fusses with lights and camera. Five minutes pass, maybe less.

Then I feel like a balloon full of water pops inside me, water shoots out of me. "Water! Water!" I shout. Stan rushes in with his camera and films while the water pours out of me. So excited we are. "Here comes some more!" "Wait a minute!" "I can't!" Clickety-clackety-buzz goes the camera. Something tremendous is happening to me. I have entered into a world of beautiful agony—agony of great beauty, joyous agony, unbearable beauty. I roar like a lion. Stan films, clickety-clackety-buzz, his hands are trembling with the camera, but clickety-clackety-buzz anyway. I roar again and pant fast like I had run a mile and roar, and Stan films, and we are so very happy because the baby is coming at last!

What? The baby is coming at last? Where's the doctor? I'm in second stage. Where's the doctor? Yes, where's the doctor? We don't know. Stan films, and I roar. Stan, call the doctor. He calls the hospital and gets the nurse who says she'll be right here. It takes ten minutes driving fast from the hospital here. Stan starts worrying. I continue roaring and panting. Stan stops filming he's so upset. He gets nervous. He tells me to relax and pant. He needs to relax; I'm doing fine. I tell him how much I love him and ask him if he's got my face when I'm roaring and this sets him off again and reassures him, and he clickety-clackety-buzzes while I roar and pant, and we are both very happy, and it is like we are doing something together each with his own task, and each task is so great and wonderful beyond telling, and then the nurse comes and sees how things are and calls and has the doctor paged and ten minutes more pass, and I ask the nurse if she could deliver the baby all right without the doctor, and she says he'll come, and I'm doing fine, and I roar and roar louder and louder and pant and pant faster and faster, and Stan talks to the nurse and films and films and, finally, the doctor comes live already there is a bit of hair born, and I go and lie on the delivery table and then doctor says I can push, which is what I've been wanting to do all along but I've been panting so as to wait for the doctor and everything to be ready because, when you pant, it comes slower so anyway I'm pushing and Stan's filming and the doctor is saying "Maneroo!" because when I push then things happen fast, and the nurse says over and over that I'm doing very well, and I push and pant and roar and always clickety-clackety-buzz and more and more and more and then the doctor says don't push anymore just pant and so I pant so fast I don't hardly get any air, and this one is very different; it's joyous relief, sort of like finally reaching the gates of heaven after an impossibly hard climb, and I hear the doctor very excited saying "The head is born-anterior shoulder—posterior shoulder—" and then there is the baby held by her heels, and she's crying, and I'm saying, "Baby, baby," over and over, and Stan is laughing and covered with sweat, and the placenta is born, and the doctor and nurse do this and that to the baby, while I take some pictures of Stan because he is so beautiful, and then they all have a drink, but I am quite drunk, and I eat a sandwich, and the baby is in the cradle and asleep, and then we were left alone and happiness everywhere.

Index

P. Adams Sitney (1944–2025) was one of America's foremost film scholars. His *Visionary Film: The American Avant-Garde*, first published in 1974, established the canon of the American art film. He is remembered for his peerless contributions to the historiography of independent cinema and the creation of its enabling institutions. Sitney first met Stan and Jane Brakhage in 1962.

David E. James taught film studies at the University of Southern California in Los Angeles. His most recent books are *Power Misses II: Cinema, Asian and Modern* (2021) and *Rock 'N' Film: Cinema's Dance with Popular Music* (2016).

Sticking Place Books (stickingplacebooks.com) is a New York-based publisher specializing in cinema, offering interview books, memoirs, critical and historical studies, screenplays, and essay collections. Our titles include:

Lessons with Kiarostami, edited by Paul Cronin

In the Shadow of Trees: The Collected Poetry of Abbas Kiarostami

Still Film Crazy (After All These Years) by Patrick McGilligan

It's Only a Movie by Bruce Joel Rubin

Three Visionary Screenplays by Bruce Joel Rubin

Playing Among the Stars: Conversations with Damien Chazelle by Nathan Réra

The Magic Eye: The Cinema of Stanley Kubrick by Neil Hornick

A Shared Cinema: Conversations with Michael Ciment by N. T. Bihn

The Naughty Bits: What the Censors Wouldn't Let You See in Hollywood's Most Famous Movies by Nat Segaloff

Mexico: The Aztec Account of the Conquest by Werner Herzog

Werner Herzog/Rogue Filmmaker by David LaRocca

De Palma on De Palma: Conversations with Samuel Blumenfeld and Laurent Vachaud

Publication as Autobiography: Occasional and Forsaken Texts— and Endangered Cinema Species by Scott MacDonald

Filmmakers Thinking by Adrian Martin

Secret Cinema: The Rise and Fall of the Blue Movie by John Baxter

Casualties of War: An Investigation by Nathan Réra

Hollywood on the Tiber by Hank Kaufman and Gene Lerner

What Made Cinema? Essays on Visual Culture and Early Film by Ian Christie

Travels in the Cities of Cinema: Conversations with Jonathan Rosenbaum by Ehsan Khoshbakht

Camera Movements that Confound Us by Jonathan Rosenbaum

Upon Open Sky by Guillermo Arriaga

Ambrose Chapel by Brian De Palma

Russian Poland by David Mamet

The Archival Impermanence Project by Ross Lipman

These Fragments I Have Shored Against My Ruin by Caveh Zahedi

Cinema Now and Then: Conversations with James Naremore by Craig S. Simpson

Circle of Lions by Anthony Ray

Peace of Mind: A Paul Williams Anthology, edited by Paul Cronin

Flashbacks: A Passion for Film by Peter Cowie

Haneke on Haneke: Conversations with Michel Cieutat and Philippe Rouyer

Darkness Visible: The Cinema of Jonathan Glazer by John Bleasdale

Let Me Dream Again: Essays on the Moving Image by Luke McKernan

O Brother, What Might Have Been: Three Lost Screenplays by Preston Sturges

Mister Everywhere: Conversations with Pierre Rissient by Samuel Blumenfeld

Every Movie is a Miracle: A Colloquy Between Leonard Maltin and Nat Segaloff

High Contrast Hollywood by Julian Upton

Charles Chaplin's The Freak: The Story of an Unfinished Film by David Robinson
Jump Cuts, Tracking Shots, and Scherzos by David Sterritt
A Cinephile Under the Influence: Conversations with David Sterritt by Mikita Brottman
My Life is the Cinema by Esfir Shub
I Killed Bette Davis by Larry Cohen
HeadHunter by Larry Cohen
I Loved Movies, But… by Joseph McBride, Conversations with Danny Peary
A Reluctant Film Critic by Gerald Peary
The Zen of the Director by Peter Markham
Adventures in Auteurism: A Crusade for the Criminally Neglected by Daniel Kremer
Persistence of Vision: A Collection of Film Criticism, Edited by Joseph McBride
Writings and Relics 1990–95 by Michael Almereyda
My Strange Love: Selected Film Reviews and Essays, 2001–2021 by Stuart Klawans
The Autobiography of Jane Brakhage by Jane Wodening
    with P. Adams Sitney and David E. James
The Curse of Queen Kelly by Pamela Hutchinson
Lost Screenplays of the 1970s by Jim McBride
My Lunches with Henry Jaglom by Daniel Kremer